Aims and Options

A Thematic Approach to Writing

Aims and Options

A

Thematic

Approach

to

Writing

SECOND EDITION

Rodney D. Keller
Ricks College

HOUGHTON MIFFLIN COMPANY   BOSTON   NEW YORK

FOR CHRISTI, OUR SONS, AND OUR FAMILIES

Senior Sponsoring Editor: Mary Jo Southern
Senior Associate Editor: Ellen Darion
Editorial Assistant: Kate O'Sullivan
Senior Project Editor: Fred Burns
Senior Production/Design Coordinator: Carol Merrigan
Senior Manufacturing Coordinator: Sally Culler

Cover designer: Diana Coe

Cover image: Delauney, Robert: Rythm. Spirals. 1935. Coll. Sonia Delaunay, Paris, France. Giraudon/Art Resource, N.Y.

Printed in the U.S.A.

Library of Congress Catalog Card Number: 98-72052

ISBN: 0-395-89961-3

1 2 3 4 5 6 7 8 9–CW–02 01 00 99 98

CONTENTS

Chapter 3 ENVIRONMENT   *82*

Chapter 5 IDENTITY 162

PREFACE

Aims and Options: A Thematic Approach to Writing informally and simply introduces the multiple writing options available to first-year college students and encourages them to explore these possibilities to determine the most effective way to achieve a particular aim or purpose in their own writing.

Aims and Options focuses on four main goals for college writing:

To reflect by expressing self or sharing personal experiences

To inform by reporting information, explaining a concept, or describing an object

To persuade by influencing readers' beliefs and actions or appealing to readers' reasons, emotions, or values

To speculate by discussing past, present, and future possibilities or asking, What if? or, What about?

These aims are the reasons students write, and they can help students decide how best to meet their needs and the needs of their readers. The principles behind these aims can help students understand more fully *why* and *how* they write. The assumption behind this text is that the writer's purpose for writing is the most important influence that governs the writer's options regarding all aspects of writing: audience, topic, organization, examples, and language.

CONTENT AND ORGANIZATION

Aims and Options consists of eight chapters, each focusing on a theme: work, education, environment, health, identity, relationships, law, and media. This thematic focus gives students a direction for their ideas. The themes also provide continuity among the different stages of the writing process within each chapter.

Each thematically arranged chapter guides students through the writing process. Many beginning writers fail to realize that writing *is* a process, a process that involves different activities at various stages, from initial idea to finished product. And the writing process is different for different people. Therefore, students need options. Each chapter highlights and integrates its own prewriting, drafting, rewriting, and editing principle or strategy so that students can experiment and discover what method works best for them. Specifically, *Aims and Options* contains eight distinct prewriting, drafting, rewriting, and editing strategies.

An appendix provides instruction on writing a research paper and using correct documentation.

SPECIAL FEATURES

Aims and Options has several features that make the text and this edition flexible and easy to use:

Thematic organization   Organized into eight thematic chapters based on issues relevant to students' lives, all readings, examples, exercises, writing topics, and student essays are based on the chapters' themes: work, education, environment, health, identity, relationships, law, and media.

Reading–writing connection   Two professional essays introducing each chapter function as springboards for thinking and writing about the topic of the chapter as models of good writing. Questions after each selection guide students in evaluating the writer's techniques and thinking critically about the content.

Writing process   Each chapter highlights a different prewriting, drafting, rewriting, and editing strategy to allow students to explore the different options writers have for expressing their ideas. Instruction and practice in grammar and mechanics are integrated in the chapter as part of the writing process.

Expository strategies   Integrated into each chapter is one of eight different expository strategies that provide students with additional tools and options for achieving their main purpose in writing. These eight strategies include: narration, description, definition, cause and effect, classification, comparison and contrast, process, and persuasion.

Student essays   Each chapter contains a student essay in progress; that student essay becomes an example for the prewriting, drafting, and rewriting sections. An annotated student draft appears in each chapter.

"Exploring Your Options"   This feature leads students through the process of writing their own essays.

Extensive writing opportunities   Each chapter contains sixteen different suggested writing assignments that focus on the four different writing aims. Many of these assignments encourage students to actively address local social issues and to participate in or explore community service organizations.

Researching and documenting   The research and documentation section of *Aims and Options* is in the appendix. This location allows students and teachers to refer to it whenever they wish to provide researched support for any of their writing assignments. This section gives general and workable steps in organizing a formal or an informal research question and project and guides students in APA and MLA documentation.

NEW TO THE SECOND EDITION

Aims and Options, Second Edition, has been revised to make it even more useful and relevant to students today. New features include:

- 30 percent new selections. Selections by favorites such as Rachel Carson, Henry Louis Gates, and Bob Greene are joined by new selections by Martin Luther King, Jr., Tomoyuki Iwashita, Richard Rodriguez, and Elissa Ely.

- Two new chapter themes, "Identity" and "Media," engage students and stimulate their writing.

- Collaborative writing: "Writing Together" exercises and assignments, which now appear in every chapter, help students see writing as a social activity and give them the option to aid each other as they prewrite, draft, rewrite, and edit their essays.

- Peer response: In addition to collaborative writing activities, *Aims and Options* encourages the use of peer response groups and now provides questions adapted to focus on the four primary writing aims: reflect, inform, persuade, and speculate.

- Writing with Computers: Each chapter provides suggestions and strategies for using the computer as a writing tool. Also included in this edition is a brief section on using the Internet as a research option and examples of electronic documentation.

ACKNOWLEDGMENTS

Writing is a truly collaborative effort. I would like to thank those who have helped me in this writing project. Thanks goes first to the Ricks College administration, colleagues, and students who have provided me with examples, encouragement, and support.

I am also indebted to the many reviewers who have given me the benefit of their insights and suggestions at various stages of the book's development. These reviewers include:

Kathi Gardner-Bradham, Central Carolina Technical College

Beverly Burch, Vincennes University

Sandra Frazier, Kent State University—Trumball Branch

Patricia Licklider, John Jay College of Criminal Justice—CUNY

Karen Standridge, Pikes Peak Community College

Howard Walters, Mississippi Gulf Coast Community College

I am indeed grateful to the Houghton Mifflin editorial staff who kindly accepted me as a member of their own team. Many thanks to Mary Jo Southern who has believed in me from the start and to Ellen Darion who has guided me through this revision. Without their assistance, this work would not have been possible.

And finally, I express my gratitude and love to Christi for her enduring strength and encouragement and to our sons, Stephen, Kevin, and Nathan for their constant motivation.

Rodney D. Keller

Aims and Options

A Thematic Approach to Writing

INTRODUCTION

The overall purpose of *Aims and Options: A Thematic Approach to Writing,* second edition, is to provide clear and simple general instructions for writing college papers. A more specific purpose is to help you—the student writer—come up with new ideas and draw on your experiences both to enrich the writing process and to improve the quality of its product.

COMMUNICATION TRIANGLE

The most basic guideline for writing is the communication triangle (Figure I.1). It identifies the four main components of writing: the *writer,* the *reader,* the *topic,* and the *message.*

FIGURE I.1

**Communica-
tion triangle**

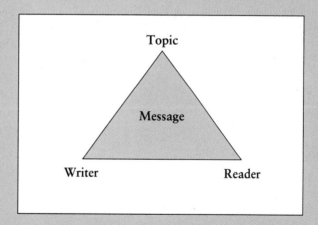

Each point of the triangle represents an important element of writing: the *writer,* the *reader,* and the *topic.* Inside the triangle is the central idea that the writer wants to communicate about the topic to the reader: the *message.*

The *writer* is you. As a writer, you bring all of your attitudes, experiences, observations, research, and, most importantly, *yourself* to the subject. Suppose your subject is civil rights. Your attitudes about civil rights are affected by the interactions you have had with other people, by what you have seen on television or at the movies, by what you have read. And you bring these attitudes to your writing.

In addition to your own attitudes and knowledge about civil rights, you have to look outside yourself and determine how your *reader* feels about the topic of civil rights. What are the reader's values? experiences? economic and social status? intellect? age? expectations? attitudes? For example, someone who grew up in a segregated rural community during the 1960s probably feels very differently about civil rights than does someone who grew up in an integrated middle-class suburb during the 1980s. What you know about the reader affects how you deal with the topic.

And because the *topic* is anything that has been thought, said, written, and believed about civil rights, you can't possibly write about, nor can your reader possibly understand, all the information there is on this topic. As a writer, then, with your reader in mind, you must determine what you want to say about the topic and how you will say it. From the process of selecting and limiting what you want to say comes your *message,* the central idea of your paper. The message is influenced by the three other elements of the communication triangle: the writer, the reader, and the topic.

WRITING AIMS

Each of the components of writing that make up the communication triangle is linked to one of the four primary purposes for writing: *to reflect, to inform, to persuade,* and *to speculate* (Figure I.2).

FIGURE I.2

Writing aims

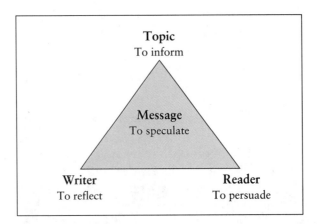

If you are writing a paper about your own experiences with and opinions on civil rights, the aim of the paper is *to reflect* (for example, retelling a personal experience with prejudice). If you emphasize the topic, your aim is *to inform* (describing different types of nonviolent demonstrations such as sit-ins, boycotts, or marches). If your emphasis is on the reader, your aim is *to persuade* (encouraging a campus organization to participate in Brotherhood Week). And if your chief focus is on the message or on possibilities—what might be or what might have been—your aim is *to speculate* (envisioning changes in civil rights over the next twenty years).

Writing to Reflect

The chief characteristic of reflective writing is self-expression. When you write to reflect, you want to share with others how you feel or think about a topic. You want to share impressions, ideas, or moments that are significant to you. Although you also may be informing or persuading your readers, your main focus is on you. Your thoughts, emotions, and experiences become the subject of the writing.

Personal experiences often are very private and often don't pertain to anyone but you. These private experiences are what you write about in your journal or in letters to close friends. You don't intend for them to be read by all people. When you're asked to write reflectively for a college assignment, however, you're being asked to share your experiences with a larger audience, usually to make a specific point. Reflective writing involves *recalling* a personal experience, *commenting* on that experience, and *providing* new insights about the significance of that experience to yourself and to others. Your comment on and the insights gained from your personal experiences can increase the understanding of your topic for a wider audience.

Writing to Reflect

Characteristics	*Examples*
Express self	Journal
Share personal experiences	Personal essay
	Autobiography
	Personal letter

An example of reflective writing is James Roberson's description of demonstrating against segregation in the mid-1950s. Roberson writes about the frustrations he felt in being forced to sit at the back of a bus simply because of his skin color and about the ways in which he and his friends dealt with that frustration.

The green sign on the Birmingham city buses was one of the most powerful pieces of wood in the city. It was about the size of a shoe box and fit into the holes on the back of the bus seats. On one side of the board it said "Colored, do not sit beyond this board." The bus driver had the authority to move that green board in any direction he wanted to at any time.

To give you an example, the bus might be headed for Collegeville in North Birmingham, where blacks lived. When the maids and chauffeurs and street sweepers—those were the jobs for blacks in those days—would get on the bus, they'd all be seated. In another mile, ten whites might get on. The driver would get the green board, move it, and the blacks would have to get up. A seventy-year old black person might have to move for a six-year-old white child.

A group of us formed a little club called the Eagles. When we would get on the buses, I would take the green sign and move it up or throw it away. I was a teenager, and that was my way of fighting the system.

Sometimes we would defy the green board. We would sit right behind the bus driver. You really had to imagine the driver as a cobra snake or a vicious dog, and you're treading on his territory. You know that if you move close to him, he's going to strike you. The driver would say, "All right, you niggers got to get up."

We'd say, "You talking to us?" There were guys who were like conductors and drove black plain cars. The bus driver would get off and call one of those guys. He would come on and say, "Get off or we're gonna call the law."

"So call them," we said. When he'd go to call, we'd get off the bus and disappear.

In this example Roberson is writing to reflect. He relies on personal memory to meet his objective: describing segregation on the Birmingham city buses and illustrating how he and others demonstrated against that segregation.

Writing to Inform

Another purpose for writing is to inform. When your purpose is primarily to report information, to explain a concept, or to describe an object, your writing is informative. The emphasis here is on the topic, not on the writer or the reader. News stories often are informative: their aim is to present facts and information objectively, without introducing reporters' opinions or personal experiences. The writers simply state the major events of an incident. Other examples of writing that informs are directions or explanations of how a computer or a satellite works. The

Writing to Reflect
Peer Response Questions

Once you have written a reflective draft, you can use the following questions to help evaluate your own work. You can also use the questions to guide your comments on a classmate's paper.

For the Writer

1. If you had twenty-four more hours to work on this paper, what changes would you make?

2. What questions do you have about your paper? Where would you like the group to focus its attention? Where do you feel you need the most direction?

For the Reader

1. State the main point of the paper in a single, concise statement. What in the paper leads you to that statement? What detracts from that statement?

2. How does the writer use details to recall and illustrate an event?

3. Where does the writer analyze that event? How is the event connected to the writer's main idea?

4. Where does the writer provide insights for the readers? How does the writer use a personal experience to make meaningful generalizations for readers?

5. Describe the insights you have gained about yourself by reading this essay.

6. Where do you get confused? Where do you want to know more? Know less?

7. Where do you think the writer has used effective examples or has written particularly well?

8. If this were your paper, what would you add? Delete?

characteristics of informative writing include accurate reporting; unbiased presentation; and clear, specific examples or explanations.

Writing to Inform

Characteristics	*Examples*
Report information	Newspaper article
Explain a concept	Research paper
Describe an object	Report of events
	Summary

Here is an example of writing that informs, from an article by Roxanne Brown. In her report, Brown describes Rosa Parks's refusal to move to the rear of a bus on December 1, 1955, in Montgomery, Alabama.

> After a long day at the Montgomery Fair department store where she worked as an assistant tailor, Mrs. Parks remained rooted to her seat when the driver of the bus she had taken home asked her to stand. The seat she was told to surrender to a White man was actually in the first row of the "colored section" of the bus. The White section was full, and, as was customary, Blacks were expected to give up their seats when White passengers boarded.
>
> Mrs. Parks was arrested for failure to comply with the city ordinance and fined $14. When E. D. Nixon, head of the state chapter of the NAACP, and her husband, Raymond Parks, came to bail her out, it was decided that this incident presented the perfect catalyst to launch a boycott of the public transportation system in Montgomery.

The author may have had personal experiences with segregation, but this writing does not recount those experiences or her opinions. Instead, Brown describes the circumstances that led to Parks's arrest and to the Montgomery bus boycott. Brown's writing is accurate, objective, clear, and specific—it's informative.

Writing to Persuade

Persuasive writing has its emphasis on the reader, not on the writer or the topic. Its purpose is to make the reader look at an issue differently or act in a particular way. Every element of persuasive writing—words, sentence structure, organization, examples—is specifically geared toward the reader. And writing to persuade can take many forms—advertisements, political cartoons, editorials, law reforms.

Writing to Inform
Peer Response Questions

Once you have written an informative draft, you can use the following questions to help evaluate your own work. You can also use the questions to guide your comments on a classmate's paper.

For the Writer

1. If you had only twenty-four hours to work on this paper, what changes would you make?

2. What questions do you have about your paper? Where would you like the group to focus its attention? Where do you feel you need the most direction?

For the Reader

1. Describe how the writer informs. Where does the writer report information; explain a concept; or describe an object, person, or situation?

2. Whom is the writer informing? Is the information geared for that audience? What other questions might that audience have that the writer has yet to anticipate or address?

3. Is the reporting complete and accurate? Where does the writer rely on statistics, opinions, examples, or authorities? Why is or why is this not effective?

4. Describe the type of knowledge the writer uses to inform. Does the writer use personal, indirect, researched knowledge or a combination? What is the most effective and why?

5. Has the writer provided an unbiased presentation? Where is there evidence of bias? Where is there evidence of objective presentation? How could the writer revise the biased elements?

6. Describe how the writer uses clear, specific examples and explanations.

7. Where do you get confused? Where do you want to know more? Know less?

8. Where do you think the writer has informed his or her audience or has written particularly well?

9. If this were your paper, what would you add? Delete?

When you write to persuade, you use one or a combination of three basic strategies: you use *reasoning* based on facts and statistics to move readers intellectually, you use *emotions* to make readers feel something strongly, or you use *values* to motivate readers with their sense of right and wrong.

Writing to Persuade

Characteristics	*Examples*
Influence readers' beliefs and actions	Advertisement
	Political speech
Appeal to readers' reason, emotions, or values	Sermon
	Editorial

One example of writing that persuades is a leaflet that was printed on the night of Rosa Parks's arrest. The leaflet called for a one-day boycott of the Montgomery bus system. The boycott lasted thirteen months.

Another Negro woman has been arrested and thrown in jail because she refused to get up out of her seat on the bus for a white person to sit down. It is the second time since the Claudette Colvin case that a Negro woman has been arrested for the same thing. This has to be stopped. Negroes have rights too, for if Negroes did not ride the buses, they could not operate. Three-fourths of the riders are Negroes, yet we are arrested, or have to stand over empty seats. If we do not do something to stop these arrests, they will continue. The next time it may be you, or your daughter, or mother. This woman's case will come up on Monday. We are, therefore, asking every Negro to stay off the buses Monday in protest of the arrest and trial. Don't ride the buses to work, to town, to school, or anywhere on Monday. You can afford to stay out of school for one day if you have no other way to go except by bus. You can also afford to stay out of town for one day. If you work, take a cab, or walk. But please, children and grownups, don't ride the bus at all on Monday. Please stay off of all buses Monday.

In this paragraph the writers use all three strategies of persuasive writing. First, they use *reasoning*. They state the facts of Parks's arrest and the earlier arrest of another woman, Claudette Colvin. They use *emotions*—in this case, fear—by suggesting that "the next time it may be you, or your daughter, or mother." And finally, the writers use *values* to persuade their readers that segregation is not right: "This has to be stopped. Negroes have rights too." When you write to persuade, you focus on your readers to influence their thinking or their actions by appealing to their intellect, their emotions, or their values.

Writing to Speculate

When you write to speculate, you are examining possibilities in the past, present, or future. You ask, What if . . . ? or What about . . . ? with regard to an issue or an idea. When you write to speculate, you use your imagination. Obviously, you can only guess how things would have turned out differently if the past or present could be changed, or what the future holds. But your speculations must be rooted in scientific evidence or human experience. You should be able to support what you're saying.

Writing to Speculate

Characteristics	Examples
Discuss past, present, and future possibilities	Proposal
Ask, What if . . . ? or What about . . . ?	Hypothetical situation or possibility
	Alternatives

An example of writing to speculate comes from Dr. Martin Luther King's famous "I Have a Dream" speech. He delivered the speech on August 28, 1963, at the Lincoln Memorial in Washington, D.C. In it, King talks about a world of peace, justice, and love.

> I say to you today, my friends, though, even though we face the difficulties of today and tomorrow, I still have a dream. It is a dream deeply rooted in the American dream. I have a dream that one day this nation will rise up, live out the true meaning of its creed: "We hold these truths to be self-evident, that all men are created equal."
>
> I have a dream that one day on the red hills of Georgia sons of former slaves and the sons of former slave-owners will be able to sit down together at the table of brotherhood. I have a dream that one day even the state of Mississippi, a state sweltering[1] with the heat of injustice, sweltering with the heat of oppression, will be transformed into an oasis of freedom and justice.
>
> I have a dream that my four little children will one day live in a nation where they will not be judged by the color of their skin but by

---

[1] **sweltering:** suffering from oppressive heat

Writing to Persuade
Peer Response Questions

Once you have written a persuasive draft, you can use the following questions to help evaluate your own work. You can also use the questions to guide your comments on a classmate's paper.

For the Writer
1. If you had twenty-four more hours to work on this paper, what changes would you make?

2. What questions do you have about your paper? Where would you like the group to focus its attention? Where do you feel you need the most direction?

For the Reader
1. Write a single, concise statement that accurately reflects the writer's position. (Be careful not to present your position—only the writer's position.) Where does the writer use a formal thesis statement or controlling idea to state that position?

2. Where does the writer use examples, statistics, scenarios, case studies, or authorities to convince you that his or her position is valid? Where does the writer need more specific support?

3. Does the writer explain other points of view that don't support her or his position? Where does the writer acknowledge other points of view? Has the writer acknowledged your own point of view? If not, what does the writer need to do?

4. Does the writer restate the primary reasons for his or her stance? Does this restatement show why this stance is desirable? Is this the best place in the paper for showing this stance? If not, where would you place it?

5. Where do you get confused? Where do you want to know more? Know less?

6. Where do you think the writer has used effective examples or has written particularly well?

7. If this were your paper, what would you add? Delete?

8. Has the writer persuaded you to consider her or his position? Has your position changed at all?

the content of their character. I have a dream . . . I have a dream that one day in Alabama, with its vicious racists, with its governor having his lips dripping with the words of interposition and nullification,[2] one day right there in Alabama little black boys and black girls will be able to join hands with little white boys and white girls as sisters and brothers.

Notice that while King speculates on what the future holds, he keeps in touch with the past and the present by referring to racial injustice in Mississippi and Alabama.

The four aims of writing often overlap. Rarely do you write just to reflect or just to inform or just to persuade or just to speculate. But the principles behind these aims can help you understand more fully *why* and *how* you write what you do. They can help you decide how best to meet your needs and those of the reader, topic, and message.

THE WRITING PROCESS

Writing is a process. It doesn't simply appear on the page, and when it is on the page, it doesn't always say what you want it to say. When you read newspapers, magazines, and textbooks, you see finished pieces of writing. You don't see the author sitting alone; struggling to get ideas on paper; experimenting with different words and examples; and slowly developing an essay, an article, or a chapter.

Annie Dillard, a talented contemporary essayist, explains in her book *The Writing Life* (1989) that writing is hard work and that it takes time:

> It takes years to write a book—between two and ten years. . . . Out of a human population on earth of four and a half billion, perhaps twenty people can write a book in a year. Some people lift cars, too. Some people enter week-long sled-dog races, go over Niagara Falls in barrels, fly planes through the Arc de Triomphe. Some people feel no pain in childbirth. Some people eat cars. There is no call to take human extremes as norms.
>
> Writing a book, full time, takes between two and ten years. The long poem, John Berryman said, takes between five and ten years. Thomas Mann was a prodigy of production. Working full time, he wrote a page a day. That is 365 pages a year, for he did write every

---

[2] **interposition and nullification:** state and local authorities' disregard for federal laws that protect civil rights

Writing to Speculate
Peer Response Questions

Once you have written a speculative draft, you can use the following questions to help evaluate your own work. You can also use the questions to guide your comments on a classmate's paper.

For the Writer
1. If you had twenty-four more hours to work on this paper, what changes would you make?

2. What questions do you have about your paper? Where would you like the group to focus its attention? Where do you feel you need the most direction?

For the Reader
1. What position or claim does the writer make about a specific possibility?

2. What assumptions does the writer make about the issue? About the reader? Explain whether those assumptions are valid.

3. Where in the paper does the writer use reasons to encourage the reader to consider a specific possibility?

4. What types of evidence and knowledge does the writer draw upon? Is it personal, indirect, or researched knowledge? How does the evidence support the writer's position?

5. Describe any other issues or assumptions about this position that you feel the writer should consider before revising.

6. Where do you get confuesd? Where do you want to know more? Know less?

7. Where are places you think the writer has used effective examples or has written particularly well?

8. If this were your paper, what would you add? Delete?

day—a good-sized book a year. At a page a day, he was one of the most prolific writers who ever lived. Flaubert wrote steadily, with only the usual, appalling strains. For twenty-five years he finished a big book every five to seven years. My guess is that full-time writers average a book every five years; seventy-three usable pages a year, or a usable fifth of a page a day. . . . On plenty of days the writer can write three or four pages, and on plenty of other days he concludes he must throw them away.

Dillard is not trying to frighten you. She wants you to know that writing is challenging, that words don't explode onto the page or monitor in polished form. Writing is a process, and the output at any stage of that process is going to be different from the output at the other stages. Moreover, the writing process is different for most people.

Prewriting is the planning stage of the writing process. In this stage you determine why you're writing, what you're going to write about, and how you're going to support your thesis. In the prewriting stage, you gather the information you are going to need as you write. The prewriting stage prepares you to begin the actual writing.

In the *drafting* stage, you begin to write words and examples on paper or to type them on a keyboard. People draft differently. A fortunate few are able to draft their ideas simply, effortlessly, and clearly. But most of us end up with a product in need of correction. That's OK. In the drafting stage you are supposed to put ideas and examples on paper without worrying about whether your writing is grammatically correct or well organized. A messy draft can be changed later in the writing process. Right now, you want to get the ideas from the prewriting stage onto paper or computer monitor.

Rewriting is the fix-it stage of the writing process, the point at which you examine the draft to determine what works well and what needs strengthening. In this stage you check that what you've written does what it's supposed to do (reflect, inform, persuade, speculate); addresses a specific audience; is organized logically; and expresses your thoughts clearly. Rewriting transforms the writer-based draft (written to get the writer's ideas on paper) to a reader-based draft (written to meet the reader's needs).

Editing is the polishing stage of the writing process. In this stage you check that sentences are grammatically sound, that words are spelled correctly, that punctuation is used correctly. Don't try to edit as you draft. If you're worrying about right and wrong, you may not get your ideas down—and that's the purpose of drafting. Editing is the final stage of the writing process. It's here that correctness counts.

The writing process doesn't always follow these stages in sequence. For instance, as you draft or rewrite, you may realize that an example doesn't work the way you'd like it to, so you go back to the prewriting stage to generate more ideas. Or in the prewriting stage, you may stop to look up a word in the dictionary, something usually done in the editing stage. Or while you're drafting, you may decide to rewrite a sentence before going on. Generally, however, the writing process moves progressively from prewriting to drafting, from drafting to rewriting, and from rewriting to editing.

Now, with a brief explanation of the communication triangle (writer, reader, topic, message), of the writing aims (to reflect, to inform, to persuade, to speculate), and of the writing process (prewriting, drafting, rewriting, editing), you are ready to begin your first writing assignment. You can do it. Good luck!

Chapter 1

WORK

——◆◆——

Five days a week, fifty weeks a year, five hundred weeks each decade. Work is the most time-consuming activity of adult life. We spend more time working than we do with family and friends, in our community or church, or at play.

To prepare for this chapter's theme, work, answer the following questions:

- How does work influence people's lives?
- How do people's attitudes about work affect their performance on the job?

READINGS on *Work*

Nonnie's Day
Mary E. Mebane

Mary E. Mebane describes growing up in North Carolina in Mary: An Autobiography *(1981) and in* Mary, Wayfarer. *In the following selection, Mebane recounts the routine of her mother's daily work at a tobacco factory and at home.*

Nonnie led a structured, orderly existence. Before six o'clock in the morning, she was up, starting her day. First she turned on WPTF and listened to the news and the weather and the music. Later, when WDNC in Durham hired Norfleet Whitted, the first black announcer in the area, she listened first to one station, then to the other. Some mornings it would be "They Traced Her Little Footprints in the Snow," and other mornings it would be black gospel-singing and rhythm-and-blues. Then she would make a fire in the wood stove and start her breakfast. She prepared some meat—fried liver pudding or fatback, or a streak-of-fat streak-of-lean—and made a hoecake of bread on top of the stove, which she ate with either Karo syrup or homemade blackberry preserves, occasionally with store-bought strawberry preserves, or sometimes with homemade watermelon-rind preserves that she had canned in the summer. Then she would drink her coffee, call me to get up, and leave the house in her blue uniform, blue apron, and blue cap—it would still be dark when she left on winter mornings—and go to catch her ride to the tobacco factory (with Mr. Ralph Baldwin at first, and then, when he retired, with Mr. James Yergan). When Miss Delilah still lived in Wildwood, before she and Mr. Leroy separated, she would come by and call from the road and the two of them would walk together to the end of the road near the highway and wait for Mr. Ralph there.

My job after she left was to see that the fire didn't go out in the wood stove, to see that the pots sitting on the back didn't burn—for in them was our supper, often pinto beans or black-eyed peas or collard greens or turnip salad. Occasionally there was kale or mustard greens or cressy salad. The other pot would have the meat, which most often was neck bones or pig feet or pig ears, and sometimes spareribs. These would cook until it was time for me to go to school; then I would let the fire die down, only to relight it when I came home to let the pots finish cooking.

After Nonnie left, I also had the task of getting Ruf Junior up so that he could get to school on time. This presented no problem to me until Ruf Junior was in high school and started playing basketball. Often he would travel with the team to schools in distant towns, sometimes getting home after midnight, and the next morning he would be tired and sleepy and wouldn't want to get up. I sympathized, but I had my job to do. If I let him oversleep, I knew that Nonnie would fuss when she got home. But on the other hand, no matter how often I called to him, he would murmur sleepily, "All right, all right," then go back to sleep. I solved this problem one bitter-cold winter morning. I jerked all the covers off his bed and ran. I knew that the only place he could get warm again would be in the kitchen. (The only fire was in the wood stove.) The fire was already out, so he'd have to make one. After that, I didn't have such a hard time getting him up.

My mother worked as a cutter, clipping the hard ends of each bundle of   4
tobacco before it was shredded to make cigarettes. At noon she ate the lunch she had brought from home in a brown paper bag: a biscuit with meat in it and a sweet potato or a piece of pie or cake. Some of the women ate in the cafeteria, but in her thirty years at the Liggett and Myers factory, she never once did. She always took her lunch. Then she worked on until closing time, caught her ride back to Wildwood, and started on the evening's activities. First she had supper, which I had finished preparing from the morning. After I got older we sometimes had meat other than what had to be prepared in a "pot." It would be my duty to fry chicken or prepare ham bits and gravy.

After supper, she'd read the Durham *Sun* and see to it that we did the   5
chores if we hadn't done them already: slop the hogs, feed the chickens, get in the wood for the next day. Then we were free. She'd get her blue uniform ready for the next day, then listen to the radio. No later than nine o'clock, she would be in bed. In the morning she would get up, turn on the radio, and start frying some fatback. Another day would have started.

Questions and Issues to Consider

Writing Process   1. Mebane uses specific details to describe her own and her mother's day. Without looking back at the essay, list several details you remember most clearly. Why are these details memorable?

2. Mebane organizes the events of her essay in chronological order. Explain why she uses this organization.

Aims of Writing   3. Mebane writes to reflect. She focuses on her own memories to make a point. But nowhere does she specifically state what her point is. What possible point can she be making about her own life? about her mother's? about work?

Critical Thinking   4. Mebane writes that her mother kept up her daily routine for thirty years. Explain why people stay in the same job year after year.

Why I Quit the Company
Tomoyuki Iwashita

———

Tomoyuki Iwashita was hired for a prestigious position by a well-respected Japanese corporation immediately after graduating from the university. He describes the working conditions that led to his quitting. He is now a journalist in Tokyo.

When I tell people that I quit working for the company after only a year,   1
most of them think I'm crazy. They can't understand why I would want to
give up a prestigious and secure job. But I think I'd have been crazy to stay, and
I'll try to explain why.

I started working for the company immediately after graduating from uni-   2
versity. It's a big, well-known trading company with about 6,000 employees
all over the world. There's a lot of competition to get into this and other similar companies, which promise young people a wealthy and successful future. I
was set on course to be a Japanese "yuppie."

I'd been used to living independently as a student, looking after myself   3
and organizing my own schedule. As soon as I started working all that changed.
I was given a room in the company dormitory, which is like a fancy hotel, with
a twenty-four-hour hot bath service and all meals laid on. Most single company employees live in a dormitory like this, and many married employees
live in company apartments. The dorm system is actually a great help because
living in Tokyo costs more than young people earn—but I found it stifling.

My life rapidly became reduced to a shuffle between the dorm and the   4
office. The working day is officially eight hours, but you can never leave the
office on time. I used to work from nine in the morning until eight or nine at
night, and often until midnight. Drinking with colleagues[1] after work is part of
the job; you can't say no. The company building contained cafeterias, shops,
a bank, a post office, a doctor's office, a barber's. . . . I never needed to leave
the building. Working, drinking, sleeping, and standing on a horribly crowded
commuter train for an hour and a half each way: This was my life. I spent all
my time with the same colleagues; when I wasn't involved in entertaining
clients on the weekend, I was expected to play golf with my colleagues. I soon
lost sight of the world outside the company.

This isolation is part of the brainwashing process. A personnel manager   5
said: "We want excellent students who are active, clever, and tough. Three
months is enough to train them to be devoted businessmen." I would hear my
colleagues saying: "I'm not making any profit for the company, so I'm not con-

———

[1]**colleagues:** co-workers

tributing." Very few employees claim all the overtime pay due to them. Keeping an employee costs the company 50 million yen ($400,000) a year, or so the company claims. Many employees put the company's profits before their own mental and physical well-being.

Overtiredness and overwork leave you little energy to analyze or criticize   6
your situation. There are shops full of "health drinks," cocktails of caffeine and other drugs, which will keep you going even when you're exhausted. *Karoshi* (death from overwork) is increasingly common and is always being discussed in the newspapers. I myself collapsed from working too hard. My boss told me: "You should control your health; it's your own fault if you get sick." There is no paid sick leave; I used up half of my fourteen days' annual leave because of sickness.

We had a labor union, but it seemed to have an odd relationship with the   7
management. A couple of times a year I was told to go home at five o'clock. The union representatives were coming around to investigate working hours; everyone knew in advance. If it was "discovered" that we were all working overtime in excess of fifty hours a month our boss might have had some problem being promoted; and our prospects would have been affected. So we all pretended to work normal hours that day.

The company also controls its employees' private lives. Many company   8
employees under thirty are single. They are expected to devote all their time to the company and become good workers; they don't have time to find a girl-friend. The company offers scholarships to the most promising young employees to enable them to study abroad for a year or two. But unmarried people who are on these courses are not allowed to get married until they have completed the course! Married employees who are sent to train abroad have to leave their families in Japan for the first year.

In fact, the quality of married life is often determined by the husband's   9
work. Men who have just gotten married try to go home early for a while, but soon have to revert[2] to the norm of late-night work. They have little time to spend with their wives and even on the weekend are expected to play golf with colleagues. Fathers cannot find time to communicate with their children and child rearing is largely left to mothers. Married men posted abroad will often leave their family behind in Japan; they fear that their children will fall behind in the fiercely competitive Japanese education system.

Why do people put up with this? They believe this to be a normal working   10
life or just cannot see an alternative. Many think that such personal sacrifices are necessary to keep Japan economically successful. Perhaps, saddest of all, Japan's education and socialization[3] processes do not equip people with the intellectual and spiritual resources to question and challenge the status quo. They stamp out even the desire for a different kind of life.

---

[2]**revert:** return
[3]**socialization:** adapting to a culture or society

However, there are some signs that things are changing. Although many   11
new employees in my company were quickly brainwashed, many others, like
myself, complained about life in the company and seriously considered leaving. But most of them were already in fetters[4]—of debt. Pleased with themselves for getting into the company and anticipating a life of executive luxury,
these new employees throw their money around. Every night they are out
drinking. They buy smart clothes and take a taxi back to the dormitory after the
last train has gone. They start borrowing money from the bank and soon they
have a debt growing like a snowball rolling down a slope. The banks demand
no security for loans; it's enough to be working for a well-known company.
Some borrow as much as a year's salary in the first few months. They can't
leave the company while they have such debts to pay off.   12

I was one of the few people in my intake of employees who didn't get into
debt. I left the company dormitory after three months to share an apartment
with a friend. I left the company exactly one year after I entered it. It took me a
while to find a new job, but I'm working as a journalist now. My life is still
busy, but it's a lot better than it was. I'm lucky because nearly all big Japanese
companies are like the one I worked for, and conditions in many small companies are even worse.

It's not easy to opt out of a life-style that is generally considered to be pres-   13
tigious and desirable, but more and more young people in Japan are thinking
about doing it. You have to give up a lot of superficially[5] attractive material benefits in order to preserve the quality of your life and your sanity. I don't think I
was crazy to leave the company. I think I would have gone crazy if I'd stayed.

Questions and Issues to Consider

Writing Process   1. Iwashita uses specific examples to describe his experience. List at
least three specific details he uses to illustrate his position that "the
company also controls its employees' private lives."

2. Iwashita organizes his essay according to ideas and not according to
chronological order. Some ideas include isolation, overwork, and
labor unions. List three other ideas Iwashita uses to direct his writing.

Aims of Writing   3. Iwashita writes to inform. Although he uses personal experience as
a basis for his discussion, what else besides his own experience does
Iwashita use to explain his ideas?

---

[4]**fetters:** chains
[5]**superficially:** not meaningful

Critical Thinking   4. Iwashita quit his job at great personal cost. Describe your desire or actual decision to quit a job you once had.

PREWRITING

MAKING A LIST

Sometimes you know right away what you intend to write about. Usually, however, you have to work to come up with an idea. There is no foolproof method for finding a topic, but one that can help is making a list.

Set aside a short amount of time (say fifteen minutes), relax, and do the following:

1. On a sheet of paper, write the statement *I am interested in*_____ or *I've always dreamed of working as a* _____. Then begin to list anything that comes to mind. Don't stop to wonder whether something is a good idea. The purpose is to write as long a list as possible. Be as free, as imaginative, as nonjudgmental as possible.

    Here's an example. A student, Joann, already has decided that she's interested in the general topic of work. She lists every idea that comes to her in five minutes. Below is just a sample of her list:

Working at a diner	Work values
Working as a babysitter	Life without work
Working through college	Job hunting
Working on the farm	Physical labor
Working at home	Mental labor
Mr. McDougall's unemployment	No job skills
Effects on the McDougall family	No job opportunities
Effects on Mr. McDougall	Reasons for working
Who helps the McDougalls	Why my family works

2. After five minutes of listing, stop and read each item. Circle the items you feel you have the most experience with through personal, indirect, or researched knowledge. *Personal knowledge* is based on your own experience; *indirect knowledge* is learned from another's

experiences; *researched knowledge* is information from other sources (books, newspapers, magazines, interviews). Joann reviews her list and determines that she's most interested in and has had the most experience with three possibilities:

Unemployment and the McDougall family

Work values

Working through college

3. Now put the list away for several hours. When you look at the list again, simply pick one of the topics you've circled—the topic you're most interested in or most knowledgeable about.

For example, Joann likes all three topics. She has had indirect experience with unemployment because of her neighbor's recent lay-off. Also she is working part-time while she is in college. But Joann feels strongly that values are learned through work, so she decides to write about work values.

EXPLORING YOUR OPTIONS

1. Complete one of the two following statements:

a. I am interested in _____

_____

b. I've always dreamed of working as a(n) _____

_____

2. Using your completed statement, quickly list twenty ideas or items that come to mind.

_____   _____

_____   _____

_____   _____

_____   _____

_____   _____

_____   _____
_____   _____
_____   _____
_____   _____

3. Circle the items you feel you have the most interest in and experience with through personal, indirect, or researched knowledge.

4. From the circled items, choose the three topics you're most interested in and have some knowledge about. _____

_____

_____

5. Select one topic and explain why you have chosen it. _____

_____

_____

WRITING TOGETHER

1. Share your topic ideas with someone else. The simple act of telling someone about your topic ideas can help focus your thinking.

2. With that person, make a list of details or examples that relate to your possible topics.

3. With your partner, identify the subject you have the most interest in and experience with through personal, indirect, or researched knowledge.

LIMITING A TOPIC

Now that you have a topic, you have to decide what you want to say about it. One of the most common mistakes students make is choosing a topic that is too broad. The broader the topic, the more work you have to do to develop the idea fully. For example, suppose you choose to write on the topic *unemployment*. Hundreds of books have been written about unemployment and its effects, and you cannot, nor do you want to, read all of them. You also cannot write everything you know about the topic because time is limited. So you have to determine exactly what you want to say about unemployment.

1. To help limit your topic, make another list. This time write your general topic—for instance, *Unemployment*—at the top of the page.

2. Write down anything that comes to mind about your general topic. Again, don't worry about whether something is a good idea. The purpose is to make as long a list as possible.

3. After several minutes, stop and read over the list. Circle the items you feel you have the most experience with through personal, indirect, and researched knowledge. Here's an example:

General Topic: Unemployment

Jobless people	Church work with unemployed
Displaced workers	Food relief
Children of unemployed	
Unemployment insurance	Unemployment in the community
Reasons for losing jobs	Job vacancies
Transient workers	Social workers and unemployed
Unemployment in state	
Labor supply	Work sharing
Seasonal unemployment	President's reactions
Effects on family	Right to labor
Technological reasons	Plant shutdowns
Social stigma	Unemployment and inflation
Unemployment/homelessness	Regional unemployment
Job searches	Effects on marriages

4. Suppose you decide to write about unemployment in the community. What are you going to say? Where do you go from here? It's

time to make yet another list. At the top of the page, write *Unemployment in the Community* and three column headings for the different types of knowledge (personal, indirect, and researched). Then list as many ideas under each category as you can.

Limited Topic: Unemployment in the Community

Personal	*Indirect*	*Researched*
Dad's layoff	Other workers' layoffs	Local newspapers
Financial effects	Church relief	Mayor's interview
Physical effects	Store owner's reactions	Boss's interview
Emotional effects	Neighbors' reactions	Social workers
Effects on marriage	Seasonal workers	Government statistics

5. Now look over the list and choose one aspect of unemployment in the community—let's say the financial effects. Your topic—what you're going to write about—is the financial effects of unemployment in the community.

Now you have a topic. But what about the other elements of the communication triangle? What do you want to say about the topic (the writer)? How should you say it (the reader)? Why are you saying it (the message)?

6. Go back to the list of personal, indirect, and researched knowledge you generated to find your final topic. What you are looking for is material—examples and details—to support the topic. Put a checkmark next to the ideas that you would like to use in your writing, or make a new list (again, set up three columns, one for each type of knowledge). For example, from the list above, you might choose to describe the impact of your father's layoff on your family's spending patterns (personal knowledge), to examine how your neighbors have tightened their belts since they've lost their jobs (indirect knowledge), or to quote material from a newspaper article about boarded-up shops on Main Street (researched knowledge).

7. Make a list of what you think are your readers' attitudes toward and experiences with the financial effects of unemployment in the community. As you examine your readers' needs, your expectations about the kinds of examples you'll use may change.

8. From your lists of support material and readers' attitudes and experiences, decide why you're writing this paper. Is your purpose to reflect? to inform? to persuade? to speculate?

9. If your final topic anticipates your readers' needs and allows you to meet your objective for writing, it is sufficiently limited. You may want to expand it or narrow it further once you begin writing, but for now your topic is focused enough to let you start writing.

Let's go back to Joann. Remember that she chose the general topic *work values*. To limit that topic, she makes a list of things she has learned from working. Among them are the following:

Working with others	Learning responsibility
Working honestly	Working when inconvenient
Working independently	Commitments to self
Working toward goals	Commitments to others
Gaining experience	Earning money

From this list, Joann chooses her limited topic: how working can encourage personal responsibility. She feels comfortable with this topic and decides not to limit it further.

To support this limited topic, Joann lists examples of personal, indirect, and researched knowledge:

Personal	*Indirect*	*Researched*
Dad's boots	Mom's work	Interview Mr. Shyu
Lisa's chores	Dad's work	Interview workers
Golf balls	Roxanne's work	Conduct survey

In the process of listing examples of how work can encourage personal responsibility, Joann remembers her experience cleaning her father's boots to earn fifty cents. Recognizing the value of that work in learning responsibility, she decides to write on that experience. Because she's relying on personal experience, the primary purpose of her writing is to reflect. (A draft of Joann's paper begins on page 36.)

✓ CHECKLIST: DISCOVERING A TOPIC

1. Is the topic meaningful to you?

2. Do you have experience with or know something about the topic?

3. Is your experience with the topic personal, indirect, or researched?

4. Does your topic meet your readers' needs?

5. Does your topic fulfill your writing's purpose?

6. Is your topic sufficiently limited?

EXPLORING YOUR OPTIONS

1. Choose one of the three topics you circled on page 22 or listed on page 23.

   _____

2. Using your chosen topic, quickly list eight ideas or items that come to mind.

   _____   _____

   _____   _____

   _____   _____

   _____   _____

3. Select one of the eight items from the list above that you want to explore further.

   _____

4. List eight ideas that occur to you about that single item.

   _____   _____

   _____   _____

   _____   _____

   _____   _____

5. Select one of the ideas above that interests you about your topic.

   _____

6. Describe a personal experience you've had with this idea or topic.

   _____

   _____

7. Describe an indirect experience you've had with this idea or topic.

   _____

   _____

8. Describe a type of research this idea or topic may require.

   _____

   _____

9. You have taken a general topic and, by making lists, have focused both your thinking and your examples. Now write your paper's limited topic.

   _____

DRAFTING

NONSTOP WRITING

Now that you have a topic that interests you, a list of ideas and experiences to choose from, a sense of your readers' needs, and an understanding of why you're writing, it's time to write. Remember that the purpose of the drafting process is to get your ideas on paper. Don't worry about organization, punctuation, complete sentences, spelling, or anything else that could frustrate you as you write. You can make revisions later. Right now you want to limber up your mind by writing nonstop.

Nonstop writing helps you warm up to the writing process and develop thoughts and examples. It also gives you no-risk writing practice.

To do nonstop writing, set aside, say, fifteen to twenty minutes. A time limit is important. You have to know that this is not going to take you hours of painstaking work. You're going to work only for a short time.

Next, at the top of a sheet of paper, write the limited topic you've chosen and the list of personal, indirect, and researched experiences you've developed. For example, if you are planning to write about the financial effects of unemployment in the community, you would write that topic at the top of the page. Below the topic you would list your personal examples (your Dad's layoff), your indirect examples (your neighbor's reactions), and your researched examples (from local newspapers). (If your example list is long, don't bother rewriting it. Just keep the original close at hand.)

Now start to write, incorporating as much of the list as you can into your writing. Don't stop to think; just keep your fingers moving. If you get stuck, don't go back to read what you've written. Instead, keep writing the last word over and over until another idea comes—it will—and then keep writing. The only thing you should be worrying about is writing as much as you can. Don't worry about what you're writing. Write nonstop.

When your time is up, take a much deserved break. You've just finished what for most people is the most intimidating part of the process. You now have a draft full of ideas and examples. Admittedly the writing needs work, but you have something to work with—and that's a significant accomplishment.

EXPLORING YOUR OPTIONS

1. Set aside a block of time for writing nonstop.

2. Write your limited topic on the line below.

_____

3. Write the topic at the top of a blank page or screen.

4. Place your list of personal, indirect, and researched experiences nearby for easy reference.

5. Write nonstop on your topic for the set time. Don't try to control your thinking, and don't worry about organization, punctuation, complete sentences, or spelling.

WRITING WITH COMPUTERS

Write nonstop on the computer with the monitor screen turned off. The blank screen helps you not worry about organization, punctuation, complete sentences, or spelling. You're writing nonstop to explore ideas and experiences.

NARRATION

Chances are that when you write nonstop, you intuitively use the most common informal pattern of organization in writing—narration, a straightforward description of events. Of course, there should be a reason why you are describing events. You must learn how, when, and where to use narration in your writing.

How to Organize Narration

Narration describes a sequence of events. It answers questions like these: What happened? What is happening? What will happen? When did it happen? Where did it happen? A narration should be organized in chronological order: You describe what happens first, second, third, until you come to the end of the series of events. Focus only on those events that meet the objectives of your paper and the needs of your readers. Give your readers only what they need to know; omit the rest.

When to Use Narration

Narration can be used to illustrate a point, support an idea, demonstrate a principle, or explain a procedure. Use narration when you want your readers to know that you have had personal experience with the topic.

Where to Use Narration

Narration can be used at any point in a paper. You can use an extended narration of an event as a writing's primary organization, or you can incorporate a shorter narration within a section or a paragraph.

Narration: An Example

In the following paragraph, Jane Jacobs narrates the events that take place each morning outside her home. Notice how she organizes the paragraph in chronological order.

Sidewalk Ballet

The stretch of Hudson Street where I live is each day the scene of an intricate sidewalk ballet. I make my own first entrance into it a little after eight when I put out the garbage can, surely a prosaic occupation, but I enjoy my part, my little clang, as the droves of junior high school students walk by the center of the stage dropping candy wrappers. (How do they eat so much candy so early in the morning?) While I sweep up the wrappers I watch the other rituals of morning: Mr. Halpert unlocking the laundry's handcart from its mooring to a cellar door, Joe Comacchia's son-in-law stacking out the empty crates from the delicatessen, the barber bringing out his sidewalk folding chair, Mr. Goldstein arranging the coils of wire which proclaim the hardware store is open, the wife of the tenement's superintendent depositing her chunky three-year-old with a toy mandolin on the stoop, the vantage point from which he is learning the English his mother cannot speak. Now the primary children, heading for St. Luke's, dribble through to the south; the children for St. Veronica's cross, heading to the west, and the children for P.S. 41, heading toward the east. Two new entrances are being made from the wings: well-dressed and even elegant women and men with brief cases emerge from doorways and side streets. Most of these are heading for the bus and subways, but some hover on the curbs, stopping taxis which have miraculously appeared at the right moment, for the taxis are part of a wider morning ritual: having dropped passengers from midtown in the downtown financial district, they are now bringing downtowners up to midtown. Simultaneously, numbers of women in housedresses have emerged and as they crisscross with one another they pause for quick conversations that sound with either laughter or joint indignation, never, it seems, anything between. It is time for me to hurry to work too, and I exchange my ritual farewell with Mr. Lofaro, the short, thick-bodied, white-aproned fruit man who stands outside his doorway a little up the street, his arms folded, his feet planted, looking solid as earth itself. We nod; we each glance quickly up and down the street, then look back to each other and smile. We have done this many a morning for more than ten years, and we both know what it means: All is well.

PRACTICE   1. List the sequence of the major events in the paragraph, from the author's "entrance" each morning to the farewell smile.

_____

_____

_____

_____

_____

_____

_____

_____

2. Could the sequence be rearranged? Explain your answer.

_____

_____

_____

✓ CHECKLIST: NARRATION

1. Are the events in your narration in the correct sequence?

2. Does your narration include only necessary events? Have you deleted unimportant events? Have you added important ones?

3. Does the narration help clarify the purpose of the paper and your central idea?

Narration and Aims

As the following writing assignments suggest, narration can be used to meet any of the objectives of writing.

Reflect

Narrate an incident that occurred on your first day at work. Explain how that event taught you something about yourself, your co-workers, or the world.

Recall a task on the job that initially seemed too difficult to accomplish. Describe the task and explain what you have learned from it.

Inform

Write an informative article for the school paper on sexual harassment in the workplace. Give a concrete example of sexual harassment perhaps by briefly describing a specific situation in which a manager keeps asking an employee for a date after the employee has declared no interest in dating.

For an article about job hunting, recount the major steps a recent graduate in your field took to find a job.

Persuade

Persuade an employer to allow flexible work schedules by narrating workers' accounts of long rides during morning and evening rush hours.

Persuade a worker to change a careless work practice by describing the possible consequences of that practice.

Speculate

Speculate on the type of work a great-grandparent did as a child to help at home by describing what may have been his or her chores on a typical day.

Imagine that because of a layoff, you've been out of work for a year. Describe how this experience would affect you and your family.

EXPLORING YOUR OPTIONS

1. Locate an example of narration in your nonstop-writing draft. Briefly describe the content of that narration.

_____

_____

_____

2. Put a checkmark next to the principal aim of your narration.

_____ To reflect   _____ To persuade

_____ To inform   _____ To speculate

3. Explain how the narration helps fulfill your purpose for writing.

_____

_____

_____

WRITING TOGETHER

1. Identify an example of narration from your nonstop writing.

2. Share the incident with two of your classmates by narrating the experience rather than by reading from your nonstop writing.

3. Notice and list the additional details and explanations you provide as your classmates listen and ask you questions about the experience.

4. Rewrite your narration by incorporating some of the new information you shared with your listeners.

REWRITING

REVIEWING

After you have written a draft, sit back and look at it objectively to see what additional information you need in order to clarify, support, or strengthen the purpose of the paper. Of course, being objective about your own paper is difficult: you already have invested a lot of time and energy in your writing. But you have to distance yourself to uncover the paper's strengths and weaknesses.

Here are steps to help you review your writing more objectively.

1. Set the writing aside for a day or two. The longer you are away from it, the more objective you will be when you go back to it. If your schedule doesn't allow you the luxury of waiting a couple of days, simply set the work aside for as long as you can, even an hour or two.

2. Review the list of your readers' attitudes, experiences, and knowledge that you developed while prewriting. Now read the paper from your readers' points of view. How do you think they are going to respond to your writing?

3. Read your paper again, looking only at your examples. Mark each example you use to illustrate or support your central idea. For example, Joann Tanner has marked three aspects she likes about her essay "Hard-Earned Money" (page 36): the way she establishes in the first paragraph her childhood desire to earn money, the good narrative example of the work involved in polishing her father's boots to earn money, and her use of personal initiative to creatively find ways to earn money.

   After you mark the examples in your paper, write different examples to illustrate the same points. Although this requires more thinking and writing, you'll end up with more options to choose from. Now decide which examples are the most effective.

4. Mark sentences, paragraphs, and sections that make you feel uncomfortable, that you think are weak. Don't try to fix them all at once; just mark them. (For instance, Joann marks the first sentence as a weak beginning for her essay. She also doesn't feel comfortable with her last paragraph because it doesn't specifically explain how her childhood experiences of earning money have continued to influence her as an adult.) Then, for each marked sentence, write two or three different sentences. Choose the sentence that best supports your paper's purpose or that best meets your readers' needs.

5. Read your draft and in *one sentence* describe the central idea you want to communicate to your readers. Read that sentence several times before you reread your draft. Then, with that idea firmly in mind, decide what to leave out and what to keep in your draft. Whatever does not advance your paper's central idea goes; whatever moves your meaning forward stays.

The more distance you have from your writing, the easier it is to uncover the writing's strengths and weaknesses. Distance gives you the time to generate new ideas for strengthening your writing.

STUDENT ESSAY

Below is the draft of Joann Tanner's essay. Joann is a mother and a returning student from Alberta, Canada, majoring in psychology. As you read the draft, ask two basic questions:

- How does Joann succeed in fulfilling her purpose for writing this essay?
- How can Joann strengthen this draft?

Hard-Earned Money

Joann provides background information that sets up her paper's topic.

weak opening sentence

Sometimes I chuckle at the thought of the things that made me happy as a child. Back then true happiness was a tightly gripped quarter in hand that could be spent on anything I wanted at the corner store. Looking back quarters were not like the quarters of today. They actually bought something. With a quarter, I could purchase enough candy to fill a brown paper lunch bag to the brim. Oh, how my mouth would water for that sweet candy. How excited I would feel as I carefully scanned the shelves for just the right morsels! Cigar bubble gum was my favorite, and it didn't take long for the whole cigar to enter my mouth, bulging my cheek, making it almost impossible to speak coherently. Yes, a quarter could buy me a great deal of candy or gum. Unfortunately, getting the quarter was the hard part. Quarters just didn't get handed out in my home. I had to figure out different methods to earn my money.

establishes childhood desire for money

Dad always seemed to supply one possible job a month. I'll never forget his muddy cowboy boots left outside the door. At the very sight of the thickly caked boots, I could envision the money I

Joann narrates an incident that illustrates her willingness to work hard for money.

would make. I didn't see dirty leather but silver. It became my job to clean the monstrous boots. Scrubbing and polishing them to meet my dad's standard was hard work. By the time I finished, my small red hands ached so much I could barely hold the cloth. Yet, satisfied that I had made every inch shine, I would proudly show my finished product to my dad. His eyes twinkled, and a warm smile would cross his face as his hand would slide deep down into his pocket, rummaging around for two quarters. Although my hands ached, it was at those moments that I learned the value of money.

good narrative example

As my appreciation for the value of money grew, so did my instinct for finding money-earning opportunities. I had an older sister who loved dodging her responsibilities at home--especially the days she worked at the local cafe. On those days, she primped endlessly in front of the mirror, and I knew if I hung around her until our chores were assigned, nine times out of ten she would offer me a quarter to do her job.

Joann uses details here to illustrate her initiative in earning money.

Many times I used my own initiative to earn money. Saturdays were the most profitable. Early in the mornings, with my gunny sack flung over my shoulder, I would head out for the ditches. These were thickly overgrown ditches that surrounded a beautiful golf course. For a ten year old, they were like a jungle. The grass was so tall it would sometimes brush my shoulders as I hunted for anything of value. Luckily for me, the ditch was a dumping ground for long-necked beer bottles, pop bottles, and, of course, golf balls. Each item I could find brought in a whole nickel at Kelly's Corner Store. From eight in the morning until early afternoon, I endlessly scoured the ditches. I seemed to have the strength of an adult as I slowly dragged the full sack to the corner store, anticipating my bubble gum cigars.

good examples of initiative

She concludes by explaining the significance of these experiences in her life.

Over the years, I have come to value highly my money-making experiences. They taught me that

there is a delicate balance between the opportunities that our parents give us and our own initiative. If my parents had supplied me with all the
money I desired, or all the jobs with which to
earn the money, I would have never learned to use
my own initiative. I'm glad I was a child who recognized the value of hard-earned money.

✓ CHECKLIST: REVIEWING

1. Have you distanced yourself from your writing?

2. Have you read your paper from your readers' points of view?

3. Have you marked examples that support your topic?

4. Have you marked words, sentences, or paragraphs that make you feel uncomfortable?

5. Have you written in a single sentence the central idea you want to communicate to your readers?

EXPLORING YOUR OPTIONS

1. Read your paper from your readers' points of view.

2. Mark the passages in your draft that seem to work well—a good example or a clear sentence.

3. Mark the passages in your draft that trouble you. Do you need to flesh out certain examples so that your readers can clearly understand what you mean?

4. On the lines below, rewrite a sentence that bothers you.

_____

_____

_____

_____

5. In a single sentence, write the central idea you would like to communicate to your readers through this paper.

_____

_____

_____

EDITING

SUBJECTS AND VERBS

Identifying Subjects and Verbs

Subjects and verbs are the basic structural elements of sentences. To be complete, a sentence must have *someone* or *something doing* or *being* something. The someone or something is the *subject,* and what the subject does is the *verb.*

subject verb

People work.

You can check your sentences for completeness by finding subjects and verbs. In each sentence, underline the subject once and verb twice. Because action is often easy to spot, try locating the verb first. Then, to locate the subject, ask *who* or *what* is doing the action.

Alicia works in the library on Mondays.

The action in this sentence is the word *works,* so it is the verb. The person doing the working is Alicia, so *Alicia* is the subject of the sentence.
Locate the subjects and verbs in the following sentences:

Randy starts work every morning at seven o'clock.

Senator Fresen worries about unemployment each election year.

Often the verb doesn't show action; instead it tells what the subject *is* or *was*. The most common verbs that state existence are the *be* verbs, which include *am, are, is, was, were, being,* and *been*.

I <u>am</u>	We <u>are</u>	She <u>is</u>
He <u>was</u>	They <u>were</u>	

The *be* verbs convey the least meaning of all verbs, which means that they are not very interesting. The verbs in the following sentences are *be* verbs:

<u>Scott</u> <u>is</u> a hard worker.

<u>They</u> <u>were</u> the last to leave the job site.

Some verbs have an auxiliary verb that helps create tense or form questions. The helping verb plus the main verb becomes the complete verb of the sentence. In the sentence

Alfredo <u>will ride</u> to work with us.

will is the helping verb and *ride* is the main verb. The complete verb is *will ride*.

HELPING VERBS

am, is, are	may, might, must
can, could	shall, should
do, does, did	was, were
has, have, had	will, would

Here are two more sentences that use common helping verbs:

Technology *has* changed manufacturing procedures.

Employers *should* provide adequate health benefits.

Sentences also can have more than one subject and one verb:

The <u>university</u> and local <u>businesses</u> <u>cooperate</u> to provide work experience for students.

<u>Employers</u> <u>hire</u> and <u>train</u> students as interns.

Sometimes a subject is difficult to locate because it looks like another part of the sentence. In the following sentence, is the subject *most* or *workers*?

Most of the workers arrive early.

The word *of* is a *preposition* (a word that shows relationships—for instance, of time or space—between words). The preposition and the words that follow it through the next noun or pronoun make up a *prepositional phrase*. In the sentence above, *of the workers* is a prepositional phrase. Prepositional phrases are *never* a part of the subject. Below is a list of some common prepositions.

PREPOSITIONS

about	beyond	onto
above	by	outside
across	down	over
after	during	past
against	except	since
along	for	through
among	from	to
around	in	toward
at	inside	under
before	into	until
behind	like	up
below	near	upon
beneath	of	with
beside	off	within
between	on	

If you are having trouble locating the subject of a sentence, look for prepositional phrases in the sentence and cross them out.

Many ~~of the employees~~ were late.

~~From their position~~ the problem was significant.

The words *there* and *here* are rarely the subjects of sentences. When a sentence begins with either of these words, the subject should be placed after the verb.

There <u>was</u> a <u>question</u> concerning employee benefits.

Here <u>are</u> the <u>work schedule</u> and <u>pay sheets</u> for next week.

In commands, the subject of the sentence—*you*—is understood; it is not written.

<u>Come</u> to work on time. (<u>You</u> <u>come</u> to work on time.)

<u>Submit</u> your suggestions to the supervisor. (<u>You</u> <u>submit</u> your suggestions to the supervisor.)

More about Verbs

Verb tenses   A verb's tense indicates when the verb's action takes place. There are three simple tenses in English: present, past, and future. *Present* tense is action that is occurring now.

Fumiko *works* in the bookstore this year.

Past tense is action that has occurred before now.

Fumiko *worked* in the cafeteria last year.

Future tense is action that will occur in the future. We indicate the future tense with the helping verbs *will* and *shall*.

Fumiko *will work* in the recruiting office next year.

Regular and irregular verbs   Most verbs are *regular*. You create their past tense and past participle (a form of the verb used with a helping verb) by adding *-d* or *-ed* to the present tense of the verb.

Present tense	Past tense	Past Participle
work	worked	worked
study	studied	studied

The past tense and past participle of *irregular* English verbs are formed in some other way than by adding *-d* or *-ed* to the present tense. If you have a question about a verb's forms, check a dictionary under the verb's present tense. For irregular verbs, dictionaries list the present tense, the past tense, and the past participle—in that order (*blow, blew, blown*). Below is a chart of some common irregular verbs.

IRREGULAR VERBS

Present tense	Past tense	Past participle
arise	arose	arisen
begin	began	begun
bite	bit	bitten, bit
blow	blew	blown
break	broke	broken
buy	bought	bought
catch	caught	caught
cut	cut	cut
drink	drank	drunk
drive	drove	driven
eat	ate	eaten
fall	fell	fallen
find	found	found
get	got	got, gotten
hear	heard	heard
hold	held	held
lay	laid	laid
lie	lay	lain
ring	rang	rung
rise	rose	risen
see	saw	seen
set	set	set
sing	sang	sung
sit	sat	sat
swim	swam	swum
write	wrote	written

EXERCISE 1   In the following sentences, underline the subject once and the verb twice. Cross out prepositional phrases as you look for subjects. Be sure to double-underline all the verbs.

1. Some believe in a six-hour work day and a thirty-hour work week.

2. There would be more time for families, friends, self, and community.

3. Shortened work days improve productivity.

4. Extend paid vacations for all American workers.

5. Most workers have only two weeks of paid vacation each year.

6. Employers should discourage overtime work.

7. With fewer people overworking, more jobs become available for the unemployed.

8. American workers with shorter work hours can still compete in a world economy.

EXERCISE 2   In the paragraph below, underline the subject of each sentence once and the verb twice. Cross out prepositional phrases as you look for subjects. Be sure to double-underline all the verbs.

Joseph spends hours each day with his children. Joseph arrives home from work when his children return home from school. He helps them with homework. He shuttles them to their after-school activities. He spends time with them. Joseph has arranged a flexible schedule with his employer. Because Joseph leaves work early, he arrives at work earlier than his fellow workers. Because Joseph feels freshest in the early mornings and because the office is still quiet, Joseph is extremely productive at work. Consequently, Joseph's flexible schedule helps him be both a better employee and a better parent.

EXERCISE 3   Using the current draft of your essay, do the following:

1. Select ten sentences.
2. Underline the subject of each sentence once and the verb twice.
3. Cross out prepositional phrases as you look for subjects.

OPTIONS FOR WRITING

Reflect

1. On the basis of an experience you had with your first job, offer advice to someone just starting work.

2. Explain how both parents' working outside the home affects their children. Support your opinions with personal examples.

Inform

3. Interview two or three employers about the effect an employee's absenteeism has on other employees and the business. Use the interviews as the basis for a paper.

4. Narrate examples of sexism in the workplace.

Persuade

5. Persuade a workaholic friend not to work overtime.

6. A friend can't decide whether to work full-time or to enroll in college. Write a letter in which you explain your thoughts about this dilemma.

Speculate

7. Using your chosen field of study, describe your ideal working conditions. In your narration, discuss hours, benefits, the work environment, and recognition.

8. Write a narration of a grandparent's work life in which you speculate on the details of his or her job.

Chapter 2

EDUCATION

~

One problem many students entering college face is too much freedom. Throughout high school, their lives have been organized, controlled, and structured by parents, teachers, and administrators. For example, when a test was scheduled, the teacher would remind students and coach them on what they needed to know. In college, however, an instructor might announce a test in five weeks and then never mention it again.

College instructors assume that students are responsible for their own education. To survive in college, then, students have to keep themselves organized, motivated, and disciplined.

To prepare for this chapter's theme, education, answer the following questions:

- In what ways are college students responsible for their own education?
- How does a student's questioning the information and ideas presented in class contribute to his or her education?

READINGS on *Education*

Advice That Can Help You Succeed on Campus
U.S. *News and World Report* Staff Writers

The staff writers of U.S. News and World Report *have compiled the following article by interviewing college counselors, faculty advisors, and a successful student who all offer suggestions to students on how to succeed in college. This article was first printed in 1985.*

The fat letter has finally arrived welcoming you as a member of the class   1
of 1990. You're about to become a college freshman.

Most students enter college expecting to leave with a bachelor's degree;   2
only half ever do. The others drop out.

"Half of a college education has to come from the student," advises Fred   3
Hargadon, former dean of admissions at Stanford University. But how?

College counselors, faculty advisers and one very successful student offer   4
the following tips on how to get the most out of your college education.

INVOLVEMENT. The most successful students are those actively involved   5
in their education. By interacting with classmates and faculty and participating
in activities, you become part of the college community, developing support
groups that you can turn to for help. Get involved, but not overcommitted. In
the first term, focus on adjusting to the new academic demands.

Consider study groups in which you meet regularly with a few classmates   6
to discuss course material. Find an upperclassman, someone from your home-
town or down the hall who can be a mentor. Older students can offer advice
on courses plus activities to join.

TIME MANAGEMENT. "Man is first a social animal, then a rational one,"   7
says E. Glenn Griffin, a professor emeritus at Purdue University. So you may
find it hard to say "No" each time your roommate wants to see "Beverly Hills
Cop" when you need to read *Paradise Lost.*

College is known for its distractions. In those first months, you'll meet peo-   8
ple whose values and priorities are different from yours. The newness of the
situation and the range of decisions you'll face could leave you confused.

Think about what you want from college—and from friends. Study after   9
breakfast, between classes, whatever works best for you. Don't cut off all
social contacts. They're as vital to surviving in college as reading. Study Hegel
first, then catch the late showing of "Rambo."

STUDY METHODS. Would you take a trip by stopping for directions at   10
every filling station instead of reading a map? Of course not, but that's how
most people study, says Griffin, who teaches a course on preparing for college.

Studying in college demands more reading and thinking, less memorization than in high school. Survey the material first to get a sense of it; formulate some questions. Jot down key ideas, tell yourself the essence of what you've read and review it. Does it make sense? Were your questions answered?

Get copies of old exams from the library so you can see what types of questions each professor asks. Preparing for an exam on the Civil War will be easier if you know whether to study broad themes or specific battles.   11

KEEPING CURRENT. Professors may not notice whether you attend a large lecture, but you could notice later on, says Lawrence Graham, a 1983 graduate of Princeton University who as a senior wrote *Conquering College Life: How to Be a Winner at College.*   12

Some professors use lectures to discuss material not found in the reading on which they will base an exam. Others stress key points. Skip at your own risk. If you must miss a lecture, get the notes promptly. If too much time elapses, the notes will make less sense than secondhand notes normally do. Never fall more than a week behind in reading. If you don't do the reading, you won't understand the lecture.   13

SEEKING HELP. You may attend every calculus class, do each assignment and still watch your grade plummet. Or maybe you missed more classes than you should have. Get help. Most professors are very willing to talk about their courses. Just don't wait until a week before the midterm exam.   14

THE MAJOR CHOICE. For a minimum of $4,000 a year and four years of your life, you expect a degree—and a job—when it's over. Why not major in computer science or business and be more assured of work after graduation?   15

"When choosing a major, look inside yourself as well as at the economic pattern," advises Ernest Boyer, president of the Carnegie Foundation for the Advancement of Teaching. If you're genuinely interested in computers, major in them. If you're happiest reading *Beowulf,* don't force yourself to study business. Think carefully before choosing a major. What excites and intrigues you? Knowing that may help you avoid changing disciplines several times.   16

It is quite appropriate to view college as a broadening experience, a preparation for life. Indeed, many college students do not select their ultimate career path until *after* they graduate. So take occupational courses if you like, but don't feel compelled to mold your major to the market.   17

FINDING TOP TEACHERS. On every campus, there are professors noted for their inspirational teaching style, for their way of making a course an exciting voyage into the unknown. Don't spend four years on campus without taking their classes. So what if the professors teach modern art and Chinese history, subjects you know nothing about? When Hargadon was admissions dean at Stanford, he told parents to worry if their children were earning all A's by the end of the first quarter, which showed they were only taking subjects they would do well in. "College is a great feast from which to choose," he says. "Don't order the same meal every day."   18

Questions and Issues to Consider

Writing Process   1. Describe the audience the staff writers for *U.S. News and World Report* are addressing. What are their attitudes towards that audience? What specific references from the article illustrate the authors' concern for their audience?

2. Identify a single sentence that summarizes the entire article. This sentence can function as a thesis statement.

Aims of Writing   3. The authors are writing to inform. Identify characteristics of writing to inform that are evident in this article.

Critical Thinking   4. From your own experiences and your past successes and failures, come up with your own list of tips to help students succeed in college.

Let's Tell the Story of All America's Cultures
Ji-Yeon Mary Yuhfill

Yuhfill immigrated with her family to the United States from Seoul, Korea, when she was five years old. She attended schools in Chicago and then entered Stanford University in California. She feels strongly about America as a multicultural country. Yuhfill writes about her experiences as a multicultural student in the following editorial essay, which originally was printed in the Philadelphia Inquirer *(1991).*

I grew up hearing, seeing and almost believing that America was white—albeit with a little black tinged here and there—and that white was best.   1

The white people were everywhere in my 1970s Chicago childhood: Founding Fathers, Lewis and Clark, Lincoln, Daniel Boone, Carnegie, presidents, explorers and industrialists galore.[1] The only black people were slaves. The only Indians were scalpers.   2

I never heard one word about how Benjamin Franklin was so impressed by the Iroquois federation of nations that he adapted that model into our system of state and federal government. Or that the Indian tribes were systemati-   3

---

[1] **galore:** in abundance

cally betrayed and massacred by a greedy young nation that stole their land and called it the United States.

I never heard one word about how Asian immigrants were among the first to turn California's desert into fields of plenty. Or about Chinese immigrant Ah Bing, who bred the cherry now on sale in groceries across the nation. Or that plantation owners in Hawaii imported labor from China, Japan, Korea and the Philippines to work the sugar cane fields. I never learned that Asian immigrants were the only immigrants denied U.S. citizenship, even though they served honorably in World War I. All the immigrants in my textbook were white.   4

I never learned about Frederick Douglass, the runaway slave who became a leading abolitionist[2] and statesman, or about black scholar W.E.B. Du Bois. I never learned that black people rose up in arms against slavery. Nat Turner wasn't one of the heroes in my childhood history class.   5

I never learned that the American Southwest and California were already settled by Mexicans when they were annexed[3] after the Mexican-American War. I never learned that Mexico once had a problem keeping land-hungry white men on the U.S. side of the border.   6

So when other children called me a slant-eyed chink and told me to go back where I came from, I was ready to believe that I wasn't really an American because I wasn't white.   7

American's bittersweet legacy of struggling and failing and getting another step closer to democratic ideals of liberty and equality and justice for all wasn't for the likes of me, an immigrant child from Korea. The history books said so.   8

Well, the history books were wrong.   9

Educators around the country are finally realizing what I realized as a teenager in the library, looking up the history I wasn't getting in school. America is a multicultural nation, composed of many people with varying histories and varying traditions who have little in common except their humanity, a belief in democracy and a desire for freedom.   10

America changed them, but they changed America too.   11

A committee of scholars and teachers gathered by the New York State Department of Education recognizes this in their recent report, "One Nation, Many Peoples: A Declaration of Cultural Interdependence."   12

They recommend that public schools provide a "multicultural education, anchored to the shared principles of a liberal democracy."   13

What that means, according to the report, is recognizing that America was shaped and continues to be shaped by people of diverse backgrounds. It calls for students to be taught that history is an ongoing process of discovery and interpretation of the past, and that there is more than one way of viewing the world.   14

---

[2] **abolitionist:** someone fighting against slavery
[3] **annexed:** joined to the United States

Thus, the westward migration of white Americans is not just a heroic set-   15
tling of an untamed wild, but also the conquest of indigenous[4] peoples. Immigrants were not just white, but Asian as well. Blacks were not merely passive
slaves freed by northern whites, but active fighters for their own liberation.

In particular, according to the report, the curriculum[5] should help children   16
"to assess critically the reasons for the inconsistencies between the ideals of the
U.S. and social realities. It should provide information and intellectual tools
that can permit them to contribute to bringing reality closer to the ideals."

In other words, show children the good with the bad, and give them the   17
skills to help improve their country. What could be more patriotic?

Several dissenting members of the New York committee publicly worry   18
that America will splinter into ethnic fragments if this multicultural curriculum
is adopted. They argue that the committee's report puts the focus on ethnicity
at the expense of national unity.

But downplaying ethnicity will not bolster[6] national unity. The history of   19
America is the story of how and why people from all over the world came to
the United States, and how in struggling to make a better life for themselves,
they changed each other, they changed the country, and they all came to call
themselves Americans.

E pluribus unum. Out of many, one.   20

This is why I, with my Korean background, and my childhood tormentors,   21
with their lost-in-the-mist-of-time European backgrounds, are all Americans.

It is the unique beauty of this country. It is high time we let all our children   22
gaze upon it.

---

[4] **indigenous:** native to an area
[5] **curriculum:** course of study
[6] **bolster:** support, encourage

Questions and Issues to Consider

Writing Process **1.** Yuhfill organizes her essay by dividing it into two major parts. In
the first part she focuses on her previous knowledge, on what she
learned in school; in the second part she reveals her new understanding and attitudes. Explain how this organization supports her
purpose for writing.

2. Yuhfill supports her position by citing specific events that are not
taught in traditional history classes. Explain how these examples
reveal the author's attitude toward her topic.

Aims of Writing **3.** Explain how Yuhfill writes to persuade in the second half of the essay.
What attitudes is she trying to persuade her audience to change?

Critical Thinking   4. Describe the content of an American history class you took in college or high school. Does that content support or conflict with Yuhfill's position? Explain your answer.

PREWRITING

QUESTIONING

Prewriting helps you choose a topic. It also helps you determine what you do and do not know about the topic. One effective technique for developing insights about a topic is *questioning*. If you are having difficulty deciding how you want to approach your topic, try asking and answering some of the following *questions.** Insert your own topic into the blank where the word *education* is now. Choose the questions that seem important to you.

Definition

1. How does the dictionary define education?

2. What words did education come from?

3. What do *I* mean by education?

4. What group of things does education seem to belong to? How is education different from other things in this group?

5. What parts can education be divided into?

6. Does education mean something now that it didn't years ago? If so, what?

7. What other words mean approximately the same as education?

8. What are some concrete examples of education?

9. When is the meaning of education misunderstood?

Comparison

1. What is education similar to? In what ways?

---

*These questions are based on Elizabeth Cowan Neeld's heuristic in *Writing* (2d ed., Scott Foresman, 1986, pp. 46–55).

2. What is <u>education</u> different from? In what ways?

3. <u>Education</u> is superior to what? In what ways?

4. <u>Education</u> is inferior to what? In what ways?

5. <u>Education</u> is most unlike what? (What is it opposite to?) In what ways?

6. <u>Education</u> is most like what? In what ways?

Consequences

1. What are the effects of <u>education</u>?

2. What is the purpose of <u>education</u>?

3. When does <u>education</u> happen?

4. What is the consequence of <u>education</u>?

5. What comes before <u>education</u>?

6. What comes after <u>education</u>?

Evidence

1. What have I heard people say about <u>education</u>?

2. What facts or statistics do I know about <u>education</u>?

3. What famous proverbs (for example, "A bird in hand is worth two in the bush") do I know about <u>education</u>?

4. What songs, articles, books, movies, or TV shows do I remember about <u>education</u>?

5. What research would I like to do on <u>education</u>?

After writing brief five-minute responses to several questions, you'll find that your ideas and examples are more concrete. Now sort through your responses to limit your topic. Select the response that interests you the most, or that you have had the most experience with, or that has given you new insight into the topic. This response will be the beginning point for your draft.

For example, a student, Nicole, has chosen the general topic of education for her paper. She inserted that topic into each blank of the questions above. To begin limiting her topic, she selects five questions that interest her:

What do *I* mean by <u>education</u>?

What is <u>education</u> similar to? In what ways?

What are the effects of <u>education</u>?

What comes after <u>education</u>?

What have I heard people say about <u>education</u>?

After taking several minutes to write each answer, Nicole decides to focus on a single question: What are the effects of education? Here is her brief response:

```
I remember as a child going to Cottonwood Heights
elementary school where I was put in Level I English
and history (advanced classes) and Level III math
(basic math for those who need the most help). I did
best in the Level I classes, and I did worse in my
Level III math class. Looking back, I think one rea-
son for doing well in my advanced classes was I felt
good about myself and thought myself smarter for
being placed in the advanced classes. Because I was
in the lowest level math class, I felt dumb and
would put only limited effort into the work sheets
or math problems.
```

Answering the question has helped Nicole remember being placed in classes because of her test scores. She decides to use her experience to make readers aware of the possible consequences of using test scores to place students. Her aim, then, probably is to inform. Nicole now has a starting point for her draft: she knows generally what she wants to discuss and what her chief aim is—to inform. (A draft of Nicole's paper begins on page 71.)

EXPLORING YOUR OPTIONS

1. Insert your topic choice into five of the questions listed above, and then write the five questions below.

   a. _____

   b. _____

c. _____

d. _____

e. _____

2. On a separate sheet of paper, write brief responses to the five questions you've chosen.

3. Look over your responses and choose the one you like best. In the space below, write the question again.

   _____

4. Now briefly answer the following questions about your topic question.

   a. Why do this topic question and your response interest you?

   _____

   _____

   b. What experience have you had with this topic question?

   _____

   _____

   c. What new insights into your topic have you gained through this question?

   _____

   _____

5. Begin to limit your topic. List more specifically what you would like to accomplish by writing on this topic.

   _____

   _____

6. Put a checkmark next to the aim that best represents your reason for writing this paper.

   _____ To reflect   _____ To persuade

   _____ To inform   _____ To speculate

DEVELOPING A THESIS STATEMENT

Once you have decided on a topic, the next step is to decide what you want to say about it; you must develop an opinion or a stance. Your stance makes the topic uniquely yours because your knowledge and experience are uniquely yours. Others may agree with you that a college education is valuable, for example, but if you're the first person in your family to go to college, you have insights that others may not have. Those insights strengthen your stance; they also affect your approach to the topic education. Your topic and your stance are fundamental to your paper's thesis statement.

The *thesis statement* is the central idea on which you will build your paper. It forces you to determine what you're going to say and how you're going to say it. A thesis statement also alerts readers to your aim and stance.

A formal thesis statement has three elements:

Topic + Stance + Plan = Thesis statement

The *topic* is the central issue or subject you choose to write about. The *stance* is the point you want to make about the topic. The *plan* is how you decide to organize your support material or to explain or defend your stance.

Suppose you decide to write about succeeding in college:

Topic: Success in college

You now must decide what you want to say about success in college—your stance on the topic.

Topic: Success in college

Stance: Success in college is possible for me.

You have a topic and a stance, but you need to cut them down to manageable size. Success in college is too broad a topic. There are many different areas to succeed in while at college: you can have academic success, social success, financial success, emotional success, or athletic success, for example. Even the more limited topic of academic success may be too broad because so many different factors—from taking notes to managing your time and studying—contribute to academic success. In fact you probably could write an essay on any one of those factors. So, instead of writing on the broad topic of success in college, suppose you limit your topic to success in taking tests:

Success in taking tests is possible for me.

At this point, your topic is limited sufficiently to allow you to write an essay. Or you could limit it even more by focusing on one type of test, say essay exams:

Success in taking essay exams is possible for me.

Finally, you can list the steps that make it possible for you to succeed in taking essay exams:

Success in taking essay exams is possible for me by reading instructions carefully, outlining ideas, explaining examples, and allowing time for proofreading.

Notice that these steps set out the organization—the plan—you'll use in the essay. Your limited topic, your stance, and the plan form a tightly focused, formal thesis statement.

Nicole used this same process to arrive at her paper's thesis statement. Through the prewriting questions, she selected a topic: test-score placement. On the basis of her own experience, she believes that placing students in classes according to their test scores can affect children. Her stance, then, is that test-score placement can affect children. Nicole chose to support her stance with examples of how being placed in a low-level class gave her a label, how that label affected her self-esteem, and how her self-esteem affected her learning.

Topic: Test-score placement

Stance: Test-score placement affects children.

Plan: Classes label a student.
         Labeling affects a student's self-esteem.
         Self-esteem affects a student's learning.

Nicole combined this information in a single sentence—her thesis statement:

Thesis statement: The way children view themselves because of test-score placement in school not only labels them but also affects their self-esteem and learning.

Writing Thesis Statements

A thesis statement must be a sentence, not simply a topic or a sentence fragment. Segregation is a topic, not a thesis statement. *Being familiar with bilingual education* is a sentence fragment, not a thesis statement.

> Racial segregation in schools is morally wrong.

and

> Bilingual education prevents students from interacting with those who speak other languages.

are both thesis statements.

A thesis statement must be a sentence that you can explain or defend, not simply a fact that no one would deny. *Most college students do not attend summer sessions* is a statement of fact that requires no opinion or defense. A thesis statement would look like this:

> Because most college students do not attend summer sessions, they do not benefit from smaller classes and lower student-teacher ratios.

Finally, a thesis statement cannot be a question. *Do we need grades in school?* is a question, not a thesis statement. But, an answer to a question can be the basis for a thesis statement.

> Grades are necessary to mark achievement and motivate students.

PRACTICE   Rewrite the following thesis statements to include topic, stance, and plan.

1. A college education is expensive.

   _____

   _____

2. Lifetime learning

   _____

   _____

3. Can stress in school encourage learning?

_____

_____

4. Daily study goals are helpful in achieving academic success.

_____

_____

5. This paper discusses the success of adult education.

_____

_____

EXPLORING YOUR OPTIONS

1. Write your paper's topic.

_____

2. Write what you want to say about your topic (your stance).

_____

3. List one or more examples or details you intend to use to support your topic and stance (your plan).

a. _____

b. _____

c. _____

d. _____

4. Rewrite the information above on your topic, stance, and plan in a single, clear thesis statement.

_____

_____

_____

Thesis Statements and Controlling Ideas

A *formal thesis statement* specifically states the topic, stance, and plan you've chosen for your paper. Nicole's thesis statement is an example of a formal thesis statement:

> The way children view themselves because of test-score place-ment in school not only labels them but also affects their self-esteem and learning.

A formal thesis statement works well when you want your reader to know early on how you feel about your topic.

What do you do when you're not sure exactly what you want to write? When your draft is simply an exploration of your ideas? You can use a *working thesis statement*—a general informal statement that guides your writing but that can change as you learn more about your topic or change the focus of your paper. The working thesis statement eventually will evolve into a formal thesis statement.

Here's a working thesis statement for Nicole's paper:

> Schools should not place students into specific classes based on test scores.

She could have used this working statement to guide her writing until she was able to say more specifically why she feels this way.

At times you may not have a specific point to make; you simply want to describe an event. One possibility is to use a *controlling idea* instead of a thesis statement. There won't be a single sentence that expresses your limited topic, your stance, and your plan, but you clearly suggest these elements to the reader through the writing itself. If you do use a controlling idea, the idea must be clear enough so that you and your readers could write a formal thesis statement if necessary. For example, Nicole does not directly state, "I'm against test-score placement," but because of the examples she's chosen to use, her audience clearly understands her stance.

Thesis Statements and Aims

Thesis statements also can suggest your aim for writing in addition to your topic, stance, and plan.

Reflect

These two thesis statements suggest that the purpose of the writing is to reflect: they focus on reactions to personal experiences.

My sixth-grade teacher, Ms. Reinwand, helped me work diligently, develop patience, and gain self-confidence.

I've returned to college twenty years after high school because I'm tired of dead-end jobs and of feeling inadequate.

Inform

These two thesis statements imply that the purpose of the writing is to inform because they explain specific issues to specific audiences:

Local school officials are investigating how year-round school can save money and ease overcrowding.

Parents can show an interest in their college students' learning by asking them questions about courses, professors, and major assignments.

Persuade

The next two thesis statements indicate that the writing aim is to persuade. They are written to influence readers' opinions.

Athletic scholarships should include a weekly allowance because lengthy practice schedules, extensive travel time, and high academic standards prevent most athletes from working part-time to earn spending money.

Placing mentally challenged children in a traditional classroom stretches and stimulates their abilities and also promotes understanding among the other children.

Speculate

Finally, these two thesis statements suggest that the purpose of the writing is to speculate. They discuss issues that have not yet happened.

If college students wore school uniforms, they would place less emphasis on what others wear and more emphasis on what others think.

Students and instructor together would develop realistic yet challenging standards to indicate different levels of performance if students could determine their own grades in a course.

✓ CHECKLIST: THESIS STATEMENT

1. Does your thesis statement describe your paper's topic?

2. Does your thesis statement suggest your stance or position?

3. Does your thesis statement suggest the plan for your paper?

4. Does your thesis statement suggest your aim for writing?

5. Is your thesis statement a complete sentence?

6. Can you defend your thesis statement?

7. Is your thesis statement a statement rather than a question?

WRITING TOGETHER

1. With a classmate, review each other's thesis statements against the checklist above.

2. Discuss the strengths of your thesis statements.

3. Explain how you each plan to develop your individual essays on the basis of your current thesis statements. Describe the examples you plan to use to support your thesis statements.

DESCRIPTION

Description is another effective method of organizing information. Description illustrates, elaborates, or portrays in detail a person, a place, an object, or an idea. Usually description is a part of other organizational styles. Narration, for instance, often incorporates extensive description to recount events. And, although by definition description would seem to inform, it can be used to reflect, to persuade, and to speculate as well. Nicole is writing to inform her readers that test-score placement is not a sound practice. She uses an extended description to show how this kind of placement affected her self-esteem and learning.

Patterns

The pattern of description you use can make your descriptions more effective. Common patterns relate to the senses or to space, or make use of repetition and lists.

The Senses   One way of describing something is by writing about how it looks, feels, tastes, sounds, or smells. The more accurate and plentiful the sense details, the more concrete and clear the description. Here's a sentence that lacks sensory description:

> After winter, students do homework in the sunshine.

See how much clearer the description is when you add details of touch, sight, smell, and sound:

> After months of below-freezing temperatures, strong gusty winds, and seemingly endless snowstorms, students are stretched out in the warm March sunshine on the new green grass, near the blooming lilacs, doing homework while they listen to CDs.

Space   A spatial description describes an object from left to right, right to left, bottom to top, top to bottom, clockwise, counterclockwise, inside to outside, or outside to inside. This sentence lacks spatial description:

> The learning center has different floors.

By describing each floor of the learning center, the writer makes it easier for the reader to "see" the different parts of the building. In this example, the learning center is described from the bottom floor to the top floor:

> The McDougal Learning Center has four floors, known as libraries. The first floor is the reference and periodicals library, the second floor is the social sciences library, the third floor is the natural and technological sciences library, and the fourth floor is the humanities library.

Repetition   One effective means of description is to use a particular word or image several times, each time adding information. This sentence doesn't tell the reader very much:

> The student is frustrated.

By using a stronger word than *frustrated,* by repeating that word, and by describing more specifically why the student is disheartened, the writer makes it easier to understand how the student feels.

> The student is disheartened: disheartened by long lines, disheartened by homework, disheartened by deadlines, disheartened by lectures, disheartened by tight finances, disheartened by school.

Lists Another way to describe is to list details and images. This sentence lacks description:

> Her backpack is now ready for the day.

Notice how simply listing what's inside the backpack helps clarify the description of the backpack:

> Her seam-stretched backpack is now stuffed for the day: chemistry, English, psychology textbooks; a math workbook; three number-two pencils; a blue Bic pen; a black pen; a billfold; a comb; a tuna salad sandwich; student identification; two letters to mail; a daily planner; and today's school newspaper.

Description: An Example

In the following paragraph, Thomas S. Whitecloud describes his reaction to returning home for Christmas break. Notice that his description appeals to the senses by using sight, sound, smell, and touch (particularly temperature).

Blue Winds Dancing

Christmas Eve comes in on a north wind. Snow clouds hang over the pines, and the night comes early. Walking along the railroad bed, I feel the calm peace of snow-bound forests on either side of me. I take my time; I am back in a world where time does not mean so much now. I am alone; alone but not nearly so lonely as I was back on the campus at school. Those are never lonely who love the snow and the pines, never lonely when the pines are wearing white shawls and snow crunches coldly underfoot. In the woods I know there are the tracks of deer and rabbit; I know that if I leave the rails and go into the woods, I shall find them. I walk along feeling glad because my legs are light and my feet seem to know that they are home. A deer comes out of the woods just ahead of me and stands silhouetted on the rails. The North, I feel, has welcomed me home. I watch him and am glad that I do not wish for a gun. He goes into the woods quietly, leaving only the design of his tracks in the snow. I walk on. Now and then I pass a field, white under the night sky, with houses at the far end. Smoke comes from the chimneys of the houses, and I try to tell what sort of wood each is burning by the smoke; some burn pine, others aspen, others tamarack. There is one from which comes black coal smoke that rises lazily and drifts out over the tops of the trees. I like to watch houses and try to imagine what might be happening in them.

PRACTICE 1   1. In the selection, the author uses sensory details.

   a. List several examples related to sight.

   _____   _____

   _____   _____

   b. List several examples related to sound.

   _____   _____

   _____   _____

   c. List one example related to smell.

   _____

   d. List several examples related to touch.

   _____   _____

   _____   _____

   2. How does the author use space in his description?

   _____

   _____

   _____

   3. How does the author use repetition in the paragraph?

   _____

   _____

   _____

PRACTICE 2   The following sentences lack descriptive detail. Use sensory detail, spatial detail, repetition, or lists to flesh out the descriptions.

1. My biology professor is a good teacher.

   _____

   _____

2. I need a quiet place to study.

   _____

   _____

3. I have a few minutes between classes to walk across campus.

   _____

   _____

4. We have a multicultural campus.

   _____

   _____

5. Our campus is certainly beautiful this time of year.

   _____

   _____

WRITING WITH COMPUTERS

Rewrite on the computer the above sentences that lack descriptive detail. Use sensory detail, spatial detail, repetition, or lists to flesh out the descriptions. With a class partner, share each other's sentences and together incorporate descriptions from both of your sentences into a new single, descriptive sentence.

Description and Aims

Description can be incorporated into the different purposes for writing, as the following writing assignments suggest.

Reflect

Describe in detail an experience you've had when learning that nature conceals the unexpected in the ordinary.

Describe a stressful experience in college and explain what that experience has taught you about yourself and about life.

Inform

Describe in detail the services that a study skills lab offers to new college students.

Describe how a learning disability such as dyslexia is diagnosed.

Persuade

Describe the characteristics of an adult who cannot read as you persuade a fellow student to volunteer in the adult basic education program.

Describe the learning environment of home-taught children as you persuade a parent to consider or reconsider home schooling.

Speculate

Describe the types of organizations or types of individuals who would benefit from President Clinton's plan to allow the repayment of student loans through community service.

Describe in detail the type of college classroom you envision twenty-five years from now.

EXPLORING YOUR OPTIONS

You are ready to write the first draft of your essay. You already have determined the following:

Your topic _____

Your working thesis statement _____

_____

_____

Your main writing aim _____

Your major examples _____

_____

_____

Set aside a block of time and write your first draft. Don't worry about being right or wrong. The object is to get your ideas on paper.

DISCOVERING THE PURPOSE OF YOUR PAPER

A critical component of writing is understanding *why* you're writing. Yes, it's an assignment. But that's your motivation for writing, not your purpose. To understand *why* you write, you have to be able to answer these questions:

Why do you spend time choosing a topic?

Why do you work to get your idea across to the reader?

Why do you select a particular example?

Why is your information important to the reader?

The more precise your answers, the more focused your writing.

Before you write your first draft, you may have a sense of your purpose for writing. But the act of writing itself can generate new ideas and purposes. After writing the draft, then, you need to reevaluate your purpose for writing. Do some examples need expanding? Has your stance begun to change? What about your working thesis statement? An example: You begin a paper arguing for bilingual education. But as you research the issue, you start to question your position. When you've finished the draft, then, you have to reexamine the purpose of the paper and make sure that all the components of your writing directly contribute to that purpose.

To clarify your purpose, you have to ask several questions and answer them with examples from your writing. The questions below demand thoughtful answers. Following each question is the response Nicole wrote after her first draft.

1. **What is the most important thing I want to say about my topic?**

   The purpose of this paper is to let people know through my own experience how test-score placement can affect children's learning.

2. **Why do I think this topic is worth writing about?**

   This topic is worth writing about because as adults or as siblings we can do something to actually help someone who is going through school with low-self-esteem because of labeling. And one can also recognize schools that use placement programs that label children.

3. **Why do I think my reader needs to be aware of this topic?**

   Readers should be aware that self-esteem can affect learning, and that as adults and students, they are entitled to learn about different educational programs and how these programs are directly and indirectly affecting them or their families.

4. **How do I achieve my purpose?**

   I achieve my purpose by describing my personal experience of being in advanced-level (Group I) classes and a lower-level (Group III) class.

5. **How does each paragraph support my revised purpose or thesis statement?**

   Each paragraph has a sentence that suggests the point I want to make, followed by an example to support that point. The paragraphs also support my thesis statement.

6. **How do I clearly state my purpose in the introduction?**

   My thesis statement is in the introduction: "The way children view themselves because of test-score placement in school not only labels them but also affects their self-esteem and learning."

STUDENT ESSAY

Below is the draft of Nicole Claudio's essay. Nicole is from Utah and is majoring in psychology. As you read the draft, ask two basic questions:

- How does Nicole succeed in fulfilling her purpose for writing this essay?

- How can Nicole strengthen this draft?

Class Labels and Self-Esteem

Nicole uses a formal thesis statement.

Children need to believe in themselves. To succeed, they need to have self-esteem. Children develop their self-esteem through the support of their immediate family members, close friends, and school teachers. The way children view themselves because of test-score placement in school not only labels them but also affects their self-esteem and learning.

She uses a personal experience to support her thesis statement.

Classes label students. I remember the beginning year of my fifth grade math class at Cottonwood Heights elementary school. Twenty-one children took a test consisting of multiplication, addition, subtraction, and long division problems. The test, our math teacher said, would determine the level of math we would be placed in. I scored relatively low (C grade) and was placed in the lowest math group (Group III). Five more children scoring C grades or lower were placed in the same group as I. Group II consisted of eight classmates who had scored a B grade on the test, and Group I consisted of the seven children who scored an A on their math test. Throughout the same day, we also took placement tests in our history and English classes. In English, I scored an A, and, therefore, was labeled under Group I.

Nicole discusses how the experience ties in with her thesis statement.

I learned then that labeling affected my self-esteem. I noticed that in my Group I English class, the children interacted more with each other and with their teacher, unlike the Group III students. I also liked attending my higher history and English group classes because I felt I was smarter and was able to do the assignments, reports, and tests. I had a good attitude in those classes. However, in my Group III math class, we did not care how well we did. For example, I would fail tests and not care. I believed I was already dumb in math, so

why try. I felt inadequate and worthless in that
class.

So my self-esteem did affect my learning. In my
Group I classes, I felt good about myself and knew
the teachers were also proud of me. This enabled
me to try harder and to earn A's on tests and on
homework. On the other hand, in my Group III math
class, I achieve no more than a C grade. In my
math class, I did not want to try, and I did not
want to believe in myself, and would, therefore,
not do above C work. My will to learn had vanished
in my low math class. I was not the only one who
felt this way. My five other peers felt the same
as I. We did not do work sheets given to us, did
not study for the tests, and did not pay attention
to the teacher--we learned nothing.

Fortunately, learning came easier to me when
my family moved across town. In my new school,
classes such as math, history, and English were
never divided into groups. These subjects were
taught to the entire class. The whole class interacted with one another; questions that were asked
by other students helped answer my own questions.
I no longer felt like a part of the dumb group but
rather like an equal. This helped me gain self-
esteem along with a will to learn. In math, I no
longer had C grades, but eventually A grades in
assignments and tests. It was good to know I could
do it.

Labeling children does indeed affect their self-
esteem and learning. I believe children should not
be labeled or put in groups. Labeling causes not
only low self-esteem but a feeling of inadequacy.
Schools need to strive for programs which uplift
children's self-esteems, programs that let the
child feel as adequate as his or her peers. With
these programs, children will not only build self-
esteem to help them through their schooling years,
but they will have the knowledge that they can do
whatever they work hard enough for.

She continues to support her thesis statement with her personal experience.

She shares another experience to illustrate her main point.

Nicole concludes by emphasizing her position on this topic.

EXPLORING YOUR OPTIONS

To help you determine the purpose of your paper, write specific, detailed responses to the following six questions.

1. What is the most important thing I want to say about my topic?

   _____

   _____

   _____

2. Why do I think this topic is worth writing about?

   _____

   _____

   _____

3. Why do I think my reader needs to be aware of this topic?

   _____

   _____

   _____

4. How do I achieve my purpose?

   _____

   _____

   _____

5. How does each paragraph support my purpose or my thesis statement?

   _____

   _____

   _____

6. How do I clearly state my purpose in the introduction?

_____

_____

_____

With your purpose clearly in mind, rewrite the sections of your draft that do not express or help you meet your objective.

WRITING TOGETHER

Ask two of your classmates to read your paper's draft. Then to help you determine whether your paper's purpose is clear, ask them to respond to the following six questions:

1. What is the most important thing I have said about my topic?

2. Why do you think this topic is worth my writing about?

3. Why do you as my reader need to be aware of this topic?

4. How do you see that I have achieved my purpose?

5. How does each paragraph support my purpose or my thesis statement?

6. How have I clearly stated my purpose in the introduction?

EDITING

CLAUSES AND COMMAS

Clauses

Sentences consist of *clauses*, groups of words with subjects and verbs. There are two types of clause: *independent* (also called *main*) and *dependent* (also called *subordinate*).

Independent clauses   An independent clause is a group of words that contains a subject and a verb and that is a complete sentence (a discussion of subjects and verbs begins on page 39).

Students <u>need</u> adequate sleep.

The subject of this example is *students,* and the verb is *need.* It is an independent clause because it is a grammatically complete thought.

Dependent clauses   A dependent clause is a group of words that contains a subject and a verb but that requires more words to be grammatically complete.

When <u>students</u> <u>sleep</u> in class

The subject of this example is *students,* and the verb is *sleep.* This example is also a clause. But this clause is dependent; it needs more information to be a sentence. In other words, this clause is *dependent* on another clause for completion.

            dependent clause   *independent clause*
When <u>students</u> <u>sleep</u> in class, <u>they</u> <u>miss</u> valuable information.

The dependent clause *when students sleep in class* requires the independent clause *they miss valuable information* to complete the thought.

Subordinating conjunctions are tip-offs for dependent clauses (see the list on page 76). When a subordinating conjunction begins a clause, the clause is dependent.

Subordinating conjunctions signal the reader that the dependent clause relies on the independent clause to be a grammatically complete thought. Subordinating conjunctions also clarify the relationship between independent and dependent clauses. For instance, the following sentence contains an independent and a dependent clause:

Joaquin attends college at night because he works during the day.

Independent clause: <u>Joaquin</u> <u>attends</u> college at night

Dependent clause: *because* <u>he</u> <u>works</u> during the day

In this sentence, the subordinating conjunction *because* establishes a cause-and-effect relationship between Joaquin's attending college at night and his working during the day. The chart on page 77 describes

SUBORDINATING CONJUNCTIONS

after	provided that	whenever
although	since	where
as	so	whereas
as if	so that	wherever
because	than	whether
before	that	which
even if	though	whichever
even though	unless	while
ever since	until	who
how	what	whom
if	whatever	whose
in order that	when	why

the relationships certain subordinating conjunctions establish between independent and dependent clauses.

Commas

Commas are the most used (and misused) form of punctuation. Many writers agonize over when and where to insert commas. But there are just four basic rules for using commas within sentences.*

1. **Place a comma before a coordinating conjunction.** Coordinating conjunctions are words that can join two independent clauses. The seven coordinating conjunctions are *and, but, for, nor, or, so,* and *yet.*

   Bryan has an exam today, *and* he is prepared.

   April will go to the computer center, *or* she will go to the library.

---

*These four rules do not include using commas in dates (December 7, 1941, . . .) or certain other specific situations.

SUBORDINATING CONJUNCTIONS AND THE RELATIONSHIPS THEY ESTABLISH

To express contrast   although, as if, even though, though

To express cause   because, since

To express time   after, as, before, once, since, until, when, whenever, while

To express condition   even if, if, provided that, unless

To express place   where, wherever

To express purpose   in order that, so that, that

Together, the comma and the coordinating conjunction signal the reader that a new independent clause is about to begin.

Coordinating conjunctions also can suggest relationships between independent clauses. *And* suggests joining by addition, *or* and *nor* imply positive and negative choice, *but* and *yet* establish a contrast, *for* shows the cause of an event, and *so* indicates the result of an action.

2. **Place commas between items in a series.** Commas are required visually and grammatically to separate individual items in a list of words, phrases, or clauses.

Words: Tricia's comments are insightful, logical, and concise.

Phrases: The history study group will highlight several of the significant events, key figures and authorities, and influential laws that lead to the Civil Rights Act.

Clauses: Our literature class will discuss authors who reveal insights on human nature, who demonstrate different literary techniques, and who represent some of the world's most creative minds.

To prevent confusion, place a comma before the *and* or the *or* that precedes the final item in a series. (The comma before the final *and* in the phrases example above separates the last two items in the series. Without the comma, *key figures and authorities* and *influential laws* become the same item.)

3. **Place a comma after an introductory element.** Any clause, phrase (group of words without a subject or a verb), or word that precedes an independent clause should be set off with a comma. The comma alerts the reader to the upcoming independent clause.

> Yes, <u>I</u> <u>can study</u> tonight.

> After going to the game, <u>we</u> <u>returned</u> to the writing center.

4. **Place commas around parenthetical information.** Parenthetical information is information that is not necessary for understanding the sentence but that clarifies something within the sentence. Parenthetical information can include transition words (*therefore, however*) and appositives (an appositive is a word or group of words that renames the item before it).

Place commas around parenthetical information when it appears within a sentence:

Within:	The professor approved, for the most part, my proposal.
Transition within:	My proposal, therefore, requires more work.
Appositive within:	Dr. Adams, my professor, has interesting insights.

Place a comma after the information when it precedes (introduces) an independent clause:

Precedes: However, those insights are sometimes controversial.

Place a comma before the information when it follows an independent clause:

Follows: Those insights are sometimes controversial, however.

Using commas to distinguish nonessential information from essential information is similar to using commas to set off parenthetical information. Don't place commas around essential information. Here are two examples:

Correct:	All students who do not submit this major assignment will fail the course.
Incorrect:	All students, who do not submit this major assignment, will fail the course.

By setting off the modifying clause *who do not submit this major assignment,* the commas in the second sentence change the meaning of the sentence:

All students will fail the course.

Obviously only those students who do not submit the assignment will fail. *Who do not submit this major assignment* is essential information; it should not be set off by commas.

EXERCISE 1 Punctuate the following sentences by applying the four comma rules. Some sentences may be correct.

1. Although cultural learning is a good reason for attending college developing thinking skills may be a more important reason.

2. People without a college education obviously do think.

3. But college students who read widely write often and discuss ideas are enhancing their thinking skills.

4. In addition to better thinking skills a college education encourages self-discovery.

5. Students are often challenged intellectually emotionally morally and socially while at college.

6. These challenges often result in growth and growth leads to more interesting lives.

7. A college education should help students stretch their limits and discover their strengths and weaknesses.

8. A career therefore is only one reason for attending college.

EXERCISE 2   Punctuate the following paragraph by applying the four comma rules. Some sentences may be correct.

In *Hunger of Memory* Richard Rodriguez shares his experiences with education and learning English. When he entered elementary school he did not speak English. He spoke only the language of his home Spanish. His teachers came to his house and they insisted that his parents require young Rodriguez to speak English at home. Rodriguez his two sisters and his brother began to speak only English while their parents continued to speak Spanish. Rodriguez describes growing up in two worlds the world of Spanish and the world of English. Because he wanted to please his teachers Rodriguez quickly adopted English as his new language. Unfortunately he gradually forgot how to speak Spanish.

EXERCISE 3   Using the current draft of your essay, do the following:

1. Identify and label five sentences by placing a comma before a coordinating conjunction.

2. Identify and label five sentences by placing a comma between items in a series.

3. Identify and label five sentences by placing a comma after an introductory element.

4. Identify and label three sentences by placing a comma around parenthetical information.

OPTIONS FOR WRITING

Reflect

1. Briefly describe one unforgettable experience—positive or negative—that you have had with a teacher. Then discuss the effects that experience has had on your life.

2. From your personal experience as a parent or as a child, explain the role you believe parents play in the education process. Comment on when parents should step up or hold back their involvement. Give specific examples to support your position.

Inform

3. Interview a nontraditional student (for example, someone beginning college years after graduating from high school). Report on the individual's motivation for being in college, or describe the challenges of being a nontraditional student.

4. Report on how students can relieve the stress of going to college.

Persuade

5. Argue the case for abolishing or reforming the current grading system in your composition class. Describe the current system and offer at least one viable alternative.

6. A growing number of parents are opting to withdraw their children from public or private schools and to teach them at home. Persuade a school administrator to either encourage or discourage home schooling.

Speculate

7. Think about a teacher with whom you were frustrated. If you were that teacher, describe how you would handle a student like you. Remember that you're writing from the teacher's perspective here, so take into account the teacher's personality and background.

8. Consider a controversial issue in the local schools—perhaps dropouts, multicultural education, or funding. Speculate on and present a possible solution to the issue.

Chapter 3

ENVIRONMENT

Today we are experiencing the consequences of centuries of environmental misuse. At the same time, we are doing more than ever to preserve the environment. Never before have we been so aware of our responsibilities to the planet. Never before have technology and science been more helpful in treating environmental ills. Never before has the international community worked so well together in the single cause of improving the quality of all aspects of the environment.

To prepare for this chapter's theme, the environment, answer the following questions:

- How are individuals responsible for improving the environment?
- How does environmental neglect affect people individually?

READINGS on *Environment*

Baby Birds
Gale Lawrence

Gale Lawrence is a freelance writer, teacher, and naturalist and has written numerous naturalist books. This article is from her book The Beginning Naturalist *(1979).*

Every spring the "baby bird crisis" occurs. By May many birds have   1
hatched their first broods and are feeding them in the nest while they
grow their feathers and learn to fly. Baby birds have a way of tumbling out of
their nests, and children have a way of finding them and bringing them home.
What should a family do if faced with this "crisis"?

First, take the baby bird back to the exact spot where it was found. Look   2
carefully for a nest nearby. If you find the nest and it is accessible, put the bird
gently back into the nest. Contrary to popular belief, the mother bird will not
reject a baby that has been handled by human beings. A deer, which has a
keen sense of smell and fears the human scent, will reject a fawn that has been
handled, but birds are different. If you find the nest and return the baby, you
have done the best you can do.

As a next-best measure, tie a small box onto a branch of a tree or shrub   3
near where the bird was found, and put the baby bird in the box. The bird will
thus be off the ground and out of the reach of neighborhood cats and dogs.

The third best thing you can do is simply to leave the bird in the exact spot   4
where it was found. Parent birds are accustomed to having their young fall out
of the nest, and they will feed them on the ground. Of course, the baby bird is
more vulnerable on the ground than it is in the nest or in a box, but it still
stands a better chance of surviving under its own parents' care than under
human care. If the baby bird is found near a house, it is better to keep pet dogs
and cats indoors than to bring the baby bird indoors in an attempt to protect it.

If the baby is truly abandoned or orphaned—something you can learn   5
only by watching it from a distance for an hour or more—you have a decision
to make. You can leave it there to die a natural death—which might in fact be
the most humane thing to do. Or you can take it indoors. If you decide to care
for it yourself, you are making a substantial commitment. And, even if you live
up to your commitment, there is no guarantee that the bird will survive.

Two major problems are involved in trying to parent a baby bird. One is   6
feeding it, and the other is preparing it for life in the wild. Parent birds do it

all as a matter of course, but a human parent will have to drop other activities for a period of weeks and perhaps install a screened porch or aviary to do the job right.

Before you can even address yourself to the problem of feeding, however, you have the more immediate problem of the bird's shock and fright to contend with. Perhaps this is the time to send one member of the family for a book on the care of wild animal young, while another rigs up a heating pad or hot water bottle to warm the baby bird. One good book is *Care of the Wild Feathered and Furred: A Guide to Wildlife Handling and Care* (Santa Cruz: Unity Press, 1973) by Mae Hickman and Maxine Guy. Another is Ronald Rood's *The Care and Feeding of Wild Pets* (New York: Pocket Books, 1976). A third book that is specifically about birds is *Bird Ambulance* (New York: Charles Scribner's Sons, 1971) by Arline Thomas.   7

Now comes the problem of feeding. The warm milk in an eye dropper that seems to be everyone's immediate impulse when it comes to feeding animal young may be appropriate for baby mammals, but it will come as a complete surprise to the baby bird. Its parents were probably feeding it mashed worms, caterpillars, insects, and other delicious odds and ends. Therefore, you'll need to do the same. At first you should supply the baby bird with protein-rich foods. Eventually you're going to have to identify the species and learn something about its food habits in the wild if you want the bird to grow up properly. Whether the bird is a seed eater, an insect eater, or a predator will make a difference.   8

Parent birds feed their babies about every ten or fifteen minutes from sunrise to sunset. They also feed them exactly what they need to keep their bowels regulated and their bodies growing properly. They also keep the nest clean by removing the babies' excrement, which usually appears shortly after each feeding. In brief, between finding and preparing appropriate food, feeding, and cleaning up after meals you're not going to have much time for anything else for a while if you decide to parent a baby bird.   9

If you do manage to keep the young bird fed properly and growing, your next problem is providing it with enough space for it to practice flying. You cannot expect a bird to go from your kitchen to the wild with one swoop of its wings. You will need to continue feeding and protecting the bird while it is adjusting to the outdoors. If it had stayed with its parents, it would have had adult birds to follow and imitate, but, with nothing but human beings to encourage it, it will have to make sense out of its environment alone. The young bird that has been raised by humans is at a disadvantage when it comes to competing for food and avoiding the attacks of predators. So even if you do manage to raise a fledgling to adulthood, you have not guaranteed its survival in the wild.   10

If you think I'm trying to sound discouraging, I am. The adoption of a baby bird will probably result in failure. You might even cause a death that would not have occurred had you left the baby bird where it was. Your intentions might be good; the ethical impulse that motivates your actions might be of the   11 best kind. But you should know that even experienced veterinarians have a low success rate in caring for wild animals.

Perhaps the most important thing a child or adult can learn from an encounter with a baby bird is the difference between wild animals and domestic pets. Whereas puppies and kittens warm to human attention and become very much a part of the family, a wild bird never will. Attempting to make a pet out of a wild animal is a serious disservice to that animal—so serious, in fact, that there are laws against it. Life in the wild does not consist of friendly humans, readily available meals, and a protected environment. Wild animals must remain wild to survive.   12

Rather than adopt a baby bird, why not "adopt" a whole bird family— from a distance? Chances are there is a bird's nest somewhere near your home. Or you can build birdhouses to attact birds to your yard. Learn to watch the bird family from a distance. If human beings get too close, the parent birds won't come to the nest. So practice sitting quietly, perhaps with a pair of binoculars, far enough away from the nest that the adult birds won't feel threatened.   13

Watching birds in the wild is a much healthier and more realistic activity than fantasizing that a bird will become your special friend because you raised it. Unfortunately, movies, television, and children's books have created a "Bambi syndrome" in us. The young of most species are precious and adorable, but the desire to fondle and caress and make pets out of wildlings is dangerously romantic. It should not be encouraged. We'd be much wiser if we were content to be observers of wildlife. If we truly care about wild animals, we should be protectors of their wildness, which enables the best of them to survive.   14

Questions and Issues to Consider

Writing Process   1. Who is Lawrence's intended audience? What kind of readers would find this essay interesting?

2. Lawrence ends her first paragraph with a question. Why do you think she does this?

Aims of Writing   3. In your own words describe Lawrence's purpose in this essay. Why does she discuss this issue? Does she have more than one purpose? If so, what is her main purpose?

Critical Thinking   4. If you were faced with the decision to leave a baby bird to die a natural death or to bring it indoors, what would you do? Why?

A Fable for Tomorrow
Rachel Carson

In 1962, Rachel Carson's influential book Silent Spring *was a significant factor in the government's decision to ban the insecticide DDT. Carson, a biologist, was able to explain complicated scientific concepts simply and clearly to a general public. In the following excerpt from* Silent Spring, *Carson speculates on the effects chemicals have on the environment.*

There was once a town in the heart of America where all life seemed to live in harmony with its surroundings. The town lay in the midst of a checkerboard of prosperous farms, with fields of grain and hillsides of orchards where, in spring, white clouds of bloom drifted above the green fields. In autumn, oak and maple and birch set up a blaze of color that flamed and flickered across a backdrop of pines. Then foxes barked in the hills and deer silently crossed the fields, half hidden in the mists of the fall mornings.   1

Along the roads, laurel, viburnum and alder,[1] great ferns and wildflowers delighted the traveler's eye through much of the year. Even in winter the roadsides were places of beauty, where countless birds came to feed on the berries and on the seed heads of the dried weeds rising above the snow. The countryside was, in fact, famous for the abundance and variety of its bird life, and when the flood of migrants was pouring through in spring and fall, people traveled from great distances to observe them. Others came to fish the streams, which flowed clear and cold out of the hills and contained shady pools where trout lay. So it had been from the days many years ago when the first settlers raised their houses, sank their wells, and built their barns.   2

Then a strange blight[2] crept over the area and everything began to change. Some evil spell had settled on the community: mysterious maladies swept the flocks of chickens; the cattle and sheep sickened and died. Everywhere was a shadow of death. The farmers spoke of much illness among their families. In the town the doctors had become more and more puzzled by new kinds of sickness appearing among their patients. There had been several sudden and unexplained deaths, not only among adults but even among children, who would be stricken suddenly while at play and die within a few hours.   3

There was a strange stillness. The birds, for example—where had they gone? Many people spoke of them, puzzled and disturbed. The feeding sta-   4

---

[1] **laurel, viburnum, alder:** various shrubs and trees
[2] **blight:** a plant disease

tions in the backyards were deserted. The few birds seen anywhere were mori-bund;[3] they trembled violently and could not fly. It was a spring without voices. On the mornings that had once throbbed with the dawn chorus of robins, catbirds, doves, jays, wrens, and scores of other bird voices there was now no sound; only silence lay over the fields and woods and marsh.

On the farms the hens brooded,[4] but no chicks hatched. The farmers com-plained that they were unable to raise any pigs—the litters were small and the young survived only a few days. The apple trees were coming into bloom but no bees droned among the blossoms, so there was no pollination and there would be no fruit.

5

The roadsides, once so attractive, were now lined with browned and with-ered vegetation as though swept by fire. These, too, were silent, deserted by all living things. Even the streams were now lifeless. Anglers[5] no longer visited them, for all the fish had died.

6

In the gutters under the eaves and between the shingles of the roofs, a white granular powder still showed a few patches; some weeks before it had fallen like snow upon the roofs and the lawns, the fields and streams.

7

No witchcraft, no enemy action had silenced the rebirth of new life in this stricken world. The people had done it themselves.

8

This town does not actually exist, but it might easily have a thousand counterparts[6] in America or elsewhere in the world. I know of no community that has experienced all the misfortunes I describe. Yet every one of these dis-asters has actually happened somewhere, and many real communities have already suffered a substantial number of them. A grim specter[7] has crept upon us almost unnoticed, and this imagined tragedy may easily become a stark reality we all shall know.

9

Questions and Issues to Consider

Writing Process   1. Carson uses vivid description to help make her point. Without looking back to the essay, list as many details as you can remember. Return to any one paragraph in the essay and underline all the spe-cific details. Explain how these details help support Carson's pur-pose for writing.

---

[3]**moribund:** about to die
[4]**brooded:** sat on chicken eggs
[5]**anglers:** people who fish with hooks
[6]**counterparts:** locations with similar characteristics
[7]**specter:** a haunting possibility

Aims of Writing   2. Carson writes to speculate: She is imagining the consequences of environmental pollution. Still she makes her description of the consequences of environmental neglect seem realistic. How does Carson do this?

Critical Thinking   3. Carson describes the effects of a "strange blight" that destroys the environment. Suppose a native plant or animal in your region suddenly became extinct. How would the absence of that life form affect people and the environment?

4. Think about a time when you were exposed to or noticed pollution. Describe in detail what you saw, smelled, tasted, felt, or heard. Explain how that experience has affected your stance toward pollution.

PREWRITING

ASKING JOURNALISTS' QUESTIONS

One method for generating and organizing ideas is asking pointed questions—Who? What? When? Where? How? Why?—the kind of questions journalists ask to be sure that they have all the information they need for an article.

You can ask journalists' questions to generate ideas and to develop a more thorough understanding of your topic. For example, suppose your topic is wood-burning stoves. Begin by writing your topic at the top of a sheet of paper. Then ask these questions:

Who?

Who uses wood-burning stoves in the United States?

Who determines the environmental impact of wood-burning stoves?

Who, if anyone, should set standards for wood-burning stoves?

Who installs wood-burning stoves?

Who misuses wood-burning stoves?

What?

What happens when wood burns in a stove?

What pollutants escape into the air from wood-burning stoves?

What impact do wood-burning stoves have on the environment?

What difference is there between an efficient and an inefficient wood-burning stove?

What effects do wood-burning stoves have on people in the home?

When?

When do wood-burning stoves become environmentally dangerous?

When should government agencies place restrictions on wood-burning stoves?

When should homeowners not use their wood-burning stoves?

Where?

Where should wood-burning stoves be allowed?

Where should wood-burning stoves be banned?

How?

How is an environmentally efficient wood-burning stove engineered?

How can a homeowner affect the efficiency of a wood-burning stove?

How can a homeowner best maintain the efficiency of a wood-burning stove?

How can government agencies enforce wood-burning stove regulations?

How does an environmentally efficient wood-burning stove operate?

Why?

Why do homeowners invest in wood-burning stoves?

Why are environmentalists concerned about wood-burning stoves?

Why should the government regulate wood-burning stoves?

Why should wood-burning stoves be cleaned regularly?

Why should people who don't own wood-burning stoves be interested in this subject?

These questions and their answers identify what you know about wood-burning stoves and expand your understanding of them. Usually the more you know about a topic or the more perceptions you have about a topic, the more options you have to choose from as you write.

For instance, Dawn Walquist, a student, decides that the broad topic of her essay will be environmental policies. She begins by asking journalists' questions to determine her own knowledge and to expand her perceptions of the topic. Here are some of the questions she asks:

Who?

Who should create policies for the environment?

Who should not manage policies for the environment?

What?

What happens when someone manages the environment?

What effects do policies have on the environment?

When?

When should someone enact a policy for the environment?

When, if ever, should the environment need a policy?

Where?

Where does an environmental policy need to be implemented?

Where does an environmental policy not need to be implemented?

How?

How do ordinary citizens learn about environmental policies?

How did I become aware of environmental policies?

Why?

Why would someone try to enact an environmental policy?

Why is environmental policymaking right or wrong?

Dawn initially plans to write on the general topic of environmental policies. But in the process of asking journalists' questions, her focus and perceptions begin to change. She notices that her questions place an emphasis on individuals' understanding and misunderstanding of environmental policies. In fact, she asks herself, "How did *I* become aware of environmental policies?" At this point, Dawn remembers the fires in Yellowstone National Park in 1988, breathing and seeing the smoke-filled air at her home more than a two-hour drive from the park. She also remembers the extensive news coverage of the fires and a visit to Yellowstone the following year. She decides to write her paper on the "natural burn" policy, a controversial policy of allowing fires within a national park to burn naturally rather than controlling them. Again Dawn asks journalists' questions, this time about her more limited topic:

Who was responsible for making the natural burn policy that affected the fires in Yellowstone in 1988?

What effects have the natural burn policy had on Yellowstone National Park?

When, if ever, is a natural burn policy justified?

Where did the natural burn policy work effectively?

How did the natural burn policy come about?

Why did the fires in Yellowstone National Park even happen?

Journalists' questions have helped to expand Dawn's perception of environmental policy and to limit her topic to the effects of the natural burn policy on the fires in Yellowstone Park in 1988. Dawn assumes her main purpose in writing this essay is to inform her readers about the policy and the fires. (A draft of Dawn's paper begins on page 110.)

EXPLORING YOUR OPTIONS

1. On the line below write your topic.

    _____

2. Using your topic, write three questions for each of the journalists' questions:

    Who?

    _____

    _____

    _____

    What?

    _____

    _____

    _____

    When?

    _____

    _____

    _____

    Where?

    _____

    _____

    _____

    How?

    _____

    _____

    _____

Why?

_____

_____

_____

3. Choose one question you would like to explore further. This question is your limited topic. On the lines below, write your limited topic.

_____

_____

4. Using your limited topic, write another question for each of the journalists' questions.

Who?

_____

_____

_____

What?

_____

_____

_____

When?

_____

_____

_____

Where?

_____

_____

_____

How?

_____

_____

_____

Why?

_____

_____

_____

5. Describe more specifically what you would like to accomplish by writing on this topic. This can be your working thesis statement.

_____

_____

6. Put a checkmark next to the aim that best represents your reason for writing this paper.

_____ To reflect   _____ To persuade

_____ To inform   _____ To speculate

DRAFTING

ORGANIZING IDEAS

You have a good idea, and you want to present that idea effectively. The key to effective presentation is effective organization. Some writing in college—and some in the workplace—must follow a predetermined structure. Lab reports, business letters, legal briefs, annual reports, proposals, summaries, and technical reports are all examples of formally structured writing.

However, most college writing, and much professional writing, calls for less formal types of organization. The writer uses the type of organization that fits the paper's topic and intended audience and the author's own purpose for writing. This means that no single type of organization is appropriate for all writing. Still, most forms of organization are designed to arrange information logically, both to meet the writer's goal and to make the reader's task easier.

Ideas and Form

Allow your ideas to determine your form. It is not uncommon to write without knowing exactly what you want to say, especially when you are writing nonstop. You may know, for instance, that you want to write about the general topic of conserving water, but the specific ideas may not come to you until you actually put pen to paper. This is natural because as you write you generate new ideas. So the act of writing helps determine a paper's organization. Flexibility is important here. Try not to construct a rigid, detailed organization before you draft a paper. Instead begin writing with some general ideas and supporting examples in mind; then let the organization begin to establish itself.

Dawn, for instance, has decided to let her ideas determine her paper's organization. She's not sure where her topic will go, but she chooses to begin by writing more detailed responses to her journalists' questions on the natural burn policy and the 1988 fires in Yellowstone. She assumes her answers will reveal the direction and organization of the paper. Here, for example, is Dawn's response to the question, Why did the fires in Yellowstone National Park even happen?

> I remember the Yellowstone fires through August and September 1988. The normally clear summer skies were hazy and smoky. I even remember local newscasts advising people with health problems to stay indoors to avoid breathing the air, but since we farm, we were always outside. I don't know yet why the fires happened. I do know we were in the middle of a drought, and it was hot that summer. I also know some careless campers started a fire in Targhee that spread into the park. I remember people being upset with the idea that Yellowstone Park officials didn't allow the fires to be put out because of some policy. I want to learn more about this policy—how it has come about and how it has affected Yellowstone. I'll probably discuss the policy first, then the Yellowstone fires, and finally how the policy affected the 1988 Yellowstone fires.

Organization and the Thesis Statement

Work with a tightly focused thesis statement. Because a well-developed thesis statement includes topic, stance, and plan, it naturally organizes the writing. A thesis statement on landfills might look like this:

> Madison County's landfill is environmentally unsafe because
> of the damage it could do to the underground water supply,
> the lack of a lining, and the lack of dumping regulations.

According to this thesis statement, the author plans to discuss the possible impact of the landfill on the underground water supply before discussing the lining and the dumping regulations.

The thesis statement is an effective organizer *if* it is well developed. A broad thesis statement—*landfills are environmentally unsafe,* for example—does not suggest an organization. But don't be discouraged if you don't have a strong thesis statement at the outset. It may be that a well-organized thesis statement won't emerge until after you've finished the initial draft. Often writers use a working thesis statement until later revisions help them formulate a final one.

Dawn at this point doesn't want to use a formal thesis statement because she wants to let her ideas determine the paper's organization. However, she does choose to use a working thesis statement: People often blame the "natural burn" policy for the vast destruction of the 1988 Yellowstone fires, but there were probably other reasons.

Developing an Organization

There are different methods for establishing a paper's organization. One method is to draw up informal outlines or sketches. Another method is to use a "blueprint."

Draw up informal outlines or sketches. An informal outline helps you organize your ideas before you write. Suppose you've chosen to write on college students' responsibilities to conserve resources by recycling. After you've completed a list of journalists' questions on the topic, put a checkmark next to the questions you feel are most important in terms of your purpose and your audience's needs. Then number the checked questions in the order you plan to discuss them. Remember that this is a preliminary plan; it can change as you actually draft the paper.

Dawn reviews the journalists' questions she asked about the natural burn policy. She sees that the questions do suggest an informal organization. That is, she realizes she probably has to answer the questions in this order:

1. How did the natural burn policy come about?

2. When, if ever, is a natural burn policy justified?

3. Why did the fires in Yellowstone National Park even happen?

4. What effects has the natural burn policy had on Yellowstone National Park?

Use a "blueprint." Particularly if your writing time is limited, consider using a "blueprint," like the one in Figure 3.1, to organize your ideas. A blueprint saves time because it helps generate and organize ideas and a thesis statement before you begin drafting your paper.

Suppose your general topic is solar energy in homes. In the key ideas boxes, list general concepts you would like to cover—for example, how solar energy works, how effective solar energy is, and what solar energy costs. Then limit the topic, say, to solar energy in homes in Helena, Montana.

FIGURE 3.1

"Blueprint" organization

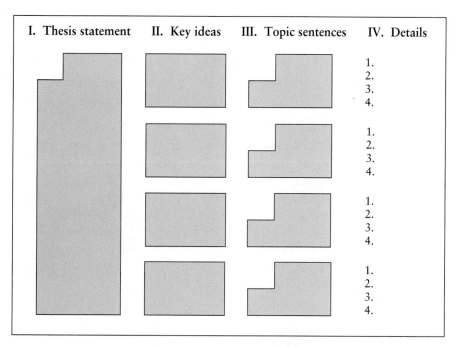

Next, incorporate all your key ideas into a single sentence. This sentence is your working thesis statement. Write the statement in the thesis statement box. Here's an example:

Solar heating systems are possible, effective, and economical for homes in Helena, Montana.

Now put each key idea into a complete sentence and write the sentences in the topic sentences boxes. A *topic sentence* is the controlling idea of a paragraph. It plays much the same role in a paragraph as a thesis statement plays in an essay: It states the subject of the paragraph. Not every essay has a formal thesis statement, and not every paragraph has a formal topic sentence. But topic sentences are common in college writing because they directly state what the paragraph is about. A topic sentence can appear anywhere in the paragraph; usually, though, it comes at the beginning. Here are three key ideas from one example and the topic sentences derived from those ideas:

Key idea: How solar energy works

Topic sentence: The two main types of solar heating systems are active and passive.

Key idea: How effective is solar energy

Topic sentence: Solar energy systems can be incorporated effectively into most home designs.

Key idea: What solar energy costs

Topic sentence: Many residential solar energy systems earn back their initial costs within five years because of increased energy savings.

Notice that the sentences do function as topic sentences and that each can get a paragraph started, a paragraph with something specific to say.

Finally, in the details column, list several examples, statistics, or incidents to support each key idea.

A blueprint can help you limit your topic and organize your ideas. But it can leave you with an organization that is stiff and artificial. If you can, let your topic, audience, or purpose determine the organization of your paper.

PRACTICE   1. Suppose your topic is excessive noise. Add examples of excessive noise to the following list:

Construction   Music   Neighbors

Traffic   Television   Animals

Emergency vehicles	Appliances	Children
_____	_____	_____
_____	_____	_____

2. Arrange the examples of excessive noise according to location—that is, inside noise or outside noise.

Inside noise		_Outside noise_	
_____	_____	_____	_____
_____	_____	_____	_____
_____	_____	_____	_____
_____	_____	_____	_____

3. Arrange the examples of excessive noise according to time—that is, daytime noise or nighttime noise.

Daytime noise		_Nighttime noise_	
_____	_____	_____	_____
_____	_____	_____	_____
_____	_____	_____	_____
_____	_____	_____	_____

EXPLORING YOUR OPTIONS

1. Allow your ideas to determine your paper's form. List either the journalists' questions you'd like to answer or the ideas you'd like to discuss in your paper.

_____

_____

_____

_____

_____

2. Ask yourself what your readers need to know first, next, and last. Then arrange your questions or ideas in the order in which you want to present them.

First: _____

Second: _____

Third: _____

Fourth: _____

Fifth: _____

WRITING TOGETHER

Share your organization plans with a classmate. Discuss your reasons for planning the paper the way you have. Determine together if your paper suggests other types of organization. Choose the organization that best meets the purpose of your paper and the needs of your audience.

DEFINITION

To help your readers understand your terms and concepts, you must define them effectively. This is particularly important when you're writing to inform or to persuade. A definition should clarify, explain, and enhance the meaning of a word or concept. For instance, the *American Heritage Dictionary* defines the word *environmentalist* as "a person who seeks to protect the natural environment." In the Pacific Northwest, both the timber industry and ecology activists consider themselves *environmentalists* because both groups want to preserve the forests. Yet each group has a different definition of the term. Because they plant new trees after they harvest a forest, lumberjacks believe that they are protecting the natural environment. Ecology activists, on the other hand, believe that environmentalists would never destroy the environment in order to protect it.

As a writer, your meaning of *environmentalist* may differ from your reader's definition. Your task, then, is to clearly define what you mean by *environmentalist.* You want your reader to understand, not necessarily accept, your definition. To use definitions most effectively in writing, you should know how to use formal and informal definitions and the various methods of extending definitions.

Formal and Informal Definitions

Words can be defined formally and informally.

Formal definitions. A formal definition provides three types of information: word, family, and qualifiers. The *word* is simply the term being defined. The *family* is the general category the word belongs to. The *qualifiers* are the qualities or differences that distinguish the word from other members of the family.

Word	=	Family	+	Qualifiers
Pollution	is	a waste product		such as a harmful chemical in a solid, liquid, or gas state that is discharged into the air, water, or soil.

The word *pollution* belongs to the general family of waste products; it differs from other waste products that are not expelled into the atmosphere, water, or ground.

Because formal definitions are complex, use them sparingly in your writing. Too many formal definitions make reading difficult. (Formal definitions are used most frequently in scientific and technical writings.)

Informal definitions. Shorter, easier to write, and easier to understand than a formal definition, an informal definition generally is used to explain a term. An informal definition simply substitutes an explanatory word, phrase, or clause for the term. Here is an informal definition of *human ecology:*

Human ecology is the relationship between people and their environment, how they affect each other.

Notice how the definition substitutes the words *people* and *environment* for *human ecology* and emphasizes the relationship between them.

Extended Definitions

When a sentence-length definition does not explain a term adequately, you may have to extend or expand the definition. There are many ways to extend a definition.

Further definition. Often when you're defining a term, especially in a formal definition, you have to use terms or principles within the definition that the reader may not know. These terms also need defining. For example, one definition of *desertification* is "desert expansion." What does *desert expansion* mean? Notice how the following example both explains what *desert expansion* is and extends the definition of *desertification*:

> *Desertification* is desert expansion. Because of warming weather patterns, long extended droughts, overgrazing, inefficient land cultivation, and extensive timber cutting, productive land has fast become unproductive desert. These deserts are increasing at an alarming rate all over, even in places where there were no deserts just a few years ago. So the deserts of the earth are expanding, and desertification continues to occur.

Concrete examples. Perhaps the most effective method of extending a definition is providing concrete examples. Suppose, for instance, that you want to extend the informal definition of *human ecology*. Notice how specific examples sharpen the meaning of the term:

> A century ago a homesteader chopped trees for a home or plowed the ground for crops. Each felled tree or each plowed furrow changed both the environment and the homesteader. Neither remained the same; they affected each other. Or consider today's hiker who leaves a beverage can on the trail, or the driver who tosses a hamburger wrapper from the car window. Or consider that every person in the United States produces more than twice his or her weight in waste every day. Each individual has an impact on the environment, and, in turn, this changed environment directly or indirectly affects each person. This is *human ecology*.

Comparison. Another method of extending a definition is to compare the term with a principle or experience with which the readers are familiar. Your readers may not know anything about the greenhouse effect of global warming, but they probably have sat in a car with the windows up:

> The greenhouse effect is like the interior of a warm car on a cold but sunny winter's day. The sun shines through the windows and heats the car, and the rolled-up windows prevent the heat from escaping. Therefore, the car's interior is warmer than the outside temperature. This is known as the *greenhouse effect*. Similarly, the sun shines through the earth's polluted atmosphere and heats the earth,

and the pollution prevents the heat from escaping. The greenhouse effect, then, contributes to global warming.

Cause and effect. To extend a definition by using cause and effect, you explain how something happened and what the consequences are. In the following example, the term *deforestation* is easier to understand if you explain the factors that can cause deforestation.

> As the world's need for food, lumber, and energy has continued to grow, many nations have allowed their forests to be destroyed. For example, farmers burn the forests to create more pastures for cattle or land for cultivation. The timber industry clears huge forests for lumber. And communities dam rivers to generate hydroelectric power. Activities like these are the cause of *deforestation*, the depletion of forests.

Dawn's topic is the natural burn policy and the Yellowstone fires. Instead of using a formal definition of *natural burn policy*, she decides to develop an informal definition. She plans to extend that definition with concrete examples and cause and effect. She'll give specific examples of both the cause of the fire and the effects the policy has had on Yellowstone.

✓ CHECKLIST: DEFINITION

1. Is the definition formal?

2. If your definition is formal, have you clearly identified the *family* or general category the word belongs to?

3. If your definition is formal, have you accurately distinguished the word with specific *qualifiers* or qualities that distinguish the word from other members of the family?

4. Is your definition informal?

5. Does your definition simply substitute an explanatory word, phrase, or clause?

6. Is your definition extended?

7. If your definition is extended, do you use further definition, concrete examples, comparison, or cause and effect?

DEFINITION: AN EXAMPLE

In the following paragraph from his book *Earth in the Balance: Ecology and the Human Spirit* (1992), Vice President Al Gore defines the term *deforestation*. Notice that he combines concrete examples with cause and effect to extend his definition.

Deforestation

At the current rate of deforestation, virtually all of the tropical rain forests will be gone partway through the next century. . . . They are being burned to clear land for pasture; they are being clear-cut with chain saws for lumber; they are being flooded by hydroelectric dams to generate power. They are disappearing from the face of the earth at the rate of one and a half acres a second, night and day, every day, all year round. And, for a number of reasons, the destruction of tropical rain forests is still picking up speed: the rapid population growth in tropical countries is leading to relentless pressure for expansion into marginal areas; shortages of fuel confronting an estimated [one] billion people in large areas of the Third World lead many to ravage the surrounding forests; mounting debts owed by developing countries to the industrial world encourage the exploitation of all available natural resources in a short-term effort to earn hard currency; massive, often misguided development projects that are inappropriate for tropical countries are opening formerly inaccessible vast areas to the civilized world; and livestock farming, with its insatiable demand for cleared pasture land every year, continues to spread. The list of reasons is long and complex, but the essential point is simple: in the daily battle between a growing, always ravenous civilization and an ancient ecosystem, the ecosystem is losing badly.

PRACTICE 1   1. In one sentence, write an informal definition of *deforestation*.

_____

_____

2. Identify four concrete examples Gore uses to define and illustrate *deforestation*.

_____   _____

_____   _____

3. Gore identifies several causes of deforestation. List two of them.

_____   _____

4. Gore identifies several effects of deforestation. List two of them.

_____   _____

5. Explain how Gore indirectly uses comparison to define *deforestation*.

_____

_____

_____

PRACTICE 2   1. Write a one-sentence formal definition (Word = Family + Qualifiers) for one of the following words: *waste, conservation, recycle.*

_____

_____

2. Write a one-sentence informal definition for the word you defined formally in question 1.

_____

_____

3. Use your informal definition (question 2) as the first sentence of a paragraph. Then extend that definition by using one or more of the following methods: further definition, concrete examples, comparison, cause and effect.

_____

_____

_____

_____

_____

_____

_____

WRITING TOGETHER

1. After completing Practice 2 on your own, share your definitions with a class partner who has also defined the same term.

2. As a pair, repeat Practice 2 and include details from each of your definitions.

EXPLORING YOUR OPTIONS

1. List three terms or concepts that you want to define in the paper you are working on now.

   _____   _____   _____

2. Write a one-sentence formal definition (Word = Family + Qualifiers) for one of the terms or concepts you listed in question 1.

   _____

   _____

3. Write a one-sentence informal definition for one of the terms or concepts you listed in question 1.

   _____

   _____

4. Use your informal definition (question 3) as the first sentence of a paragraph. Then extend that definition by using one or more of the following methods: further definition, concrete examples, comparison, cause and effect.

   _____

   _____

   _____

   _____

   _____

Definition and Aims

As the following writing assignments show, definition can be used with all the different writing aims.

Reflect

Chances are your definition of *recycling* has changed over the years. At one time, *recycling* probably meant wearing hand-me-down clothes and may have been an "embarrassing" experience. Later, when recycling meant having the old family car at your disposal, you may have added the concepts of "freedom" and "responsibility" to your changing definition of *recycling*. Explain how your definition of *recycling* has evolved.

Using a personal experience, define *environmental abuse*.

Inform

Explain the concept of *landfills* by describing for your classmates the journey trash takes from your trash can to its final destination, the community landfill.

Define *plastics* by describing for your classmates how the properties of plastics can be beneficial or hazardous to the environment.

Persuade

Persuade local homeowners to incorporate solar energy alternatives into their present heating systems by defining *solar energy* and writing specific examples or physical descriptions of the systems that are available for installation.

Persuade local homeowners to test their homes for radon gas by defining *radon gas*. Consider explaining how to test for radon gas or how to remove radon gas from a home.

Speculate

Speculate on the state of the environment one hundred years from now by defining and providing examples of fuel sources, manufacturing techniques, waste emissions, or changed lifestyles.

What do you think *population control* will mean one hundred years from now?

EXPLORING YOUR OPTIONS

You are now ready to write your first draft. You already have determined the following:

Your limited topic: _____

Your working thesis statement: _____

_____

_____

Your main writing aim: _____

The order you plan to use for your key ideas:

First: _____

Second: _____

Third: _____

Fourth: _____

Fifth: _____

Set aside a block of time, and write your first draft. Don't worry about right and wrong. The objective is to get your ideas onto paper.

REWRITING

ANALYZING YOUR AUDIENCE

The element of the communication triangle that many inexperienced writers overlook is the reader. Good writers choose examples, words, a tone, and a structure that best meet the needs, assumptions, and attitudes of their audience. To help you determine those needs, assumptions, and attitudes, try answering these three questions:

Why does my audience *need* to be better informed about this subject?

What does my audience *assume* or already know about this subject?

What is my audience's *attitude* toward, or feelings and beliefs about, this subject?

Describing Your Audience

After reading your draft, answer the three questions about your audience in as much detail as possible. Here are Dawn's responses to the three questions about her audience:

1. Why does my audience *need* to be better informed about this subject?

> I'd like my audience to recognize that poli-
> cies currently exist that do have an impact on
> the environment. These policies for the most
> part continue to affect the environment signif-
> icantly. But, unfortunately, many of us are
> unaware of the policies or their impact. For
> example, I vividly remember genuinely believing
> the sensational news reports of the 1988 Yel-
> lowstone fires saying that the park authorities
> were allowing the entire park to burn rather
> than put out fires. The more I learn about the
> natural burn policy, I realize how little I
> understood it before. My audience needs to
> understand it also.

2. What does my audience *assume* or already know about this subject?

> I have had some experience with these
> fires because we live a couple hours from
> Yellowstone Park. I assume others from my
> area won't have difficulty remembering the
> smoke-filled air, the brilliant red sunsets,
> or young people joining fire crews. I assume
> those outside the area have some memories
> because of the extensive national news cover-
> age. Even if readers know nothing about the
> 1988 fires or even about Yellowstone, they
> can imagine fires burning more than a million
> acres of woods and grassland.

3. What is my audience's *attitude* toward, or feelings and beliefs about, this subject?

> My audience, I assume, is like I was,
> believing that any fire is bad. Fire needs
> to be put out. People are generally afraid

```
of fire because it has such uncontrollable
destructive power. We also have images of
peaceful, beautiful mature trees growing for
generations suddenly gone up in flame. And we
may even have images of animals fleeing for
their lives from the flames as we remember
Bambi and his mother running to escape fire.
But fire can also be good. It can warm us,
cook for us, create an industrial age for us.
And fire can rejuvenate a forest. I need to
inform my audience about that renewal.
```

Rewriting for an Audience

Now incorporate your awareness of your audience into your paper. Review your answers to the questions about your audience's needs, assumptions, and attitudes. Then reread and rewrite your draft to reflect those needs, assumptions, and attitudes. Often your best papers are those in which you focus on your audience.

STUDENT ESSAY

Below is a draft of Dawn Walquist's essay. Dawn is from Idaho and is majoring in general studies. As you read the draft, ask yourself two basic questions:

- How does Dawn succeed in fulfilling her purpose for writing this essay?

- How can Dawn strengthen this draft?

Natural Burn Policy: Can It Take the Heat?

Dawn begins by giving readers background information on her topic.

```
    The year of 1988 will be remembered as one of
the driest summers ever recorded in the history of
Yellowstone National Park. People will remember
crops shriveling and rivers shrinking while forest
and meadows burned under a cloudless sky for
months on end. People driving through Yellowstone
at this time encountered black charred trees on
both sides of the road. Flames raced down moun-
tains and across landscape destroying everything
in their path. People were enraged that park offi-
```

cials would allow the natural and scenic setting in Yellowstone Park to be destroyed in this manner. Many people blamed "natural burn" policy for this disastrous scene. They claimed that "If fires had been fought from the beginning, the losses would have been far less" ("What About" 112). Dr. Bob Murch, Program Manager of the Forest Service's Disaster Assistance Program, argues, "Even if we could stop all fires, considering their ecological value, I would not recommend such a policy. We must find a way for such fires to exist" (qtd. in Wuerthner, "Flames," 42-43). I believe the "natural burn" policy did not cause the rapid progression of the fires in Yellowstone during the 1988 fire season. The combination of wind, dry weather, and low moisture content contributed to the damage, but this policy itself did not harm the park's wildlife, vegetation, or scenic features in any way. Nature should be allowed to take its course.

Most people were initially against the "natural burn" policy because they did not understand what it stated. People assumed that "natural burn" meant that fires are allowed to burn uncontrolled over landscape, no matter what the circumstances. This assumption is incorrect. "Natural burn" allows agencies to develop a fire management plan that specifically outlines under what conditions a fire is allowed to burn. Any fires which do not meet these conditions are immediately suppressed.

Four conditions were developed under the "natural burn" policy in 1972. First, as often as possible, any lightning-caused fires were allowed to burn naturally. Second, fire was to be suppressed if it threatened people or natural features. It was also to be suppressed if it threatened or endangered wildlife or burned outside the park boundaries. Third, all human-caused fires were to be suppressed. Fourth, prescribed or controlled burning was permitted in areas where there was a buildup of fuels, such as dead and fallen trees (Vogt 19). These conditions under the "natural

Dawn uses outside sources to explain and support her topic.

She defines natural burn policy for readers.

burn" policy were designed to protect the park, not harm it.

In the first sixteen years after the "natural burn" policy had been enacted, there had never been any serious problems. Two hundred thirty-five fires were allowed to burn which consumed a total of 34,157 acres (Wood 162). The largest of these fires burned an area of 7,400 acres. At this rate, it would have taken 675 years for every area of the park to be renewed (Conniff 43).

Dawn describes the factors that together caused the 1988 fires.

Many unusual circumstances converged in 1988 to create ideal conditions for a severe forest fire. These factors included heavy drought, high winds, an unusual number of lightning strikes, and the low moisture content of downed branches, grasses, and timber. The summer of 1988 was the driest ever recorded in the park's history. In a typical "Yellowstone summer," June and July are without rain, but storms arriving in August usually bring the necessary moisture to extinguish the fires which started earlier in the summer. However, this did not happen in the summer of 1988. The first precipitation that summer was recorded on September 11. This lack of precipitation caused extremely low moisture content in downed branches, grasses, and timber. The moisture content in previous years averaged around twelve percent. In 1988 it was as low as two or three percent. The fuels also dried out much earlier in the season and stayed much drier than in previous years (Wuerthner, *Yellowstone,* 18).

The second unusual factor was the wind, which sometimes reached the strength of a hurricane. High winds frequently pushed fires as fast as two miles per hour. The fire often advanced as much as 5-10 miles per day. The combination of wind and low humidity was the primary reason for the uncontrollable fires (Ekey 11).

The third unusual condition in 1988 was the larger number of lightning strikes. In an average year, there are about 22 lightning strikes during the summer. During this summer, the amount was double its previous average. Forty-eight of the

fifty-two fires caused by lightning burned less
than one acre (Zumbo 87).

She describes the
effects the fires had
on the park.

This combination of unusual factors led to the
destruction of 1.5 million acres within the boundaries of Yellowstone Park. This sounds like an
incredible amount of land, but this figure actually represents only one-tenth of the park's
acreage (Simpson 70). It is true that some of the
beauty of the park was lost when these fires raged
through in 1988, but this destruction was necessary for the renewal of vegetation and wildlife
within the park. George Wuerthner, a chief ecologist for Yellowstone Park, argues, "Fires did not
'destroy' 1.5 million acres of Yellowstone; they
'created' 1.5 million acres of new ecological
opportunity" ("Flames" 42).

Some of this ecological opportunity which was
created included many new varieties of plants and
animals. A total of 261 large mammals were found
dead in the burned areas. Most of these animals were
killed from excessive smoke inhalation. This number
was comprised of 246 elk, 2 moose, 4 mule deer, and
9 bison (Romme and Despain 44). This seems like a
large number of elk, but this number represents only
1% of the total population in the park. None of the
68 radio-collared park elk were killed (Singer and
others 717). Most of the large animals were not
affected by the fires. They just moved out of the
way. Within days after the fires' occurrence, animals had migrated back to their now burned homes.

These fires appeared to have caused major destruction to the vegetation; however, recovery took
place the following summer. For example, the burned
meadows recovered by the summer of 1989. Burned forest floors also recovered in 3-5 years. John Varley,
Yellowstone Park's chief of research, concedes,
". . . we can look forward to a great increase in
plant species, as much as tenfold in 20 years" (qtd.
in Jeffery 271). This kind of regrowth has not
occurred in the park for 300 years.

An example of vegetation which cannot survive
without fire is the lodgepole pine. Fire is

necessary for its survival. Its pinecones are serotinous which means that the cones remain closed at maturity, opening and releasing their seeds only after they have been burned (Romme and Despain 44). Don Despain, a park plant ecologist, shows that immediately after a fire, the ground is covered with seeds in a density of 50,000 to 1 million seeds per acre. Within 5 years there will still be approximately 1000 seedlings per acre, depending upon how much competition these seedlings face from grasses, wildflowers, and shrubs (Simpson 43). The survival of these trees is impossible without a fire.

Dawn concludes by returning to the natural burn policy and her own position.

These fires were a natural event in the ecological history of Yellowstone Park. An event such as these fires only occurs about every 200–300 years. A study by an ecological research team showed that these fires behaved very similarly to the fires that burned through the park around 1700 (Ekey 124). Yellowstone was not harmed in any permanent way by the fires that raged through the park in 1988. Yes, there was some temporary damage relating to animals and vegetation, but they will recover. Therefore, the "natural burn" policy was not responsible for the damage caused by the fires in 1988. We should feel proud that we were around to witness a historical event such as this.

Works Cited

Conniff, Richard. "Yellowstone's 'Rebirth' Amid the Ashes Is Not Neat or Simple, but It's Real." *Smithsonian* September 1989: 36–48.

Ekey, Robert. *Yellowstone on Fire*. Billings: Falcon Press, 1989.

Jeffery, David. "Yellowstone, the Great Fires of 1988." *National Geographic* February 1989: 250–275.

Romme, William H., and Don G. Despain. "Yellowstone Fires." *Scientific American* November 1989: 36–46.

Simpson, Ross W. *The Fires of '88*. Helena: American Geographic Publishing, 1989.

Singer, Francis J., et al. "Drought, Fires, and Large Mammals." *Bioscience* November 1989: 716–723.

Vogt, Gregory. *Forests on Fire.* New York: Franklin Watts, 1990.

"What About the 'Natural Fire' Policy." *Sunset* May 1989: 112.

Wood, Wilbur. "Political Fires Still Smolder." *The Nation* 7 August 1989: 162–165.

Wuerthner, George. "The Flames of 1988." *Wilderness* Summer 1989: 41–54.

Wuerthner, George. *Yellowstone and the Fires of Change.* Salt Lake City: Haggis House Publications, Inc., 1988.

Zumbo, Jim. "The Year Yellowstone Burned." *Outdoor Life* December 1988: 53, 87–89.

EXPLORING YOUR OPTIONS

1. To better identify your audience, answer the following three questions:

   Why does my audience *need* to be better informed about this subject? _____

   _____

   _____

   What does my audience *assume* or already know about this subject? _____

   _____

   _____

   What is my audience's *attitude* toward or feelings and beliefs about this subject?

   _____

   _____

   _____

2. Now reread your draft. Rewrite any sentence or paragraph that does not take into account your audience's needs, assumptions, or attitudes.

EDITING

CORRECTING COMMON SENTENCE ERRORS

When your ideas are strong and your organization is effective, you don't want common sentence errors to detract from them. Fortunately, correcting fragments, run-ons, and comma splices becomes easier with practice and with an understanding of what you can do to correct errors.

Fragments

A complete sentence must have an *independent clause,* a group of words that contains a subject and verb and that is a grammatically complete thought. A group of words that does not have a subject or a verb or that is not a complete thought is a *dependent clause* or *fragment.* Fragments are not acceptable in most writing.

A fragment can be a *phrase*—a group of words without a subject or without a verb:

> threw away the newspaper (no subject)
>
> they burning wood in the wood stove (unacceptable verb; *-ing* words by themselves require a helping verb)
>
> throwing away plastic cartons (no subject; unacceptable verb)
>
> the gasoline that we always use (no verb)

To correct these kinds of fragments, add a subject or a complete verb to make a complete sentence:

> We threw away the newspaper.
>
> They were burning wood in the wood stove.
>
> People are throwing away plastic cartons.
>
> The gasoline that we always use is unleaded.

To help spot dependent clauses, look for clauses that begin with subordinating conjunctions such as these. For a discussion of subordinating conjunctions, see pages 76–79.

SUBORDINATING CONJUNCTIONS

after	provided that	whenever
although	since	where
as	so	whereas
as if	so that	wherever
because	than	whether
before	that	which
even if	though	whichever
even though	unless	while
ever since	until	who
how	what	whom
if	whatever	whose
in order that	when	why

The following fragments are dependent clauses because they begin with a subordinating conjunction:

when my neighbor uses insecticides

because the household tries to recycle paper

One way of correcting a fragment is to make the clause independent by removing the dependent word:

My neighbor uses insecticides.

The household tries to recycle paper.

The more common method of correcting a dependent-clause fragment is to add an independent clause to the fragment, at either the beginning or the end of the dependent clause:

My neighbor always asks questions *when he uses pesticides.*

Because the household tries to recycle paper, the wastebasket is often empty.

When the independent clause comes first, as it does in the first example here, no comma is necessary. When the independent clause comes second, as it does in the second example, a comma must separate the independent clause from the dependent clause (see the comma rules in Chapter 2).

Run-ons and Comma Splices

Independent clauses can be joined in one of three ways:

Connected with a comma plus a coordinating conjunction
(*and, but, for, nor, or, so, yet*)

Connected with a semicolon

Separated by a period

A *run-on sentence* fuses two independent clauses together without any punctuation:

Incorrect: The students recycle their soda cans and the student body donates the money to various charities.

Correct: The students recycle their soda cans, and the student body donates the money to various charities.

Incorrect: Ford is developing an electric car it is pollution-free.

Correct: Ford is developing an electric car; it is pollution-free.

Notice that the first example may not seem to be a run-on sentence because the coordinating conjunction *and* connects the clauses. But remember that a coordinating conjunction requires a comma. If there is no comma before a coordinating conjunction, then the sentence is a run-on.

A *comma splice* incorrectly joins two independent clauses with just a comma. To correct a comma splice, separate the clauses with a period (make two sentences) or a semicolon:

Incorrect: The Mojave Desert is polluted, it is littered with trash from passing cars.

Correct: The Mojave Desert is polluted. It is littered with trash from passing cars.

Incorrect: Researchers are saving the California condor, they breed and raise the young in captivity.

Correct: Researchers are saving the California condor; they breed and raise the young in captivity.

WRITING WITH COMPUTERS

Try the grammar function of your computer's word processing program. Identify only the major sentence errors of fragments, run-ons, and comma splices. If you disagree with the computer's suggestions, check with a classmate. Determine what makes the sentence incomplete or what proper punctuation will alleviate the error. Make the corrections in your draft.

EXERCISE 1   Underline the subject once and the verb twice in both independent and dependent clauses. Circle dependent clauses. Then correctly punctuate the run-on sentences and comma splices, and make fragments into complete sentences.

1. The earth has an envelope of atmospheric gases, it acts like a greenhouse on a sunny day.

2. Light energy passes in but infrared radiation is trapped inside.

3. Because carbon dioxide in the atmosphere has increased 25 percent in this century.

4. The earth's temperature risen 0.5 degree Celsius.

5. Results from burning coal, oil, and gasoline.

6. The burning of tropical rain forests another major source of gas.

7. Some carbon dioxide dissolves in the ocean but much of it enters the atmosphere and blocks escaping radiation.

8. Temperatures may rise two to four degrees Celsius, this is sometime between the years 2025 and 2075.

EXERCISE 2   In the paragraph below, underline the subject once and the verb twice in both independent and dependent clauses. Circle dependent clauses. Then correctly punctuate the run-on sentences and comma splices, and make fragments into complete sentences.

Increased global warming changing fertile croplands into deserts. The dust bowl conditions would return they would affect the American Midwest, Canada, and Europe. Irrigation would not help, ground water reserves quickly would be depleted. Can decrease our consumption of fossil fuels. Emphasizing conservation and renewable energy sources. One renewable energy source is wind power another source is solar energy. Using public transportation, riding bicycles, and walking. We could use the air conditioner less, we could turn down heaters. We must halt global warming.

EXERCISE 3   Using the current draft of your essay, do the following:

1. Identify ten sentences and underline the subject once and the verb twice in both independent and dependent clauses.
2. Circle dependent clauses.
3. Correctly punctuate any run-on sentences.
4. Correctly punctuate any comma splices.
5. Make fragments into complete sentences.

OPTIONS FOR WRITING

Reflect

1. Remember a place you've been where the natural beauty of the surroundings has brought you peace or an insight about life—a place you would like to go back to. Describe in detail one aspect of the experience or the place. Use detail and vivid examples to help the reader share your reactions.

2. Using your perception or experience, define any term that pertains to an environmental issue (for example, *pollution, environmentalist, acid rain, recycling,* or *conservation*). Don't consult a dictionary or other source; simply explain the term as you understand it. Then extend your definition with concrete examples from your experience.

Inform

3. Observe the activity at a landfill for several hours. Record in detail what takes place there, what people dump, what your sensory experience is. Then write a paper describing your observations to someone who has never been to a landfill.

4. Interview a person in your community who is involved with environmental issues—a member of an environmental group or a citizens' awareness group, or someone who works for a government agency. Describe how this person defines *environment*.

Persuade

5. Determine where a public park (of any size) would make a valuable contribution to your community. In a letter to the city council, give your reasons for creating the new park.

6. Develop a plan for encouraging students to carpool, to take public transportation, to ride bicycles, or to walk to school. Draw up a proposal in which you persuade the administration or student body to incorporate your plan in ongoing transportation programs.

Speculate

7. From where you are sitting right now, describe what the environment around you may have looked like one hundred years ago.

8. From where you are sitting right now, describe what the environment around you may look like one hundred years from now.

Chapter 4

HEALTH

❧

There are conservative studies that claim that more than two-thirds of Americans are in poor health and poor physical shape. We overeat, and we eat poorly. We don't exercise. We abuse our bodies with tobacco, alcohol, prescription drugs, and over-the-counter remedies. We don't sleep well. We don't relieve alarmingly high buildups of psychological, emotional, mental, and social stress. No wonder we're tired, miserable, and unhealthy!

Does this sound like you? Well, you can do something about it. The human body usually responds readily to only minor changes in lifestyle. Try eating sensibly—balanced meals in moderate quantities. Set aside thirty minutes three times a week for exercise. Don't smoke. And spend some time developing relationships. You have only one body. Treat it well.

To prepare for this chapter's theme, health, answer the following questions:

- How does good or poor health affect one's life?
- How are individuals responsible for their health?

READINGS on *Health*

A Giant Step

Henry Louis Gates, Jr.

Henry Louis Gates, Jr., grew up in the Appalachian Mountains of West Virginia. Despite poverty and an injury that limited his physical activities for twenty-six years, Gates excelled academically in high school and at Yale and Cambridge. He was a writer for Time *magazine before becoming a professor at Harvard University. In the following magazine article (1989), Gates describes the consequences of receiving a hairline fracture while playing a game of touch football.*

"What's this?" the hospital janitor said to me as he stumbled over my right shoe. 1

"My shoes," I said. 2

"That's not a shoe, brother," he replied, holding it to the light. "That's a brick." 3

It *did* look like a brick, sort of. 4

"Well, we can throw these in the trash now," he said. 5

"I guess so." 6

We had been together since 1975, those shoes and I. They were orthopedic shoes built around molds of my feet, and they had a 2¼-inch lift. I had mixed feelings about them. On the one hand, they had given me a more or less even gait for the first time in 10 years. On the other hand, they had marked me as a "handicapped person," complete with cane and special license plates. I went through a pair a year, but it was always the same shoe, black, wide, weighing about four pounds. 7

It all started 26 years ago in Piedmont, W. Va., a backwoods town of 2,000 people. While playing a game of touch football at a Methodist summer camp, I incurred a hairline fracture. Thing is, I didn't know it yet. I was 14 and had finally lost the chubbiness of my youth. I was just learning tennis and beginning to date, and who knew where that might lead? 8

Not too far. A few weeks later, I was returning to school from lunch when, out of the blue, the ball-and-socket joint of my hip sheared apart. It was instant agony, and from that time on nothing in my life would be quite the same. 9

I propped myself against the brick wall of the schoolhouse, where the school delinquent found me. He was black as slate, twice my size, mean as the day was long and beat up kids just because he could. But the look on my 10 face told him something was seriously wrong, and—bless him—he stayed by my side for the two hours it took to get me into a taxi.

"It's a torn ligament in your knee," the surgeon said. (One of the signs of   11
what I had—a "slipped epiphysis"[1] —is intense knee pain, I later learned.) So he scheduled me for a walking cast.

I was wheeled into surgery and placed on the operating table. As the doc-   12
tor wrapped my leg with wet plaster strips, he asked about my schoolwork.

"Boy," he said, "I understand you want to be a doctor."   13

I said, "Yessir." Where I came from, you always said "sir" to white people,   14
unless you were trying to make a statement.

Had I taken a lot of science courses?   15

"Yessir. I enjoy science."   16

"Are you good at it?"   17

"Yessir, I believe so."   18

"Tell me, who was the father of sterilization?"   19

"Oh, that's easy, Joseph Lister."   20

Then he asked who discovered penicillin.   21

Alexander Fleming.   22

And what about DNA?   23

Watson and Crick.   24

The interview went on like this, and I thought my answers might get me a   25
pat on the head. Actually, they just confirmed the diagnosis he'd come to.

He stood me on my feet and insisted that I walk. When I tried, the joint   26
ripped apart and I fell on the floor. It hurt like nothing I'd ever known.

The doctor shook his head. "Pauline," he said to my mother, his voice   27
kindly but amused, "there's not a thing wrong with that child. The problem's psychosomatic.[2] Your son's an overachiever."

Back then, the term didn't mean what it usually means today. In   28
Appalachia, in 1964, "overachiever" designated a sort of pathology:[3] the over-straining of your natural capacity. A colored kid who thought he could be a doctor—just for instance—was headed for a breakdown.

What made the pain abate was my mother's reaction. I'd never, ever heard   29
her talk back to a white person before. And doctors, well, their words were scripture.

Not this time. Pauline Gates stared at him for a moment. "Get his clothes,   30
pack his bags—we're going to the University Medical Center," which was 60 miles away.

Not great news: the one thing I knew was that they only moved you to the   31
University Medical Center when you were going to die. I had three operations

---

[1] **epiphysis:** cartilage that has slipped from a bone
[2] **psychosomatic:** showing physical symptoms that are the product of emotional conflict
[3] **pathology:** abnormal condition

that year. I gave my tennis racket to the delinquent, which he probably used to club little kids with. So I wasn't going to make it to Wimbledon. But at least I wasn't going to die, though sometimes I wanted to. Following the last operation, which fitted me for a metal ball, I was confined to bed, flat on my back, immobilized by a complex system of weights and pulleys. It was six weeks of bondage—and bedpans. I spent my time reading James Baldwin, learning to play chess and quarreling daily with my mother, who had rented a small room—which we could ill afford—in a motel just down the hill from the hospital.

I think we both came to realize that our quarreling was a sort of ritual. We'd argue about everything—what time of day it was—but the arguments kept me from thinking about that traction system.   32

I limped through the next decade—through Yale and Cambridge . . . as far away from Piedmont as I could get. But I couldn't escape the pain, which increased as the joint calcified[4] and began to fuse over the next 15 years. My leg grew shorter, as the muscles atrophied[5] and the ball of the ball-and-socket joint migrated into my pelvis. Aspirin, then Motrin, heating pads and massages, became my traveling companions.   33

Most frustrating was passing store windows full of fine shoes. I used to dream about walking into one of those stores and buying a pair of shoes. "Give me two pairs, one black, one cordovan," I'd say. "Wrap 'em up." No six-week wait as with the orthotics in which I was confined. These would be real shoes. Not bricks.   34

In the meantime, hip-joint technology progressed dramatically. But no surgeon wanted to operate on me until I was significantly older, or until the pain was so great that surgery was unavoidable. After all, a new hip would last only for 15 years, and I'd already lost too much bone. It wasn't a procedure they were sure they'd be able to repeat.   35

This year, my 40th, the doctors decided the time had come.   36

I increased my life insurance and made the plunge.   37

The nights before my operations are the longest nights of my life—but never long enough. Jerking awake, grabbing for my watch, I experience a delicious sense of relief as I discover that only a minute or two have passed. You never want 6 A.M. to come.   38

And then the door swings open. "Good morning, Mr. Gates," the nurse says. "It's time."   39

The last thing I remember, just vaguely, was wondering where amnesiac[6] minutes go in one's consciousness, wondering if I experienced the pain and sounds, then forgot them, or if these were somehow blocked out, dividing the   40

---

[4] **calcified:** built-up hard calcium deposits
[5] **atrophied:** wasted away
[6] **amnesiac:** forgotten

self on the operating table from the conscious self in the recovery room. I didn't like that idea very much. I was about to protest when I blinked.

"It's over, Mr. Gates," says a voice. But how could it be over? I had merely   41
blinked. "You talked to us several times," the surgeon had told me, and that was the scariest part of all.

Twenty-four hours later, they get me out of bed and help me into a "walker."   42
As they stand me on my feet, my wife bursts into tears. "Your foot is touching the ground!" I am afraid to look but it is true: the surgeon has lengthened my leg with that gleaming titanium and chrome-cobalt alloy ball-and-socket joint.

"You'll need new shoes," the surgeon says. "Get a pair of Dock-Sides; they   43
have a secure grip. You'll need a 3/4-inch lift in the heel, which can be as discreet as you want"

I can't help thinking about those window displays of shoes, those elegant   44
shoes that, suddenly, I will be able to wear. Dock-Sides and sneakers, boots and loafers, sandals and brogues. I feel, at last, a furtive sympathy for Imelda Marcos,[7] the queen of soles.

The next day, I walk over to the trash can, and take a long look at the brick.   45
I don't want to seem ungracious or unappreciative. We have walked long miles together. I feel disloyal, as if I am abandoning an old friend. I take a second look.

Maybe I'll have [it] bronzed.   46

---

[7]**Imelda Marcos:** former First Lady of the Philippines, who achieved a special notoriety for the size of her shoe collection

---

Questions and Issues to Consider

Writing Process   1. Gates writes about the consequences of receiving a hairline fracture while playing a game of touch football. Discuss the sequence in which Gates describes those consequences.

2. Gates does not use a formal thesis statement. In a single sentence, write what you think Gates's controlling idea is.

Aims of Writing   3. People can have a variety of purposes for writing about their lives. Some hope to understand themselves better. Others simply want to share their experiences. Still others have a personal or political message. What is Gates's purpose in this essay? Cite a particular passage to support your explanation.

Critical Thinking   4. Gates claims that his shoes had marked him a "handicapped person." What do you think marks a person "handicapped"?

Dreaming of Disconnecting a Respirator
Elissa Ely

Elissa Ely is a science columnist and national radio commentator who is also a practicing psychiatrist. In the following article first printed in the Boston Globe *(1989), Ely describes her conflicting professional and personal feelings on euthanasia, or assisted suicide.*

L ate one night in the Intensive Care Unit, one eye on the cardiac monitor and one on the Sunday paper, I read this story: 1

An infant lies in a hospital, hooked to life by a respirator.[1] He exists in a "persistent[2] vegetative state" after swallowing a balloon that blocked the oxygen to his brain. This "vegetative state," I've always thought, is a metaphor[3] inaccurately borrowed from nature, since it implies that with only the proper watering and fertilizer, a comatose[4] patient will bloom again.   2

One day his father comes to visit. He disconnects the respirator and, with a gun in hand, cradles his son until the infant dies. The father is arrested and charged with murder.   3

In the ICU where I read this, many patients are bound to respirators. I look to my left and see them lined up, like potted plants. Some will eventually be "weaned" back to their own lung power. Others will never draw an independent breath again.   4

In Bed No. 2, there is a woman who has been on the respirator for almost two months. When she was admitted with a simple pneumonia, there were no clues she would come apart so terribly. On her third day, she had a sudden and enigmatic[5] seizure. She rolled rapidly downhill. Her pneumonia is now gone, but her lungs refuse independence: she can't come off the machine.   5

I know little about this patient except that she is elderly and European. (It is the peculiar loss of hospital life that patients often exist here with a medical history, but not a personal one.) I sometimes try to picture her as she might have been: busy in a chintz kitchen smelling of pastries. She might have hummed, rolling dough. Now there is a portable radio by the bed, playing Top Ten, while the respirator hisses and clicks 12 times a minute.   6

The family no longer visits. They have already signed the autopsy request, which is clipped to the front of her thick chart. Yet in their pain, they cannot   7

---

[1] **respirator:** a medical machine that helps a patient to breathe
[2] **persistent:** unchanging
[3] **metaphor:** comparison
[4] **comatose:** unconscious
[5] **enigmatic:** unexplained

take the final step and allow us to discontinue her respirator. Instead, they have retired her here, where they hope she is well cared for, and where she exists in a state of perpetual mechanical life.

I have dreamed of disconnecting my patient's respirator. Every day I make   8
her death impossible and her life unbearable. Each decision—the blood draws, the rectal temperatures, the oxygen concentration—is one for or against life. No action in the ICU is neutral. Yet many of these decisions are made with an eye toward legal neutrality—and this has little to do with medical truth. The medical truth is that this patient exists without being alive. The legal neutrality is that existence is all that is required.

Late at night, reading in the ICU, the story of that father—so dangerous   9
and impassioned—puts me to shame. I would never disconnect my patient from her respirator; it is unthinkable. But this is not because I am a doctor. It is because I feel differently toward her than the father toward his son.

I do not love her enough.   10

Questions and Issues to Consider

Writing Process   1. Ely uses two specific examples of families with comatose loved ones. Explain how these examples illustrate her conflicting feelings on euthanasia.

2. Ely does not use a formal thesis statement but has a strong controlling idea. Write a formal thesis statement that clearly describes Ely's position. What are some possible reasons for her to use a controlling idea and not a formal thesis statement?

Aims of Writing   3. Ely uses personal and indirect knowledge to inform readers of the controversy with euthanasia. How does her experience as a practicing psychiatrist (psychiatrists are medical doctors specializing in mental and emotional health) establish her as an authority on this topic?

Critical Thinking   4. Are you like Ely? Do you have conflicting feelings on euthanasia? What experiences and knowledge do you have to support your position?

PREWRITING

CUBING

Cubing is a prewriting activity that translates abstract ideas into tangible experiences or examples.* It helps writers examine a topic from different angles. Each side of a cube (there are six) represents a way of looking at a topic: description, comparison, association, analysis, application, and argument (Figure 4.1).

FIGURE 4.1

Cubing

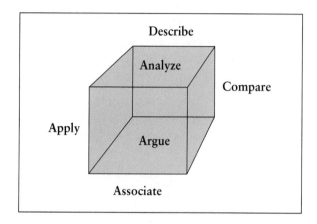

To do cubing, write nonstop for several minutes "from" each side of the cube. In the examples below we apply cubing to the general topic of stress.

Describe   Begin with a description of the topic. Describe the physical characteristics of someone experiencing stress. List the sights, sounds, tastes, textures, smells, shapes, and colors associated with stress. For example, a flashing red light, a screeching siren, blood, smoke—all can induce stress in people.

Compare   Compare your topic with an object. Is stress like a river? a roller coaster ride? a mountain? a fall? a computer? a journey? a marriage? an illness? a car? a comforter? Each of these comparisons is more concrete than the general term

---

*Elizabeth and Gregory Cowan developed the cubing technique. See *Writing* (John Wiley & Sons, 1980), pp. 25–26.

stress, and an explanation of your comparison can give you new insights into the topic.

Associate   Think about the events, ideas, concepts, people, times, and places you associate with the topic. The associations can be personal or indirect experiences. Ambulances, hospitals, doctors, disease, unexplained symptoms, cancer, medications, pain, and death are all associated with stress.

Analyze   Divide your topic into parts or categories, and explain how those parts relate to one another. Stress often is manifested through emotion. Other manifestations of stress are physical, intellectual, or social. Explain how anxiety affects you emotionally, physically, intellectually, and socially.

Apply   Explain how your topic can be used or what you've learned from it. How has stress affected your life? Think about ways to manage and prevent stress.

Argue   Choose a position on your topic and defend it. Everyone knows about the negative effects of stress. What about the positive effects? Try writing both sides of the argument— a good way to make your side more convincing.

After examining your topic from these six angles, decide which ideas and examples best illustrate your stance on the topic. You now have concrete examples to choose from as you begin to draft your paper.

Sandy Bybee, a student, has decided to write on caffeine as an addictive drug. She uses cubing to generate specific ideas for her paper. Here are some of the ideas she discovers about her topic through cubing.

Describe   Sandy *describes* the physical characteristics of a young caffeine-addicted woman named Nicol:

> When Nicol wakes in the morning she drinks
> a Pepsi and stops at the corner Circle K
> store to down a cup of hot cocoa on her way
> to school. At ten o'clock in the morning,
> Nicol begins to feel fatigued. At the student
> union building, she buys a large chocolate
> bar. The sugar will give her a lift to make
> it through calculus. Lunch time creeps up,
> but Nicol has a headache and decided not to
> eat. Instead she swallows two Excedrin with a

Pepsi chaser, hoping her head will stop exploding. It is now four o'clock, and Nicol drinks another Pepsi. She has a Shakespeare quiz and the caffeine in the Pepsi will make her more alert. At dinner the same scenario is played—a Pepsi and two Excedrin.

Compare   Sandy *compares* caffeine addiction with other forms of drug addiction:

Caffeine is as addictive as other drugs such as nicotine or alcohol. Dave, for example, at an early age of five or six, would pick up partially extinguished cigarettes from his mother's ashtray and experiment with smoking. He would also take sips of beer from almost-empty cans. Over the course of twenty years, Dave became more and more addicted to the nicotine and alcohol he had conditioned his body to crave. Dave spent years controlling his cravings and finally quit smoking and drinking. Years later, Dave tried to stop drinking caffeine, and he discovered that the symptoms of quitting the caffeine were almost entirely the same as those he experienced quitting smoking and drinking.

Associate   Sandy *associates* caffeine as a painkiller with her friend Jennifer's experience:

I am familiar with the effects caffeine can have with reducing pain because of my friend Jennifer. Jennifer suffered for over two years from almost constant pain from migraine headaches. Doctors had no idea what the cause of the headaches were, but they suggested she treat the pain with caffeine and wait to see if time would cure the headaches. Jennifer began taking large doses of caffeine in the forms of Excedrin and caffeinated soda pop when her migraine headaches became severe. Her pain lessened. The caffeine acted as a painkiller.

Analyze   Sandy *analyzes* various causes and effects of caffeine addiction:

Too much caffeine causes "the caffeine shakes." This condition occurs when the body has too much stimulant from caffeine. The hands develop a tremor, and the head sometimes twitches. The only cure is to quit the caffeine; but once a person has used caffeine, quitting is not so easy. When the body is conditioned to caffeine, it depends on the drug to wake it up. When caffeine is added to the body's natural stimulants, the muscles of the body overdose and the muscles shake. It is much like an electrical shock.

Apply   Sandy *applies* her knowledge of caffeine addiction through the example of Nicol:

When Nicol drinks Pepsi in the morning to wake up, the caffeine creates a shock to the nerves of her body. It is called a fast pick-up. However, the fast pick-up from caffeine is often followed by a severe headache when the caffeine quits coming. To solve her headache problem, Nicol uses more caffeine in the form of Excedrin. Of course, the headache subsides because more caffeine is added. Nicol does not know that every time she needs the drug, her body will signal her with a headache and a shaking hand.

Argue   Finally, Sandy *argues* that caffeine is addictive:

More than 80 percent of Americans take some form of caffeine each day. These Americans do not realize that drinking a caffeine drink, eating chocolate, and taking Excedrin can cause them to become addicted to caffeine. The FDA has asked Congress to declare caffeine a drug. Through tests and studies, the FDA knows the dangers of caffeine to the body; yet the lawmakers on Capitol Hill will

not take any action against the drug. The
soda pop manufacturers and chocolate industries do not want to take caffeine out of
their products, so they spend millions of
dollars each year lobbying Congress not to
name caffeine as a drug. These manufacturers
know that those few milligrams of caffeine
are addicting the American population, securing their product.

Sandy will not discuss all of these aspects of caffeine addiction in her paper, but now she has ideas to work with. (A draft of Sandy's paper begins on page 152.)

EXPLORING YOUR OPTIONS

1. On the line below, write your topic choice.

   _____

2. Now examine your topic from each side of the cube:

   Describe the physical characteristics of your topic.

   _____

   _____

   _____

   Compare your topic with one or more objects.

   _____

   _____

   _____

   Associate your topic with events, ideas, people's times, and places.

   _____

   _____

   _____

Analyze your topic by dividing it into parts or categories.

_____

_____

_____

Apply the topic to your experiences.

_____

_____

_____

Argue both sides of a position on your topic.

_____

_____

_____

3. Identify a side you would like to explore further. This side becomes your limited topic. Write your limited topic:

_____

_____

4. Identify six items you would like to discuss about your limited topic.

_____   _____

_____   _____

_____   _____

5. List more specifically what you want to accomplish by writing on this topic.

_____

_____

6. Put a checkmark next to the aim that best represents your reason for writing this paper.

_____ To reflect   _____ To persuade

_____ To inform   _____ To speculate

DRAFTING

INTRODUCTIONS AND CONCLUSIONS

Perhaps the two most important paragraphs in a paper are the introduction and the conclusion. Generally the introduction and the conclusion summarize your paper's topic, state or imply your thesis statement, and encourage the reader to participate with you, the writer. They differ in that the introduction opens the paper's possibilities to the reader while the conclusion pulls together and sums up the ideas in the paper. Here are some suggestions to help make these two paragraphs easier to write.*

Introductions

There are no gimmicks or secrets to writing strong, effective introductions. It does help to write the introduction last, when your ideas have taken form. The importance of an introduction cannot be overstated: the stronger your introduction, the more powerful your paper.

Here are some thoughts on writing introductions:

Write a rough introduction, and return to it after you've finished the first draft. Writing involves discovery. Once the first draft is finished, you'll probably have discovered several points that you'd like to include in the introduction. For

---

*The first five suggestions are based on John Trimble's discussion of "openers" in _Writing with Style: Conversations on the Art of Writing_ (Prentice-Hall, 1975), pp. 30–36.

instance, Ophelia decides to write a paper on addiction to over-the-counter medications. Because she's not sure exactly what she's going to write, her rough introduction is simply a brief list of what she plans to discuss in the paper. It will be rewritten at a later stage.

> I'm not sure where my ideas will take me, but I do want to address how over-the-counter drugs can become addictive. I plan to use Ryan as an example. He has had problems sleeping at night, so he buys brand-name sleeping aids. Yet in the morning and afternoon he has problems being alert, so he buys caffeine-rich stimulants that eventually keep him awake at night. I hope to show that this addiction can sneak up on an individual and how to guard against it.

Write a strong, tightly focused thesis statement. If possible, organize your opening paragraph so that the thesis statement is at the end. This makes the transition to the next paragraph easier. Remember that a thesis statement can appear anywhere in a paper. But most readers expect the thesis statement early. For example, here's a formal thesis statement for a paper on malnutrition and college students: *Malnutrition may be a problem for some college students because of their excessive dieting, unbalanced meals, or irregular eating habits.*

The following introduction places this formal thesis statement last, where it leads easily into the next paragraph:

> Rebecca and her roommates are not eating healthy meals. They choose to plan and prepare their meals individually rather than as a group. One roommate often skips one or two meals a day hoping to lose some weight. Another roommate who is stretching her limited money is living this month on oriental noodles and macaroni and cheese. And Rebecca's busy schedule forces her to grab whatever food is available as she dashes from work to class to service clubs. Malnutrition may be a problem for some college students because of their excessive dieting, unbalanced meals, or irregular eating habits.

Use concrete examples. An introduction certainly can be general. But you may find it effective to introduce a few concrete details in the opening paragraph, to grab the reader's attention. For example, Stephen is writing a paper on the high cost of medical care. He uses concrete examples to introduce his subject:

A safe blood pressure level is 120/80. My father's blood pressure is 168/105. Although this level is not alarmingly high, he checks with the family doctor. The doctor charges $58 for the visit and schedules tests and x-rays. The EKG for the heart costs $127, the lab work for four different blood tests costs $142, and the x-rays come to $214. This single visit to the doctor's office costs my father $541. That's unreasonable. Something needs to be done about soaring medical costs.

Talk out your introduction. If you're having difficulty getting started, stop and ask yourself, "What is it I'm really trying to say in this paper?" Then say it. The act of speaking forces words and sentences to form. After you've talked it out, write down what you've said.

Use a short—say five to eight words long—opening sentence. The average opening sentence is about eighteen words long. Shorter opening sentences help you state your point immediately, a pleasant surprise for your readers. Elspeth, for example, originally planned to begin her introduction to a paper about insomnia with this sentence:

> It's the middle of the night, and you're lying awake listening to each sound from the kitchen, the basement, and the backyard, and you can't go to sleep.

The sentence is twenty-eight words long. Instead Elspeth decided to use a short sentence. Notice how the three-word opening sentence draws the reader in immediately.

> The faucet drips. The furnace coughs. The dog barks. It's the middle of the night, and you're lying awake listening to each sound from the kitchen, the basement, and the backyard, and you can't go to sleep. The clock reads 3:17, you have a chemistry exam in less than five hours, and you're still awake. Insomnia afflicts millions each night. But there is hope and help. Therapists recommend three different techniques for getting a restful night's sleep.

Establish your qualifications and purpose for writing about your topic. Readers often want to know that you have had experience with the topic, that you are "a voice of authority." Consider explaining your background on the topic in the introduction. For instance, Tharon, who is diabetic, is writing a paper on diabetes. In the introduction he establishes his qualifications and purpose for writing the paper:

I am a diabetic. I know about blood sugars. I know about daily insulin. I know the stories about blindness and amputated limbs. But I also know that diabetes is a disease that is easy to live with, a disease that for most of my life will not interfere with any daily activity, a disease that doesn't make me any different from anyone else. Diabetes does not have to change a person's life.

Try using facts and statistics to introduce a topic. Facts and statistics provide valuable support for a topic. Kevin decides to write his paper on the sleeping habits of college students. He uses facts and statistics to introduce his topic:

Students on our campus average 5.3 hours of sleep per night. I recently conducted an informal survey of 100 students on Friday, March 11, asking them to tell within thirty minutes how much sleep they received on Wednesday and Thursday nights (March 9 and 10). Student responses ranged from 2.5 hours for one night to 11 hours for a night, but the average was 5.3 hours of sleep each night. No wonder some students find it difficult staying awake in class.

Occasionally begin an introduction with a quotation. A quotation can help involve your readers. Here's Frankie's introduction to a paper on physical fitness:

"After two months of aerobic exercise three times a week, I have more energy than I've had in years. I sleep better at nights; I don't fall asleep in class; and I can concentrate more on my studies." Carol's feelings are common among most people who stick with an exercise program. She and others have discovered that exercise generates added energy, renews their spirits, and gives them a brighter outlook on the day.

Sandy decides to introduce her topic with an extended example of Nicol, a young woman who is addicted to caffeine. Sandy wants to illustrate the characteristics of caffeine addiction in a personal way, so she decides against using statistics. A narrative introduction is easy to write because it simply relates an experience.

Conclusions

The conclusion is your last chance to influence the reader. Several methods for concluding a paper are listed below.

To remind the reader of your key ideas, summarize them.
Sandy concludes her essay with her main points:

It has been a long, hard struggle for Sarah, but things are going better for her now. She has gained back most of her weight. She continues to attend college and lead a near-normal life. Sometimes it is hard, and she occasionally has those inferior feelings, but she is becoming stronger emotionally and physically because of professional help and her family's support. Bulimia is a very serious disease. Victims need love and support. They need professional treatment. They need to know that their family and friends love them and accept them as they are.

Consider using a brief final quotation to close your paper with the voice of an authority. Ophelia concludes her paper on over-the-counter drug addiction by quoting Ryan, who recently discovered his own addiction:

Chemical dependency counselors warn us that most drugs whether legal or illegal, whether prescription or over-the-counter, are addictive. The body begins to adjust to the different chemical levels, and when those levels change, the body reacts. Ryan's example is not that unusual, and he still wonders how his addiction happened to him: "I was just trying to do it all—I wasn't listening to my body. I just needed a little sleep and a little pick-me-up. How did all of this happen to me?"

Relate an experience or anecdote to leave the reader with a strong image or emotion. Levi Liljenquist writes his student essay "Mrs. Takahashi" (see page 000) about the effect the Kobe, Japan, earthquake had upon one family. Earlier in the essay, Levi describes Mrs. Takahashi caressing her dead daughter and son. Levi finishes his essay with a general description of a temporary morgue to show the larger extent of death because of the earthquake, and he concludes with Mrs. Takahashi's image at the end to remind readers of her singular loss and of his own feelings:

I have seen such scenes on T.V. before and have never been affected by them, and now, when I hear the death count, over 5,500 killed, or see other disasters, I think only of Mrs. Takahashi.

Close with a possible solution or a warning to make a strong impression on the reader. Rachel Carson's essay "A Fable for Tomorrow" (see page 86) concludes with a warning:

This town does not actually exist, but it might easily have a thousand counterparts in America or elsewhere in the world. I know of no community that has experienced all the misfortunes I describe. Yet every one of these disasters has actually happened somewhere, and many real communities have already suffered a substantial number of them. A grim specter has crept upon us almost unnoticed, and this imagined tragedy may easily become a stark reality we all shall know.

✓ CHECKLIST: INTRODUCTIONS AND CONCLUSIONS

1. Does your introduction capture your reader's attention with a strong opening sentence?

2. Does your introduction show that your paper's topic is important and meaningful?

3. Does your introduction prepare your reader for your paper's controlling idea or thesis statement?

4. Does your introduction identify the central issue you'd like to discuss?

5. Does your introduction establish your stance or attitude toward your subject?

6. Does your conclusion sum up your ideas and provide a sense of closure?

7. Does your conclusion emphasize one or more points for a final emphasis?

8. Does your conclusion make a final appeal to your reader?

EXPLORING YOUR OPTIONS

Although introductions and conclusions are difficult to write before you draft your paper, it helps to generate ideas to guide your thinking.

1. On the line below, write your limited topic.

_____

2. Write a possible thesis statement for your topic.

_____

_____

3. List four concrete examples or details you could include in your introduction.

_____   _____

_____   _____

4. Sit back and ask aloud, "What is it I'm really trying to say in this paper?" Then talk it out.

5. Write two short opening sentences, each five to eight words long.

_____

_____

6. List two reasons you have selected this topic.

_____

_____

7. State why you are qualified to write about this topic.

_____

_____

8. List three facts or statistics you could use in your introduction.

_____

_____

_____

9. Identify a brief quotation you could use in your introduction.

_____

_____

_____

10. You will not use all of these options in your introduction. Choose just one or two of them, and on a separate sheet write a rough introduction to your paper.

_____

_____

_____

11. Determine an idea or an example that can be part of your conclusion.

_____

WRITING TOGETHER

1. Remove the introduction from your paper's draft.

2. Exchange drafts with a classmate.

3. Write a developed introduction for each other's paper.

4. Compare the new introduction with the original one.

5. Discuss suggestions for improving each paper's introduction.

WRITING WITH COMPUTERS

1. On the computer, write three different types of introductions for your current paper. For example, have one introduction establish your qualifications, another begin with a quotation, and the third use facts and statistics.

2. After writing all three introductions, select the most effective introduction for your paper's purpose or rewrite an introduction using a combination of different types.

CAUSE AND EFFECT

An examination of cause and effect is a type of analysis. Cause often answers the question *Why has something happened?* and effect generally addresses the consequence of *What* has happened? Most of us believe that things happen for reasons, and we can't help trying to determine those reasons. If you went to bed feeling fine but woke up with an aching back, you'd want to know *why* your back hurts. You remember that yesterday you helped a friend move a piano and a refrigerator. That's probably why your back is sore this morning. What you've done is analyze a cause and effect relationship.

Suppose your topic is anorexia nervosa. If you ask why anorexia nervosa affects mostly young women, your answer will be about the causes of the illness. If you address what physiological changes occur because of anorexia nervosa, your response will be about the effects of the illness.

Four kinds of cause and effect patterns help organize both your thoughts and your writing: single cause→many effects, many causes→single effect, a causal chain, and single cause→single effect.

Single Cause→Many Effects

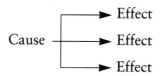

The single cause→many effects organization emphasizes the consequences associated with an event or item. Suppose you're writing a paper on the effects daily exercise has had on your life. The single cause is daily exercise; three of the many effects may be gradual weight loss, lowered heart rate, and increased stamina.

Many Causes→Single Effect

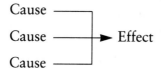

The many causes→single effect organization emphasizes the reasons that lead to a particular consequence. If, for example, in your paper you ask why you've started an exercise program (effect), your answers (causes) might include being overweight, a family history of heart disease, and frequently feeling tired.

Causal Chain

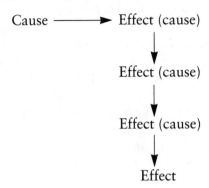

Most cause and effect organizations are not as simple as the first two. A more realistic, and more complicated, cause and effect organization is the causal chain. Each cause has an effect that is the cause of another effect, and so on, in a series.

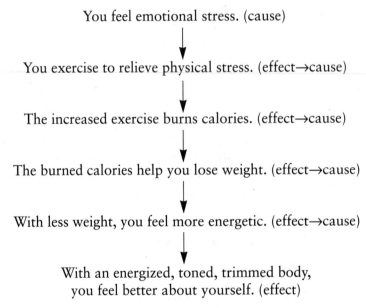

The causal chain is more difficult to use than the other organizations, but it does reflect cause and effect relationships more accurately.

Single Cause→Single Effect

Rare is the single cause that produces a single effect. Usually other factors contribute to the effect. People say that if you read a lot, you will do well in school. But everyone who reads a lot doesn't necessarily do well in school; and many people who do well in school never read anything but what they've been assigned. The single cause→single effect organization is what you find in a scientific laboratory, where variables are strictly controlled. We seldom have this kind of control in real life.

✓ CHECKLIST: CAUSE AND EFFECT

1. Does the cause fit the effect?

2. Is the connection between the cause and the effect clear?

3. Is there enough evidence to establish the cause and effect relationship?

CAUSE AND EFFECT: AN EXAMPLE

In the following paragraph, Norman Cousins uses cause and effect to explain the consequences of relieving a professional athlete's pain rather than treating the injury. Which cause and effect pattern does Cousins use?

Masking Pain

Professional athletes are sometimes severely disadvantaged by trainers whose job it is to keep them in action. The more famous the athlete, the greater the risk that he or she may be subjected to extreme medical measures when injury strikes. The star baseball pitcher whose arm is sore because of a torn muscle or tissue damage may need sustained rest more than anything else. But his team is battling for a place in the World Series; so the trainer or team doctor, called upon to work his magic, reaches for a strong dose of butazolidine or other powerful pain suppressants. Presto, the pain disappears! That could be the last game, however, in which he is able to throw a ball with full strength. The drugs didn't repair the torn muscle or cause the damaged tissue to heal. What they did was to mask the pain, enabling the pitcher to throw hard, further damaging the torn muscle. Little wonder that so many star athletes are cut down in their prime, more the victims of overzealous treatment of their injuries than of the injuries themselves.

PRACTICE 1   Cousins uses the causal chain pattern of cause and effect. The first part of the causal chain is the cause—the athlete's injury. The first effect or consequence is pain. Using details from the paragraph, diagram the rest of the causal chain showing how each effect becomes the cause of another consequence, leading to the final effect, a shortened career.

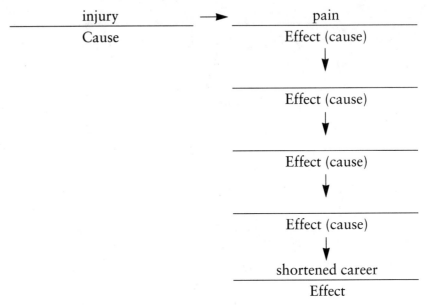

PRACTICE 2   1. Assume that diet is the single cause of many effects. In the diagram below, list three effects or consequences of your eating habits.

2. Assume that stress is the single effect of many causes. In the diagram below, list three factors that create stress in your life.

3. Assume that diet affects your health (a reasonable assumption). Complete the causal chain diagram below with effects and causes you've identified yourself.

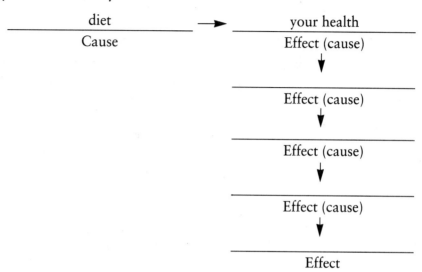

diet	→	your health
Cause		Effect (cause)

EXPLORING YOUR OPTIONS

1. Identify a possible cause and effect relationship that you may want to write about in the paper you're working on now.

   _____

   _____

2. Put a checkmark next to the pattern that best represents your cause and effect relationship.

   _____ Single cause → many effects   _____ Causal chain

   _____ Many causes → single effect   _____ Single cause → single effect

3. Using that pattern as a model, write a brief paragraph in which you describe your paper's cause and effect relationship.

   _____

   _____

   _____

_____

_____

_____

_____

Cause and Effect and Aims

Cause and effect can be used to meet all four writing objectives, as the following assignments show.

Reflect

Explain how a car accident has affected you physically or emotionally.

Identify someone you know with a chemical dependency. Using what you know about that person, explore possible causes for that dependency.

Inform

Generally those who have money receive better health care than those who do not have money. Discuss the possible consequences of economic discrimination in the provision and adequacy of health care.

Nutritionists claim that a high-fiber diet can improve a person's health. Inform your classmates about the effects a high-fiber diet can have on their health.

Persuade

Alcohol consumption is a significant factor in many car accidents. Write a persuasive article for the school paper explaining the role alcohol plays in accidents or describing the effects an alcohol-related accident has had on the lives of people you know.

Stress can have adverse effects on one's health. By explaining the effects of a stress-reducing activity, persuade a friend to relieve stress.

Speculate

Consider your current lifestyle—especially your eating, sleeping, and exercising habits. What consequences do you think your lifestyle will have on your body twenty years from now?

Many college students experience mild depression—a byproduct of the stress that comes from preparing for exams, the breakup of a relationship, or the frustrations of a busy schedule. Write about the possible causes of depression. Then speculate on specific activities to relieve depression.

EXPLORING YOUR OPTIONS

You are now ready to write your first draft. You already have determined the following:

Your limited topic: _____

Your working thesis statement: _____

_____

_____

Your main writing aim: _____

Your rough introduction:

Set aside a block of time, and write your first draft. Don't worry about being right or wrong. The object is to get your ideas onto paper.

REWRITING

MAKING A FOCUS MAP

In the drafting stage, your thoughts can take off without any control or direction. This isn't a bad thing. Sometimes a wild ride can help generate ideas and remind you of experiences. But a lack of direction and focus also can make your ideas impossible for a reader to follow. To set a course—a focus—for your revised draft, use a focus map to help you delete information that doesn't contribute to the purpose of your paper and to order information that does (Figure 4.2).

FIGURE 4.2

Focus map

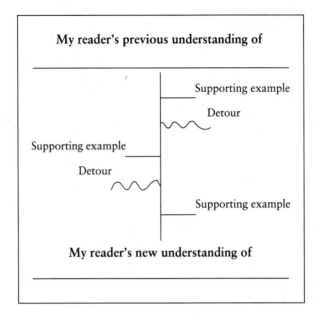

At the top of a sheet of paper write, "My reader's previous under-standing of _____ (your topic)." This is what you believe your reader knows about the topic *before* he or she reads your paper. At the bot-tom of the page write, "My reader's new understanding of _____ (your paper's topic)." This new understanding should reflect your rea-son for writing the paper.

Now draw a vertical line between the two statements. This line is the map for your revised draft. As you read your original draft, draw horizontal lines from the vertical line to represent supporting examples that clearly take the reader closer to the final destination. If an idea or an example begins to head off in another direction, place the idea off to a side with a squiggly line to show a detour. Continue reading the draft and locating the ideas on your map.

Figure 4.3 shows Sandy's map. Remember that her topic is caffeine addiction. At the top of the page she writes, "My reader's previous understanding of caffeine is that it is not an addictive drug." At the bottom she writes, "My reader's new understanding of caffeine is that many of the 80 percent of Americans who take some form of caffeine a day are addicted to that drug."

Now Sandy maps the support for her first draft. Her first example is the extended example of Nicol. Because this example helps lead readers to a new understanding, Sandy draws a straight line to it. Next Sandy wrote about Jennifer, a friend who used caffeine as a painkiller to relieve her migraine headaches. Jennifer's experience does illustrate that caffeine is a drug, but Sandy is concerned that readers will misunderstand her point and believe that caffeine is a positive drug and painkiller for most pains and not just for Jennifer's isolated circumstance. So Sandy marks the Jennifer example with a squiggly line. Sandy continues to map and mark the examples, statistics, and history she uses for support in her draft. When she's finished, she can see at a glance which information supports or detracts from her stance. She now has a direction for her rewriting.

FIGURE 4.3

Sample map

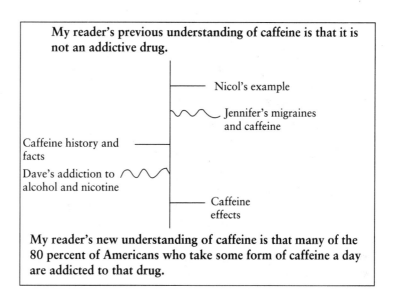

When you've finished drawing your focus map, analyze it carefully. Start at the top, with your reader's previous understanding of the subject. Then follow the line down the page. As you go, think about the sequence of the information. Do the ideas on your map follow a logical order? If not, rearrange them. Also determine whether any of your "detours" should be incorporated into the paper. Now rewrite your draft, using the map as a guide.

STUDENT ESSAY

Below is a revised draft of Sandy Bybee's essay. Sandy is a grandmother and a returning student from Idaho majoring in teacher education. As you read the draft, ask two basic questions:

- How does Sandy succeed in fulfilling her purpose for writing this essay?

- How can Sandy strengthen this draft?

Caffeine: "To Be, or Not to Be"

Nicol rises from bed each morning and grabs a Pepsi from the fridge. She dresses, brushes her teeth, and drives to school. On the way to school, she stops at the Circle K store and downs a cup of hot cocoa. Now she is ready to begin her day.

At ten o'clock in the morning, Nicol begins to feel fatigued. At the student union building, she buys a large chocolate bar. The sugar will give her a lift to make it through calculus. Lunch time creeps up, but Nicol has a headache and decides not to eat. Instead she swallows two Excedrin with a Pepsi chaser, hoping her head will stop exploding. It is now four o'clock, and Nicol drinks another Pepsi. She has a Shakespeare quiz, and the caffeine in the Pepsi will make her more alert. Nicol is addicted to caffeine, the most widely abused drug in America today.

Caffeine comes from the cola bean that is found on the mountains of tropical forests. It was first used hundreds of years ago by the natives of South America. They noticed that when the animals ate the cola berries, they acted more lively. These same natives used the cola bean to develop a hot drink that America now calls coffee. Then in the early 1900's, caffeine was extracted from the bean and used by soda pop manufacturers to create a new drink called Coca-Cola. This added a new way for Americans to ingest their favorite drug.

At first Americans did not realize that chocolate, soda pop, and over-the-counter medications were damaging their bodies. But, as the Federal Drug Administration (FDA) tested and proved the effect of caffeine on the human body, many people began to realize that caffeine was an addictive drug.

An average soda pop contains 54 milligrams (ml.) of caffeine; a chocolate bar, 50 ml.; a cup of coffee, 70 ml.; and one Excedrin 250 ml. The FDA has stated that "If a person consumes more than 750 milligrams of caffeine a day, he/she is addicted to the drug." It would not take many sodas, chocolate bars, or Excedrin to equal 750 ml.

The FDA has also stated that too much caffeine [over 1,000 mg.] causes "the caffeine shakes." This condition occurs when the body has too much stimulant from caffeine. The hands develop a tremor and the head sometimes twitches. The only cure is to quit the caffeine; but, once a person has used caffeine, quitting is not so easy. When the body is used to caffeine, it depends on the drug to wake it up. When caffeine is added to the body's natural stimulant, the muscles of the body overdose and the muscles shake. It is much like an electrical shock. When Nicol drank the Pepsi in the morning to wake up, the caffeine created a shock to the nerves of her body. It is called a fast pick-up. However, the fast pick-up from caffeine is often followed with a severe headache when the caffeine quits coming. To solve her headache problem, Nicol used more caffeine in the form of Excedrin. Of course, the headache subsided because more caffeine was added. Nicol did not know that every time her body needs a drug, it will signal her with a headache and a shaking hand.

Many American students think that drinking a caffeine drink before a test will help them test better. This is true for the person who is not addicted to caffeine, but for the drug-addicted person, it will do nothing. When caffeine is taken into the body, the blood vessels open, allowing more blood to flow to the brain. This increases recall at a faster pace. This same effect is not achieved for the caffeine-addicted individual. When caffeine is taken into the blood vessels of a caffeine addict, the recall becomes faster, but the effect does not last because the body has adapted to the caffeine use. Nicol will not benefit from the caffeine drink before her Shakespeare test. In fact, the added caffeine could cause her to get the shakes, which would disrupt her thinking processes, not aid them.

She concludes by stating her position that caffeine is an addictive drug.

More than 80 percent of Americans take some form of caffeine each day. These Americans do not realize that drinking a caffeine drink, eating chocolate, and taking Excedrin can cause them to become addicted to caffeine. Through tests and studies, the FDA knows the dangers of caffeine to the body, yet, the lawmakers on Capitol Hill will not take any action against this drug. The soda pop and chocolate industries do not want to take caffeine out of their products; they spend millions of dollars each year lobbying Congress not to name caffeine as a drug. These industries know that those few milligrams of caffeine are addicting the American population, thus securing their product.

Like 80 percent of Americans, Nicol, unknowingly, is addicted to a drug. The drug is caffeine.

EXPLORING YOUR OPTIONS

To focus your revisions, create a focus map.

1. What is your reader's previous understanding of your topic?

   _____

   _____

2. What is your reader's new understanding of your topic after reading your paper?

   _____

   _____

3. Identify and list the supporting examples you use that clearly lead your reader to a new understanding of the topic.

   _____   _____

   _____   _____

_____   _____

4. Identify and list any examples or explanations that may confuse your reader, that do not lead your reader easily to a new understanding of the topic.

_____   _____

_____   _____

5. Arrange your best examples and support in a logical sequence.

First: _____

Second: _____

Third: _____

Fourth: _____

Fifth: _____

6. Rewrite your draft, using the map as a guide.

WRITING TOGETHER

To focus the direction of your revised draft, team up with a classmate and create a focus map for each other's papers. Complete the following exercise.

1. What is my previous understanding of the writer's topic?

_____

_____

2. What is my understanding of the writer's topic now, after I've read the paper?

_____

_____

3. List the supporting examples the writer uses that lead you easily to a new understanding of the topic.

_____   _____

_____   _____

_____   _____

4. List any examples or explanations that confused you, that did not lead easily to a new understanding of the topic.

_____   _____

_____   _____

_____   _____

5. Arrange the writer's best examples and support in a logical sequence.

First: _____

Second: _____

Third: _____

Fourth: _____

Fifth: _____

6. Discuss your responses to this activity with your classmate. Then, using the map to focus and order your ideas, rewrite your paper.

WRITING WITH COMPUTERS

1. Identify the "detours" from the focus map of your paper's draft.

2. Highlight the "detour" material and cut it from your document. (If you're uncertain that you want to remove the passage, paste the cut material at the end of your document. You can paste it back into your paper if you decide to keep it.)

3. Read your draft without the detour.

4. Make the necessary adjustments to your draft to accommodate the removed material.

EDITING

AGREEMENT

If you use a singular subject, you must use a singular verb. If you use a plural subject, you must use a plural verb.

The student eats three balanced meals daily.

The students eat three balanced meals daily.

Similarly, a singular pronoun must have a singular antecedent (the word the pronoun refers to). If the antecedent is plural, its pronoun must be plural.

Singular: *Felicia* plans *her* menu carefully.

Plural: The *roommates* also plan *their* menus.

When the subject or antecedent is singular, the verb and pronoun are singular. When the subject or antecedent is plural, the verb and pronoun are plural. Verbs and pronouns must agree in number with subjects and antecedents.

To determine if a subject is singular or plural, substitute the singular pronoun *he* or *she* or the plural pronoun *they:*

Singular: The *student (she)* eats three balanced meals daily.

Plural: The *students (they)* eat three balanced meals daily.

Place the subject of the sentence next to the singular verb *is* or the plural verb *are* to determine if a verb is singular or plural:

Singular: The *student* (*is,* are) eating well.

Plural: The *students* (is, *are*) eating well.

Use these six rules to help you determine agreement:

1. **A compound subject that contains the conjunction *and* is usually plural.**

   Fly fishing *and* skeet shooting are my favorite activities to reduce stress.

   My father *and* uncle fish to reduce *their* stress.

2. **A subject that contains the conjunction *or* or *nor* can be singular or plural. The verb should agree with the subject closest to it.**

The nutritionist *or* the <u>doctors</u> <u>are</u> always late.

The doctors *or* the <u>nutritionist</u> <u>is</u> always late.

<u>Is</u> my <u>thermometer</u> *or* my tissues nearby?

<u>Are</u> my <u>tissues</u> *or* my thermometer nearby?

3. **The following words are singular and require a singular verb:**

anybody	everybody	no one
anyone	everyone	one
each	neither	somebody
either	nobody	someone

Notice that words that involve *one* and *body,* like *anyone* and *some-body,* are singular:

<u>Everyone</u> <u>has</u> *her* own health insurance.

<u>Everybody</u> <u>chooses</u> *his* or *her* health policy.

4. **A prepositional phrase cannot be part of a subject.** To determine the subject, cross out prepositional phrases:

<u>Each</u> ~~of the exercises~~ <u>sounds</u> like fun.

<u>Neither</u> ~~of the exercise bikes~~ <u>is working</u> today.

5. **Parenthetical information cannot be part of a subject** (see the comma rules in Chapter 2). To determine the subject, cross out the parenthetical information:

The <u>dietician</u>, ~~holding the cookbooks~~, <u>is</u> helpful.

Balanced <u>meals</u>, ~~unlike my potato chip sandwich~~, <u>are</u> healthy.

6. **Collective words usually function as a unit and take singular verbs.** Here are some sample collective words:

audience	dozen	jury
band	family	number
class	flock	none
committee	group	public
crowd	herd	team

My <u>family</u> <u>is supporting</u> my interest in physical therapy.

The <u>committee</u> <u>has approved</u> my physical therapy training schedule.

EXERCISE 1 Underline the correct word in each of the following exercises to make subjects, pronouns, and verbs agree in number.

1. Most of today's society (does, do) not have fun.

2. Each of my friends (exercises, exercise) to get into shape, not to have fun.

3. Either pressures from work or guilt (keeps, keep) many from having fun.

4. Everyone should have some fun in (his or her, their) day.

5. Many in the work force (wants, want) more leisure time.

6. But not everyone (knows, know) what to do with (his or her, their) free time.

7. A psychologist and a psychiatrist (insists, insist) that leisure time is essential to happiness.

8. Neither an overloaded student nor an overworked employee (is, are) productive without some regular relaxation.

EXERCISE 2 In the paragraph below make the subjects, pronouns, and verbs in each sentence agree in number.

Weekend trips or an overnight stay in a hotel help some people relax. This weekend, my friends and my family plans to go to Jackson

Hole, Wyoming. Some of them have never been there. Each have a different reason for going. All of us wants to go spring skiing. A few think they will try snowboarding. The jacuzzi or sauna always feel good after skiing all day. Our spirits along with our muscles begin to relax. Now one of us want to jog out to the elk preserve. Somebody discourages that idea, so we take the car.

EXERCISE 3   Using the current draft of your essay, do the following:

1. Identify five sentences using a compound subject. Underline the subjects once and the verb twice. Do the subjects and verb agree?

2. Identify five sentences that have prepositional phrases that cannot be part of the subject. To determine the subject, cross out prepositional phrases. Underline the subjects once and the verb twice. Do the subjects and verb agree?

3. Identify five other sentences and determine if the subjects and verbs agree by underlining the subjects once and the verbs twice.

OPTIONS FOR WRITING

Reflect

1. Recall a time in your life when you were seriously ill or in severe pain. Write a letter to someone in a similar situation, describing the positive effects the experience has had on your life.

2. Examine your life closely. Develop a plan to change what you consider unacceptable behavior with the single purpose of improving your life. Be specific. Spell out concrete goals and the steps necessary to reach them.

Inform

3. Interview a school psychologist, physician, or counselor about a prevalent emotional or physical health problem confronting college students today. Then write an essay explaining the problem.

4. Contact local health agencies to find the locations and times of alcohol support groups. Attend a meeting, and interview either administrators, participants, or family members about the effect the organization has had on their lives. Organize your findings in a coherent and informative report.

Persuade

5. Health care costs are exorbitant. Politicians continue to argue whether a national health care plan is necessary or practical. Using your own family or a family you consider typical, analyze its annual medical expenses in terms of insurance premiums, doctors' fees, hospital costs, and the like. Then write a letter to your congressional representative or senator expressing your feelings. Be as convincing as possible.

6. Research your family's health history, and create a detailed plan for improving your family's health. Develop a month's sample menu and a four-week exercise program and work schedule. Then persuade your family to try this new lifestyle for one month.

Speculate

7. Imagine the life of someone who has a chronic or terminal illness. Describe that person's day in as much detail as possible. Obviously you won't be able to include everything, so focus on what you think would be typical activities.

8. Picture yourself as eighty years old. What does your body look like? What health problems do you have (remember your family's medical history)? Which aspects of your current lifestyle would you change to improve your health in the future?

Chapter 5
Identity

It is in our nature to strive for things or experiences in our lives that will lead to personal growth and fulfillment. Unfortunately most of us experience periods, sometimes too frequently, of low self-esteem. We feel lonely, inadequate, and useless. And these defeating attitudes affect every aspect of our lives. The purpose of this chapter is to focus on our identity, to look inward at who or what forms and affects our self-concepts.

To prepare for this chapter's theme, identity, answer the following questions:

- How is the individual a product of genetics, family, and experience?
- How does each person's personality shape his or her perception of the world?

READINGS on *Identity*

Salvation

Langston Hughes

Langston Hughes was a poet, novelist, playwright, essayist, and leader in the emergence of African-American literature during the early and mid-twentieth century. His autobiography is entitled I Wonder As I Wander *(1956). "Salvation" comes from his* The Big Sea *(1940).*

I was saved from sin when I was going on thirteen. But not really saved. It happened like this. There was a big revival at my Auntie Reed's church. Every night for weeks there had been much preaching, singing, praying, and shouting, and some very hardened sinners had been brought to Christ, and the membership of the church had grown by leaps and bounds. Then just before the revival ended, they held a special meeting for children, "to bring the young lambs to the fold." My aunt spoke of it for days ahead. That night I was escorted to the front row and placed on the mourners' bench with all the other young sinners, who had not yet been brought to Jesus. 1

My aunt told me that when you were saved you saw a light, and something happened to you inside! And Jesus came into your life! And God was with you from then on! She said you could see and hear and feel Jesus in your soul. I believed her. I had heard a great many old people say the same thing and it seemed to me they ought to know. So I sat there calmly in the hot, crowded church, waiting for Jesus to come to me. 2

The preacher preached a wonderful rhythmical sermon, all moans and shouts and lonely cries and dire pictures of hell, and then he sang a song about the ninety and nine safe in the fold, but one little lamb was left out in the cold. Then he said: "Won't you come? Won't you come to Jesus? Young lambs, won't you come?" And he held out his arms to all us young sinners there on the mourners' bench. All the little girls cried. And some of them jumped up and went to Jesus right away. But most of us just sat there. 3

A great many old people came and knelt around us and prayed, old women with jet-black faces and braided hair, old men with work-gnarled hands. And the church sang a song about the lower lights are burning, some poor sinners to be saved. And the whole building rocked with prayer and song. 4

Still I kept waiting to *see* Jesus. 5

Finally all the young people had gone to the altar and were saved, but one boy and me. He was a rounder's son named Westley. Westley and I were surrounded by sisters and deacons praying. It was very hot in the church, and 6 getting late now. Finally Westley said to me in a whisper: "God damn! I'm tired o' sitting here. Let's get up and be saved." So he got up and was saved.

Then I was left all alone on the mourners' bench. My aunt came and knelt 7 at my knees and cried, while prayers and songs swirled all around me in the little church. The whole congregation prayed for me alone, in a mighty wail of moans and voices. And I kept waiting serenely for Jesus, waiting, waiting—but he didn't come. I wanted to see him, but nothing happened to me. Nothing! I wanted something to happen to me, but nothing happened.

I heard the songs and the minister saying: "Why don't you come? My dear 8 child, why don't you come to Jesus? Jesus is waiting for you. He wants you. Why don't you come? Sister Reed, what is this child's name?"

"Langston," my aunt sobbed. 9

"Langston, why don't you come? Why don't you come and be saved? Oh, 10 Lamb of God! Why don't you come?"

Now it was really getting late. I began to be ashamed of myself, holding 11 everything up so long. I began to wonder what God thought about Westley, who certainly hadn't seen Jesus either, but who was now sitting proudly on the platform, swinging his knickerbockered legs and grinning down at me, surrounded by deacons and old women on their knees praying. God had not struck Westley dead for taking his name in vain or for lying in the temple. So I decided that maybe to save further trouble, I'd better lie, too, and say that Jesus had come, and get up and be saved.

So I got up. 12

Suddenly the whole room broke into a sea of shouting, as they saw me rise. 13 Waves of rejoicing swept the place. Women leaped in the air. My aunt threw her arms around me. The minister took me by the hand and led me to the platform.

When things quieted down, in a hushed silence, punctuated by a few 14 ecstatic "Amens," all the new young lambs were blessed in the name of God. Then joyous singing filled the room.

That night, for the last time in my life but one—for I was a big boy twelve 15 years old—I cried. I cried, in my bed alone, and couldn't stop. I buried my head under the quilts, but my aunt heard me. She woke up and told my uncle I was crying because the Holy Ghost had come into my life, and because I had seen Jesus. But I was really crying because I couldn't bear to tell her that I had lied, that I had deceived everybody in the church, and I hadn't seen Jesus, and that now I didn't believe there was a Jesus any more, since he didn't come to help me.

Questions and Issues to Consider

Writing Process   1. Write a single sentence that could function as a thesis statement for Hughes's essay. Justify your sentence.

Aims of Writing   2. Is Hughes's primary appeal to reason through the use of facts, statistics, and evidence cited from authorities? Or does he appeal to emotions through his examples and language? Do you, as a reader, find his appeals effective?

Critical Thinking   3. Explain the significance of the title "Salvation." What other titles could Hughes have chosen?

4. Discuss the extent to which your religious heritage has shaped your perceptions of life, of others, of yourself.

Subtle Lessons in Racism

Kirsten Mullen

Kirsten Mullen observed her children's education and drew generalizations about often overlooked experiences with racism. She wrote this piece for the November 6–8, 1992, USA Weekend.

I f you had told me that this would happen, I wouldn't have believed   1
you. I mean, these are the '90s; ours is an integrated world.

Besides, it isn't politically correct.   2

During my child's six years attending an inner-city public elementary   3
school, the racial makeup flipped from 60 percent black pupils and 40 percent white to the reverse. The teachers were well-educated, thoughtful, enlightened. School was the last place where I expected to encounter racism.

I spent a fair amount of time volunteering at my son's school. I enjoyed   4
collaborating with his teachers, and I remain in awe of the incredible job that they do despite their charges' myriad abilities and the parents' varying levels of support. But the racial problems were there from the beginning.

During the first week of kindergarten, I observed five wiggle worms work-   5
ing at the blackboard in my son's class. Two were black. While the group's creative hum was louder than their teacher wished to condone (my presence may have had something to do with her low tolerance level), it seemed acceptable 5-year-old behavior. Still, I wasn't surprised when she shot them the eye. What floored me, though, was her calling only the two black pupils by name, insisting that they sit down. And this was a black teacher!

A month later, another parent and I observed the principal, a progressive   6
white woman, in a nearly identical situation. Three boys were skipping brightly, if noisily, down a hall. "I'll bet she reprimands the [lone] black

[child]," I said. She did. When I asked the principal why, she replied, "I know his mother, and she would not have approved of his behavior." I suppose the other boys' parents would have been oblivious?

Then there were the Christmas angels. The third-graders were busily making angels for their bulletin board. But there was only one small problem: Their teacher had provided only pink and white construction paper. My then-8-year-old came home disgruntled and not just a little confused. "I didn't think I could ask for brown," he said. "I didn't want her to get mad at me."   7

When I approached his teacher, she began somewhat defensively, saying: "I'm really surprised to hear this. [He's] a real leader in the class, and the children look up to him. If he had asked for brown paper, his classmates would have saluted his choice and probably followed." But the burden of race should not have fallen on the shoulders of an 8-year-old, I argued.   8

"There is so much everyone is asking of us," his teacher continued wearily. "We feed the children breakfast; some of them are here when we arrive and here when we leave [in before- and after-school care programs]; we teach sex education; we try not to favor boys over girls—and now this. But you're right. We need to be more sensitive to the matter of race."   9

Another teacher found herself in deep water when, in an attempt to teach the kids not to judge a book by its cover, she posted the words "Read an Ugly Book" on the wall in various colors, selecting brown and black for "Ugly." When I pointed it out, she said she had not been conscious of the implications of her choice.   10

Along that same line, my husband and I asked the school librarian to remember the global community when she produced bulletin-board designs featuring seasonal greetings or announcing coming events that included images of people. What was she thinking, we wondered, when she concocted a winter wonderland peopled with three blonds?   11

These encounters were far from painless for me. I was terrified the first time I brought up the subject of race at school. My palms were clammy, my heart was racing, and I could not have done it without rehearsing in the bathroom mirror. But all of the discussions since then have been easier. I also remember the day when our principal shared a teacher's (and perhaps her own) opinion about us: "[Those] two are never satisfied." We gave the question back to her and asked, "Are you?" This discussion became the first of many on the subject of race that the three of us came to appreciate.   12

Sometimes opportunities to spark such discussion come from unexpected quarters. This past spring, the delightful 6-year-old daughter of a friend decided to create a special card for her teacher, who was black and had just delivered her first child. But none of the periodicals in her family's collection featured brown babies. "Um . . . I hope you aren't offended by this request," my friend began nervously. "But do you have any magazine pictures of brown babies?"   13

I was touched by her request and encouraged by our conversation, because a similar situation seven years ago had led me to collect images of people of color. Take as many as you need, I told her.   14

One thing's certain: If you keep your eyes open and are willing to bring up   15
this subject, you will find ample opportunities to make a difference in your
children's lives. And as more of us embrace the subject, it ceases to be taboo.

Questions and Issues to Consider

Writing Process   1. Identify a sentence from the Mullen essay that could function as a
thesis statement. If you can't locate a sentence that you think makes
a thesis statement, write your own. Does Mullen's essay support
your thesis statement?

Aims of Writing   2. Is the writing aim of Mullen's essay to inform or to persuade? Justify
your response.

Critical Thinking   3. Describe the examples of behavior Mullen claims to be racist. Do
you think they are racist? Why or why not?

4. When you started to read Mullen's essay, to what race did you
assume she belonged? How is your first assumption about her race
supported from the reading? Did your assumption prove correct?

PREWRITING

KEEPING A JOURNAL

A good source of ideas for papers is a personal journal. A journal is a
record of your ideas, feelings, and experiences. Because you're writing
for yourself, not another reader, journal entries tend to reveal more
about your attitudes and experiences than do other forms of writing.
And your thoughts about what you see, what you think, what you
question, and what you experience are a valuable source of writing
ideas and examples to support them.

Of course entries need not focus only on deeply personal, private
moments. A journal is also a place to move from the self, to explore
broader issues. You can use a journal to record experiences that you
want to remember. You also can use a journal to:

Sketch ideas for the draft of a paper

Examine alternate solutions to a problem

Rewrite and expand notes from important lectures

React to an interesting news broadcast or article

Reflect on class reading assignments

Search out answers to perplexing questions

Look at alternatives to an instructor's or author's conclusions

Apply things you've learned in class to your own life

If you don't already keep a journal, this is a good time to start. Consider focusing your entries on one of these topics:

Heroes   Everyone has a hero. Identify a hero in your life, and explain why that person is a hero to you.

Scapegoat   At some time you must have been blamed for something you did not do. Describe an incident in which you were held responsible for something over which you had no control. Talk about the lessons you learned from that experience.

Outcast   At one time or another, you've been excluded from a group—probably because of your age, gender, beliefs, or abilities. Describe a time when you were left out of a group. How has that experience affected your life?

Devil figure   Unintentionally you may have hurt someone. Perhaps you disappointed a friend, told a lie about a boy in your class, or encouraged your sister to do something wrong. Describe a time in your life when you were the cause of someone else's unhappiness. How did you feel then? How do you feel about it now? What have you learned?

Star-crossed lovers   Think back to a romantic relationship you had in grade school, high school, or college. What did you learn from that relationship?

Quest   Identify something you've accomplished. Then describe the steps you took to accomplish it, and explain how those steps led to the final outcome.

Task   Remember a responsibility or task that seemed beyond your capabilities but actually wasn't. Describe how you overcame your feelings of inadequacy and finished the task.

Initiation   When did you become an adult? At what point did you begin to think of yourself as a man or a women?

Journey   Journeys often become central points of reference in our lives. Explain the role a journey or a certain place has played in your life.

Fall   We all make mistakes. Describe a mistake you've made, and explain how that experience has affected you.

Each of these topics should stimulate memories, thoughts, and feelings. In your journal, write about those memories, thoughts, and feelings.

Patti Dixon, a student, found the topic of her paper in a journal entry. Reading through her journal, she came across a statement she had written several months earlier: "Today I took the boys with me to Food Center so we could pay for several items we didn't get charged for." Patti had forgotten all about that simple event until she read the entry. But she realized that it would be a good topic for her paper, that she could use this personal experience to tell her children and her readers how important honesty is in her life. (A draft of Patti's paper begins on page 182.)

EXPLORING YOUR OPTIONS

1. Choose one of the journal topics listed above.

   _____

   _____

2. Write a brief journal entry about that topic.

   _____

   _____

   _____

   _____

   _____

   _____

_____

_____

3. Use the entry as a source of ideas by thinking about the different writing aims.

   a. Explain how an idea from the entry can be used to reflect.

   _____

   _____

   _____

   b. Explain how an idea from the entry can be used to inform.

   _____

   _____

   _____

   c. Explain how an idea from the entry can be used to persuade.

   _____

   _____

   _____

   d. Explain how an idea from the entry can be used to speculate.

   _____

   _____

   _____

4. As your paper's topic, choose one of the ideas you've written about in question 3. Write that topic on the line below.

   _____

5. Put a checkmark next to the aim that best represents your reason for writing this paper.

   _____ To reflect   _____ To persuade

   _____ To inform   _____ To speculate

DEVELOPING COHERENCE AND TRANSITIONS

You need to connect the ideas and examples you've generated in the prewriting stage. Sentences, paragraphs, and essays are accumulations of different ideas—ideas that pull together to achieve a single purpose. A good writer takes individual ideas and relates them to other ideas. The pulling together of multiple ideas to advance a single purpose is called *coherence*. *Coherence* comes from *cohere*, which means "to stick, to hold together firmly." To be coherent, the ideas in a sentence, paragraph, or essay must show a relationship, a clear connection.

The most common method of connecting ideas is through *transitions*. A transition can be a single word, a phrase, a sentence, or a paragraph that establishes a relationship.

Making connections through transitions doesn't just happen: Transitions have to be created. One way to create effective transitions is to use signposts. *Signposts* are words or phrases that alert readers to a change in or to a reinforcement of a thought or an argument. Many words and phrases are common signposts. This is just a partial list:

SIGNPOSTS

above all	for instance	nevertheless
accordingly	furthermore	next
admittedly	hence	nonetheless
again	however	now
also	in addition	of course
and	in comparison	on the other hand
as a result of	indeed	second
as noted	in fact	similarly
besides	in other words	so
but	in spite of	still

SIGNPOSTS *(continued)*

certainly	instead	then
consequently	in the first place	therefore
finally	likewise	though
for example	moreover	yet

Notice how a student incorporates the signposts *yet, for instance, in fact,* and *but* to make connections in this paragraph:

> I get a little weary of hearing broken homes being blamed for 96.3 percent of American youth's difficulties. Many of my friends have grown up in broken homes or have been raised by only one parent. *Yet* they are doing fine now. *For instance,* some are teachers, some are salespeople, and some are just raising families on their own. *In fact,* I'm the product of a broken home, *but* I too have been able to overcome this supposed disadvantage.

You must tell the reader what the relationships are among your ideas, and that's what signposts do. Use the list as you rewrite your draft. Don't hesitate to use signposts mechanically at first. If you need to, say, "This concludes my discussion of. . . . Next I will discuss. . . ." As you write more, you will acquire the habit of using transitions. But don't expect the process to become automatic.

Another method of creating transitions uses key words. *Key words* repeat significant or unique words in a sentence, paragraph, or section to connect two or more ideas. Notice how Dr. Wayne W. Dyer repeats the idea of failure with the key words *failure, fail, unsuccessful,* and *failed* in a paragraph from his *Your Erroneous Zones:*

> Try to imagine using *failure* as a description of an animal's behavior. Consider a dog barking for fifteen minutes, and someone saying, "He really isn't very good at barking, I'd give him a C." How absurd! It is impossible for an animal to *fail* because there is no provision for evaluating natural behavior. Spiders construct webs, not successful or *unsuccessful* webs. Cats hunt mice; if they aren't successful in one attempt, they simply go after another. They don't lie there and whine, complaining about the one that got away, or have a nervous breakdown because they *failed*. Natural behavior simply is! So apply the same logic to your own behavior and rid yourself of the fear of *failure*.

Don't be worried about transitions while you're writing a rough draft. Your purpose for writing a draft is to develop ideas. But once the first draft is finished, your purpose is to show the relationships among those ideas. Read the completed draft with the single purpose of writing the needed transitions, most often between paragraphs and between major ideas and/or examples.

PRACTICE 1   Below is a paragraph from Mortimer J. Adler's essay "How to Mark a Book." Insert transition words into the blanks to give the paragraph coherence.

There are three kinds of book owners. The _____ has all the standard sets and best-sellers—unread, untouched. (_____ deluded individual owns woodpulp and ink, not books.) The _____ has a great many books—a few of them read through, most of them dipped into, but all of them as clean and shiny as the day they were bought. (_____ person would probably like to make books his own, _____ is restrained by a false respect for their physical appearance.) The _____ has a few books or many—every one of them dog-eared and dilapidated, shaken and loosened by continual use, marked and scribbled in from front to back. (_____ man owns books.)

PRACTICE 2   Langston Hughes effectively uses transitions in his essay "Salvation" at the beginning of this chapter (see page 163). Use the essay to answer the questions below.

1. Explain how Hughes makes the transition from paragraph 1 to paragraph 2.

_____

_____

2. Explain how Hughes makes the transition from paragraph 2 to paragraph 3.

_____

_____

3. Explain how Hughes makes the transition from paragraph 4 to paragraph 5.

_____

_____

4. List some of the words Hughes uses in the first seven paragraphs that tie his ideas together, that give them coherence.

_____   _____   _____

_____   _____   _____

_____   _____   _____

_____   _____   _____

CLASSIFICATION

Using Classification

Classification is the process of sorting information into groups according to type or characteristics. Concrete objects are easier to classify than abstractions. For example, athletic shoes can be classified according to different types of soles: court soles or cleat soles.

Athletic shoes

Court soles	*Cleat soles*
Basketball	Football
Tennis	Baseball
Aerobics	Golf

You can define each subgroup more completely by explaining how each is different from the others. In other words, explain how a basketball shoe is different from a tennis shoe or an aerobics shoe.

Of course abstractions also can be classified. For example, the abstract subject emotions can be divided into these groups: anger, elation, envy, fear, grief, and joy. Each group can be defined more completely by explaining how it is different from the others. For example, describe how anger is different from elation or how fear is different from grief.

Suppose you're writing about factors that shape personality. Among these factors are genetic influences, family influences, hero identification, peer culture, and the larger society.

Personality-Shaping Factors

Genetic influences

Family influences

Hero identification

Peer culture

Larger society

Simply dividing the topic doesn't necessarily explain to your readers the relationships the parts share with one another. Classification explains these relationships. The following paragraph discusses the connections among three personality-shaping factors—genetic influences, family, and peer culture:

> Three factors that influence an individual's personality are genetics, family, and peers. All aspects of an individual's personality—lifestyle, self-concept, roles—are influenced by biological and environmental factors. Genetic factors, especially, are likely to be overlooked because people need to believe that human characteristics can be changed. However, in general, most likely to be inherited are basic abilities, including reaction speed, motor capability, sensory discrimination, and intelligence. Less likely to be inherited are temperamental traits, including evenness of mood, lethargy, and emotionality in general. Although genetics has a powerful influence on shaping personality, family experience is the most important influence. The foundations of self-concept and roles are learned within the context of the home. In the home, the individual gains beliefs, attitudes, values, and skills necessary to interact with others. And an individual's peers also influence personality. The peer culture has both positive and negative impact on personality. Peers can give the individual feelings of self-respect and belongingness. On the other hand, peers can have detrimental effects on personal growth. If the individual is not accepted by peers, then feelings of disconnectedness and inferiority emerge. Therefore, the three factors—genetics, family, and peers—are woven together to help form the individual's personality.

The basis you use to classify something should be useful. It makes no sense to group angry people into those who wear black socks and those who wear brown socks because sock color has nothing to do with anger. But you could write a meaningful paper by classifying angry people into groups based on the source of that anger—say personal frustration, abuse, or ethnic injustice. In the process, you would use concrete examples of people and circumstances to illustrate the different causes of anger and to explain this abstract emotion.

✓ CHECKLIST: CLASSIFICATION

1. Does the major group you classify have clear divisions?

2. Does the classification make the point you want for your paper's purpose?

3. Are the classifications or divisions complete, or do you select only several?

4. Are the categories separate, or do they overlap?

5. Do you explain the relationships among the classifications?

CLASSIFICATION: AN EXAMPLE

In the following paragraph, Frederick B. Knight classifies human motivation. Notice how he emphasizes the groups by numbering them.

Human Motives

A comprehensive classification of motives has been formulated by Maslow. He has proposed a theory of motivation in which motives are classified according to the basic need underlying the motives. Needs are classified into five groups or levels and arranged in a hierarchy of prepotency. This arrangement means that "the appearance of one need usually rests on the prior satisfaction of another, more pre-potent need." The five groups of needs, listed in descending order of the prepotency, are as follows:

1. **Physiological needs**   This group includes the need for food, for water, for oxygen, for constant temperature, etc.

2. **Safety needs**   These needs are concerned with seeking safety and avoiding pain, threats, and danger.

3. **Love needs**   These needs give rise to the desire to belong, to be wanted, to be loved by friends, relatives, and family.

4. **Esteem needs**   These needs give rise to the desire for self-respect, strength, achievement, adequacy, prestige, attention, and appreciation.

5. **Self-actualization needs**   This group is characterized by saying that one must do what one can do.

PRACTICE

1. List three types of lies.

_____

_____

_____

2. Explain how each lie is different from the others.

Lie 1: _____

_____

_____

Lie 2: _____

_____

_____

Lie 3: _____

_____

_____

3. List three types of frustrations.

_____

_____

_____

4. Explain how each frustration is different from the others.

Frustration 1: _____

_____

_____

Frustration 2: _____

_____

_____

Frustration 3: _____

_____

_____

WRITING TOGETHER

1. After completing the above Practice exercise on your own, share your classification with a class partner who has also classified *lies* and *frustrations*.

2. As a pair, repeat the Practice exercise by generating yet another list of classifications for *lies* and *frustrations*.

Classification and Aims

You can use classification whatever the purpose of your writing, as the following assignments show.

Reflect

Classify the types of frustrations you encounter in your life. Consider academics, work, and relationships. Reflect on how you have learned to manage your frustrations.

Identify different types of personal success. Give examples of these successes from your experience or someone else's.

Inform

Three factors that influence intellectual development are genetics, family, and schooling. Write an essay informing your audience about how these factors can affect intellectual development.

People in situations beyond their control often have to learn to cope with pain. Identify and explain the different methods people use to help them cope with pain.

Persuade

Anger often harms family relationships. Classify the different types of anger found in a family situation. Then make suggestions to persuade family members to control their anger.

To always be learning is helpful in maintaining a healthy self-concept. Identify several different areas of lifetime learning to encourage a friend to make a small change in his or her life.

Speculate

Divide adversity into different groups. Write about what you think life would be like without adversity.

Classify your educational, occupational, and personal goals. Think about what you want to achieve—in terms of each goal—in six months, in a year, in five years. Continue dividing your goals into smaller groups, formulating steps that will help you meet each goal.

EXPLORING YOUR OPTIONS

You now are ready to write the first draft of your essay. You already have determined the following:

Your topic: _____

Your main writing aim: _____

1. List your major divisions.

Division 1: _____

Division 2: _____

Division 3: _____

Division 4: _____

2. Identify two examples or supports for each major division.

Division 1:

_____

_____

Division 2:

_____

_____

Division 3:

_____

_____

Division 4:

_____

_____

3. Set aside a block of time, and write your first draft. Don't worry about being right or wrong. The object is to get your ideas on paper.

REWRITING

DETERMINING VOICE AND DISTANCE

Your voice gives your writing personality. Each person has an individual writing voice, just as each person has an individual speaking voice. We recognize the voices of friends and family members when we hear them speaking in other rooms or on the telephone. Not only can we identify them from their voices, we also can distinguish their mood and feelings by carefully listening to their voices. Your writing voice "speaks" to your readers from the written page. By carefully "listening" to that voice, your readers can tell your mood and your feelings.

Your freedom to express yourself in your own voice is limited by the nature of what you're writing. You write differently in a paper for a class than you do in a note to someone you love. You write differently on a job application than you do in a letter to your mother. In a paper or on a job application, you probably use a formal voice, a traditional follow-the-rules voice. In a note or letter, you probably use an informal voice, a casual, more colorful voice—with much less emphasis on the rules.

The circumstances in which you're writing determine not only your voice but also the distance you should keep from the readers. Distance is how near or how far you are to your reader and topic. If your voice and distance aren't compatible with the writing situation, your readers can become frustrated and confused. Often an appropriate voice and distance lie somewhere between strictly formal and informal writing voices.

This rewriting activity can help you determine an appropriate voice and distance for a particular paper. Select a single well-developed paragraph from the draft of your paper. Rewrite the paragraph for someone who knows you well, either a family member or a friend. Use language and experiences with which the person is familiar.

Now rewrite the same paragraph for someone you don't know, someone who would expect a formal voice and distance—a newspaper editor or a city council member, for example.

Finally, rewrite the same paragraph a third time, with voice and distance somewhere between the informal and formal paragraphs. This is the voice and distance you probably should be using.

To help her determine voice and distance, Patti took a paragraph from her first draft and rewrote it, first informally, then formally, and then somewhere in between. Here is her informal rewrite. Her audience for this paragraph is her young sons.

```
Just as the checker added up our groceries, Mommy
ran to get some orange juice. Remember that when I
got back, the lady totaled the bill and gave us
credit for the Frosted Flakes, Lucky Charms, Tide,
Log Cabin, and Windex coupons. I was happy that we
had $10 left after paying for the groceries because
we could then go to Burger King for lunch.
```

In the paragraph below, Patti is writing to a senator. Notice how she removes herself from the situation:

```
Just as the cashier began tabulating the pur-
chases, the customer momentarily left to make
another selection. When the customer returned, the
```

cashier did a preliminary total and deducted
coupon and recycled bag credits from the overall
purchase. The receipt was only $89.73. The cus-
tomer was pleased.

In her third rewrite, Patti has found an appropriate voice and distance, somewhere between the informal and formal paragraphs:

Just as the cashier started ringing up my groceries, I hurried off to get one more item. When I
returned, the checker subtotaled my purchases,
then subtracted the credits for using coupons and
reusing bags. The total was about ninety dollars.
I was thrilled.

STUDENT ESSAY

Below is a revised draft of Patti Dixon's essay. Patti is a mother and a
returning student from Kentucky majoring in teacher education. As
you read the draft, ask yourself two basic questions:

- How does Patti succeed in fulfilling her purpose for writing this
  essay?

- How can Patti strengthen this draft?

Making Choices

Notice that Patti uses transitions effectively throughout the essay.

It was supposed to be a "major" grocery shopping
trip. That means I stock up on canned goods, frozen
foods, and other household staples. I usually spend
over a hundred dollars.

Just as the cashier started ringing up my groceries, I hurried off to get one more item. When I
returned, the checker subtotaled my purchases,
then subtracted the credits for using coupons and
reusing bags. The total was about ninety dollars.
I was thrilled.

As I put the groceries away at home, I checked
off each item on the cash register receipt. I
couldn't find the laundry detergent or disposable
diapers on the receipt. If I had noticed in the
store that the cashier forgot to charge me for the

things on the bottom of the cart, I would have said something immediately. I hadn't been standing there the whole time, however, so I arrived home with about $15 worth of merchandise I didn't pay for.

She tells her readers about her conflict.

I considered not telling my husband, thinking he would be so impressed by my thrifty shopping. I told him anyway, because we tell each other everything (almost). We discussed my options. I said that it wasn't my fault, and the store should cover employees' mistakes. On the other hand, I had taken merchandise out of a store without paying for it. Is that shoplifting? I didn't think so, because it wasn't intentional. It would be so easy to pretend nothing had happened; however, the store employees had always been courteous and honest in their business dealings, and they deserved no less from me. I would go back and pay what I owed.

Patti identifies her controlling idea.

I decided this was a good opportunity to teach my boys about honesty and making choices. I told them what had happened, without telling them what my choice had been. I explained that the store didn't even know we had these things and that we could have lots of fun with $15. But, I reminded them, people aren't supposed to take things without paying for them. I asked what they thought I should do. My five year old looked at me and said simply, "Finish it." I wanted to be certain I understood his meaning and asked what I was supposed to finish. He said, "Go back to the store and finish paying." I was delighted that he saw this as a clear-cut issue with only one real choice. His brother wholeheartedly agreed with him.

The next day I called the store manager to ask if I needed to bring in the items to be scanned because they were rather bulky and I would have the baby with me, too. He said that wasn't necessary and told me he had never gotten a call like mine. He thanked me sincerely.

When I went back to pay for the diapers, detergent, and a few other things, I made sure I took the boys along. I wanted them to see that I did finish it.

Whenever possible, I try to teach my children values such as honesty by using examples they can understand. Examples come up frequently in everyday life, in stories, and on television. I used the riots and looting in Los Angeles recently as another teaching opportunity. We discussed whether it was all right to take things from stores if everyone else was doing it and if the police weren't arresting anyone. They decided it was never all right to steal.

She concludes by explaining how a seemingly unimportant incident can have important consequences.

I teach my children that people must always make choices. By discussing some of these options now, while they are young, I hope they will make wise choices in the future that echo my values.

EXPLORING YOUR OPTIONS

To help you discover an appropriate voice and distance for your paper, try the following:

1. Rewrite a paragraph from your draft for a close friend or family member, using an informal voice and distance.

_____

_____

_____

_____

_____

_____

_____

_____

2. Rewrite the same paragraph for someone in authority—someone you do not know—using a formal voice and distance.

_____

_____

_____

_____

_____

_____

_____

_____

3. Rewrite the same paragraph with a voice somewhere between those you used in the informal and formal paragraphs.

_____

_____

_____

_____

_____

_____

_____

_____

_____

4. Which voice and distance are most appropriate for this essay?

_____

_____

5. Explain your reasoning.

_____

_____

_____

6. Now rewrite your draft, consciously keeping your voice and distance consistent with your purpose, topic, and audience.

WRITING WITH COMPUTERS

1. Use the same paragraph you have rewritten for a close friend or family member and for someone in authority.

2. On the computer, rewrite the paragraph using sentences from the informal and formal paragraphs.

3. Rewrite the same paragraph with a voice somewhere between those used in the informal and formal paragraphs.

EDITING

CHOOSING THE RIGHT PRONOUN

Pronouns are substitutes for nouns. Pronouns can be used three different ways in a sentence: as a subject, as an object, or to show possession. Possessive pronouns rarely cause confusion, so we focus here on pronouns that function as subjects or as objects of clauses or phrases.

Subjective Pronouns

Subjective pronouns function as subjects. Use subjective pronouns for subjects of clauses; for comparisons that use the words *than, as,* or *like;* and for subjective complements.

Subjects of clauses   In the following sentences, the pronouns function as the subjects of clauses:

The technician wonders if *they* (not *them*) <u>know</u> the procedure.

She (not *her*) <u>has</u> experience with self-improvement.

People seldom make mistakes with pronouns that function as the subjects of clauses.

Comparisons that use the words *than, as,* or *like*   Comparisons with the words *than, as,* and *like* take a subjective pronoun:

Tania is more serious than *he.*

The word *he* is the subject of an unstated but understood concluding clause:

Tania is more serious than <u>he</u> <u>is</u> serious.

Here's another one:

Daniel is as smart as *she.*

Daniel is as smart as <u>*she*</u> <u>is</u> smart.

If you can complete a clause after the words *than, as,* or *like,* use a subjective pronoun.

Subjective complements   If a pronoun follows a linking verb, the pronoun functions as a subjective complement and takes the subjective case. Linking verbs are verbs that connect (link) a subject with a pronoun or adjective that follows. The most common linking verbs are forms of the verb *to be (am, are, is, was, were, being,* and *been).* The subjective complement is a word that usually follows the verb and "completes" the meaning of the subject by either renaming or describing the subject:

<u>Chinami Kudo</u> <u>is</u> a student.

Chinami Kudo is the subject of the clause, *is* is the linking verb, and *a student* is the subjective complement—it describes the subject.

Remember that a subjective complement describes or completes a subject. When the subjective complement is a pronoun, then, it also must take the subjective case:

<u>Chinami Kudo</u> <u>is</u> *she.*

<u>We</u> <u>are</u> *they.*

Objective Pronouns

Objective pronouns are pronouns that function as the object of a clause or phrase. We use objective pronouns as direct or indirect objects of clauses and as objects of prepositions.

Direct and indirect objects   An object, either direct or indirect, receives the verb's action. When a pronoun functions as an object, the pronoun must be in the objective case:

A neighbor gave *her* (not *she*) flowers.

A friend telephoned *him* (not *he).*

Objects of prepositions   Whatever follows a preposition is the object of that preposition; therefore, a pronoun that follows a preposition must be in the objective case.

Amanda shares her experiences with Lori and *me* (not *I*).

Amanda sits between *us* (not *we*).

Below is a list of some common prepositions.

PREPOSITIONS

about	beyond	onto
above	by	outside
across	down	over
after	during	past
against	except	since
along	for	through
among	from	to
around	in	toward
at	inside	under
before	into	until
behind	like	up
below	near	upon
beneath	of	with
beside	off	within
between	on	

Who and *Whom*

In formal English the words *who* and *whom* also reflect case. Use *who* or *whoever* whenever the pronoun functions as the subject of a clause; use *whom* or *whomever* whenever the pronoun functions as the object of a clause or phrase.

Russell, *who* is lonely, called tonight.

Russell, however, cheers up *whomever* he calls.

The chart below lists pronouns that indicate case. The two major sections of the chart are subjective and objective pronouns. These sections are divided into singular and plural columns. The column on the left side of the chart lists person: First person is *I*, second person is *you*, and third person is everyone and everything else. The bottom row lists the subjective *who* and the objective *whom*.

CHOOSING THE RIGHT PRONOUN

	Subjective		Objective	
	Singular	Plural	Singular	Plural
First person	I	we	me	us
Second person	you	you	you	you
Third person	he she it	they	him her it	them
	who, whoever		whom, whomever	

EXERCISE 1   Underline the correct pronoun in the following sentences. Don't choose a pronoun just because it sounds right to you. Instead, apply the rules to determine the correct form.

1. I want people laughing with (I, me) rather than at (I, me).

2. It is (I, me) (who, whom) is in control.

3. Telling the truth or pointing out the obvious also can get a laugh.

    Others may not see the obvious as well as (they, them).

4. A friend relates that (he, him) keeps a file of jokes and cartoons.

5. These cartoons make (he, him) laugh when (he, him) feels stress.

6. Usually stress is not caused by a situation itself but by how (we, us) perceive the situation.

7. Comedy and tragedy are two different ways (we, us) can view any situation.

8. For those (who, whom) laugh, their lives often feel better.

EXERCISE 2   Underline the correct pronouns in the following paragraph. Then fix the pronouns that are not correct. Don't choose a pronoun just because it sounds right to you. Instead, apply the rules on pages 186–189 to determine the correct form.

Health care professionals explain how they relieve stress through physical exercise. Dr. Deborah Jackson begins the day by stretching during her shower; it helps wake her up. After work, her returns home to a four-times-a-week, hour-long routine of cycling, calisthenics, aerobics, and more stretching. Rarely do her patients do more exercising than her. Some doctors believe they should model what they preach to their patients about stress reduction. Dr. Lynn Kennington, whom is the head of the health clinic, reduces stress through his diet and exercise program. Him claims that power walking is great for him. It is not unusual for him to walk at least nine miles a week. At sixty-one, Dr. Elizabeth Walquist has exercised regularly since medical school. She says, "I think my body begins to talk back to I when I don't exercise." And because of him and his example, Dr. Layne Harris has encouraged many tense people to begin jogging with he.

EXERCISE 3   Using the current draft of your essay, do the following:

1. Identify five sentences that contain subjective pronouns. Correctly label the pronoun rule that applies to each sentence.

2. Identify five sentences that contain objective pronouns. Correctly label the pronoun rule that applies to each sentence.

OPTIONS FOR WRITING

Reflect

1. Recall a time when you chose to be honest when it would have been easier not to be. Why did you choose honesty? Explain how this incident reveals your character and values.

2. Self-evaluation often focuses on one's strengths and weaknesses. Write an essay in which you emphasize one of your strengths and one of your weaknesses. Analyze these two traits, and explain how they affect your attitudes toward yourself, others, and life.

Inform

3. Think of a person you know, either directly or indirectly, whom you consider to be noble. Interview or do research on this person. You want to identify one or more formative incidents that strengthened him or her in later life. With those incidents as background, write a character profile of the person.

4. Select an aspect of your life that is causing you stress or anger or to behave in self-defeating ways. What advice do authorities offer to help overcome the aspect of your life that is troubling you? Write a coherent essay in which you classify the behavior and the recommended ways of dealing with it.

Persuade

5. Persuade someone to be patient by describing the rewards you associate with patience.

6. To survive in college, students have to keep themselves organized and motivated. In the absence of the network of parents, teachers,

and administrators that watches over high school students, college students must motivate themselves. Write an article for the school paper encouraging students to be internally rather than externally motivated. Use concrete examples of people who are internally motivated to support your position.

Speculate

7. Set a short-term goal for yourself and determine the steps necessary to reach that goal. Write a letter to a friend—a letter in which you divide the goal into manageable parts and explain why the goal is obtainable, what obstacles you expect to encounter, and how you plan to reach the goal.

8. All parents hope that their children's lives will be better than their own, that their children will enjoy what they themselves did not enjoy. Of course, hoping can't protect children from disappointments, even the severe disappointments their parents experienced growing up. On the basis of your perceptions and experiences, describe the childhood you envision for your own children. (Be realistic!) Explain how their lives will be different from and the same as yours.

Chapter 6

RELATIONSHIPS

Personal relationships are the most significant factor in most people's lives—more important than work, recreation, or even financial security. Yet we often spend much more time in other activities than in working to maintain and improve our relationships. In this chapter we look at the different roles we play in relationships and examine ways to improve those relationships.

To prepare for this chapter's theme, relationships, answer the following questions:

- How do different relationships influence our lives?
- How can individuals develop stronger, more meaningful relationships?

READINGS on *Relationships*

Four Words
Bob Greene

Bob Greene is a syndicated columnist for the Chicago Tribune *who combines a great reporter's skill for getting to the heart of a story with warmth and caring. "Four Words" comes from a collection of his columns and essays entitled* He Was a Mid-Western Boy on His Own *(1991).*

If anyone has ever said anything cruel to you—something that has stuck with you for a long time; if anyone has ever said anything very kind to you—something that has stuck with you for a long time. . . .   1

Well, be assured that you're feeling emotions that have nothing to do with national boundaries.   2

In the city of Fujisawa, Japan, which is near Yokohama, lives a woman named Atsuko Saeki. She is twenty-six years old; she is single and lives with her parents. She has a job as a sales clerk at the Yurindo Bookstore in her town.   3

When she was a teenager, she dreamed of coming to the United States. Most of what she knew about American life she had read in textbooks. "I had a picture of the daddy sitting in the living room," she said, "and of the mommy baking chocolate chip cookies, and of a big dog lying by the couch. In my mind, the teenage girl goes to the movies on the weekends with her boyfriend. . . ."   4

She arranged to attend a college in the United States—Lassen College, in Susanville, California. When she arrived in the United States, though, it was not the dream world she had imagined. She couldn't blame anyone; it was no one's fault, and certainly not the college's fault. She considered herself naive to have pictured American life in such storybook terms.   5

"People were struggling with their own problems," she said. "People had family troubles, and money worries, and often they seemed very tense. I felt very alone."   6

At college, one of the classes that was hardest for her was physical education.   7

"We played volleyball," she said. "The class was held in an indoors gymnasium. The other students were very good at it, but I wasn't."   8

She tried to have fun playing volleyball, and often she was able to. But the games made her nervous. "I was very short, compared to the other students," she said. "I felt I wasn't doing a very good job. To be very honest, I was a lousy player."   9

One afternoon, the physical education instructor told Atsuko Saeki that   10
she was assigned to set the volleyball up for the other players on her team. "I
was told that it was my job to hit the ball to them, so that they could hit it over
the net."

No big deal for most people, but it terrified Atsuko Saeki. For some rea-   11
son, she feared she would be humiliated if she failed—if she was unable to set
the shots up for her teammates. Undoubtedly they would have forgiven her.
But in this world each person's fears—each person's perceived humiliations—
are private and are real.

Apparently a young man on her team sensed what she was going through.   12
This was a coed class; he was on her side of the net.

"He walked up to me," she said. "He whispered to me: 'Oh come on. You   13
can do that.'

"He said it in a nice way, but he was serious. If you are the kind of person   14
who has always been encouraged by your family or your friends or somebody
else, maybe you will never understand how happy those words made me feel.
Four words: 'You can do that.'"

She made it through the phys ed class. She may have thanked the young   15
man; she is not sure.

But now five years have passed; she is out of college, and back in Japan,   16
and living in her parents' house.

"I have never forgotten the words," she said. "'You can do that.' When   17
things are not going so well, I think of those words."

She is quite sure that the young man had no idea how much his words   18
meant to her. "I'm sure that he was just a nice guy," she said. "I'm sure that he
was the kind of guy who would say those words to anyone.

"But at the same time it made a big difference to me. When I left the gym-   19
nasium I felt like crying with happiness. He probably doesn't even remember
saying the words."

Which, perhaps, is the lesson here. You say something cruel to a person,   20
you have no idea how long it will stick. You say something kind, you have no
idea how long that will stick.

"I remember the young man's name," Atsuko Saeki said. "His name was   21
William Sawyer. I do not know what happened to him, but he helped me just
by whispering to me."

She's all the way over there in Japan. But still she hears his words: 22
"You can do that."

~ ~

Questions and Issues to Consider

Writing Process   1. Greene uses narration to describe Atsuko Saeki's experience and to
draw attention to what he feels is significant. On the basis of the

details Greene chooses to include in this account, explain what you assume Greene feels is important.

2. Why does Greene use quoted speech in this essay? Why does he have Atsuko Saeki tell part of her story in her own words?

Aims of Writing   3. Greene is a journalist who reports what he observes. He carefully records this event without interjecting his own opinion. If Greene isn't writing to reflect his own experience or feelings, why is he writing?

Critical Thinking   4. A seemingly insignificant experience has had a great impact on Atsuko Saeki's life. What event that you thought at the time to be insignificant has proved to have a meaningful impact on your life?

How Do I Love Thee?

Robert J. Trotter

Robert J. Trotter, senior editor for Psychology Today, *describes a system for analyzing love. The system represented by a triangle has been developed by Robert J. Sternberg, a professor of psychology and education at Yale University.*

I ntimacy, passion and commitment are the warm, hot and cold vertices[1]   1
of Sternberg's love triangle. Alone and in combination they give rise to eight possible kinds of love relationships. The first is nonlove—the absence of all three components. This describes the large majority of our personal relationships, which are simply casual interactions.

The second kind of love is liking. "If you just have intimacy," Sternberg   2
explains, "that's liking. You can talk to the person, tell about your life. And if that's all there is to it, that's what we mean by liking." It is more than nonlove. It refers to the feelings experienced in true friendships. Liking includes such things as closeness and warmth but not the intense feelings of passion or commitment.

If you just have passion, it's called infatuated[2] love—the "love at first   3
sight" that can arise almost instantaneously and dissipate[3] just as quickly. It involves a high degree of physiological arousal but no intimacy or commitment. It's the 10th-grader who falls madly in love with the beautiful girl in his

---

[1] **vertices**: triangle points
[2] **infatuated**: an unreasonable love
[3] **dissipate**: vanish

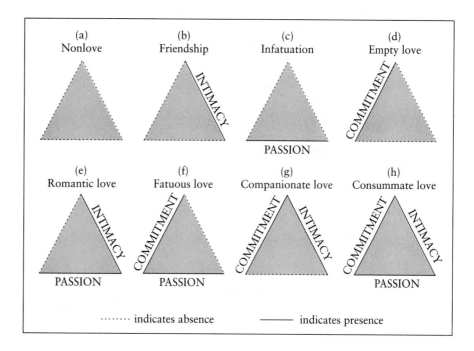

biology class but never gets up the courage to talk to her or get to know her, Sternberg says, describing his past.

Empty love is commitment without intimacy or passion, the kind of love   4
sometimes seen in a 30-year-old marriage that has become stagnant. The couple used to be intimate, but they don't talk to each other any more. They used to be passionate, but that's died out. All that remains is the commitment to stay with the other person. In societies in which marriages are arranged, Sternberg points out, empty love may precede the other kinds of love.

Romantic love, the Romeo and Juliet type of love, is a combination of inti-   5
macy and passion. More than infatuation, it's liking with the added excitement of physical attraction and arousal but without commitment. A summer affair can be very romantic, Sternberg explains, but you know it will end when she goes back to Hawaii and you go back to Florida, or wherever.

Passion plus commitment is what Sternberg calls fatuous[4] love. It's Holly-   6
wood love: Boy meets girl, a week later they're engaged, a month later they're married. They are committed on the basis of their passion, but because intimacy takes time to develop, they don't have the emotional core necessary to sustain the commitment. This kind of love, Sternberg warns, usually doesn't work out.

Companionate love is intimacy with commitment but no passion. It's a   7
long-term friendship, the kind of committed love and intimacy frequently seen in marriages in which the physical attraction has died down.

---

[4] **fatuous:** foolish

When all three elements of Sternberg's love triangle come together in a   8
relationship, you get what he calls consummate love, or complete love. It's the
kind of love toward which many people strive, especially in romantic relationships. Achieving consummate love, says Sternberg, is like trying to lose weight,
difficult but not impossible. The really hard thing is keeping the weight off after
you have lost it, or keeping the consummate[5] love alive after you have
achieved it. Consummate love is possible only in very special relationships.

---

[5] **consummate:** complete or fulfilling

⚬ ⚬

Questions and Issues to Consider

Writing Process   1. Trotter uses definition to develop his essay. Explain how Trotter
extends his definitions.

2. Trotter uses specific and general examples. Which examples are
specific, and which are general?

Aims of Writing   3. Trotter does not use personal experience and examples in this essay.
Why does he choose to use nonpersonal examples?

Critical Thinking   4. Trotter's triangle system may not include all types of love—like that
between parents and children, for example. What other examples
can you think of for the types of love that Trotter does not discuss?

PREWRITING

CLUSTERING

Clustering is a technique that can help you generate topic ideas and
examples. To make a clustering map, write and circle your general
topic in the center of a blank page. From the center circle, or hub,
branch out, writing and circling any ideas you freely associate with
your topic. Then draw lines from the topic to each major idea.

In Figure 6.1, the topic is family activities. The major ideas branching
out from the family-activities circle relate to how the activities affect the
family: physically, emotionally, mentally, financially, or socially.

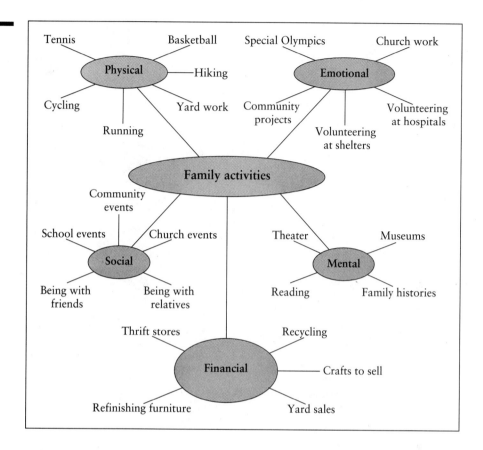

FIGURE 6.1

Clustering

From each new circle, draw lines and list examples of related activities. For example, in Figure 6.1, the Special Olympics, church work, volunteering at hospitals and shelters, and community projects are activities that affect the family emotionally. Each branch expands the original topic, giving you additional examples to choose from as you write. When you've finished clustering, choose just one of the circled ideas and write, nonstop, a short paragraph about it. This writing exercise should help you solidify your ideas and should give you a head start on your draft.

A student, Levi Liljenquist, has decided to do a paper on the Kobe, Japan earthquake. He wants to focus his paper on a single person's reaction to death that resulted from the disaster. Levi wants to organize the information he's thinking of using in the paper. He begins by writing his topic, Mrs. Takahashi, in a circle in the center of the page (Figure 6.2). From the topic circle, he draws three branches to the three main-example circles: earthquake, background, and death. Then Levi lists the details and examples that fit each category.

FIGURE 6.2

Mrs. Takahashi clustering map

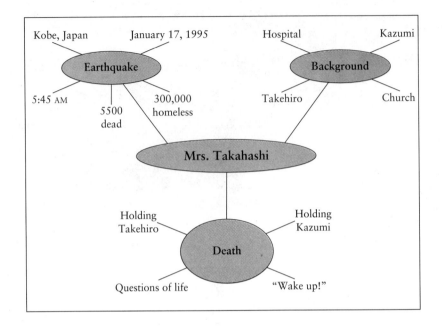

Levi decides to write, nonstop, a short paragraph about each of the major groups. He does this to get a sense of what information and perspective he wants to give to his paper. Here is Levi's response to the earthquake section. He writes about his own experience with the earthquake:

```
    It was 5:45 on the morning of January 17, 1995.
I was lying in bed asleep when I was awakened by a
loud, shrill scream, seeming to come from the cen-
ter of the earth. The sound sent a wave of fear
through my whole body. It was like the high-pitched
scream of a hawk, and it seemed to be warning of
coming danger. Sensing that something terrible was
about to happen, I lay still waiting for a sign. As
I listened closely, I heard a sound like a distant
wind, which picked up speed and intensity as it
approached. It raced toward me with great force and
velocity. I imagined that a gigantic Japanese bul-
let train was coming at me and would soon crash
through the wall by my bed. I anticipated a colli-
sion of great magnitude, and in fear, closed my
eyes and clung frantically to the sides of my mat-
tress. As the sound reached the apartment, the
```

ground gave out a scream even louder and more
piercing than the first. The earth below started to
move back and forth shaking the apartment. All of a
sudden, the shaking quickened, grew stronger, and
became more violent as the bed I was on jolted back
and forth, up and down. The sound of the cupboards
opening and closing, glass shattering as it hit the
ground, and the squeaking of the bed I was riding
on, were roaring in my ears.

Levi uses his clustering map and short paragraphs to generate ideas
and examples for his paper. (A draft of that paper begins on page 217).

EXPLORING YOUR OPTIONS

Use the clustering map below as a model to generate ideas and examples for your paper.

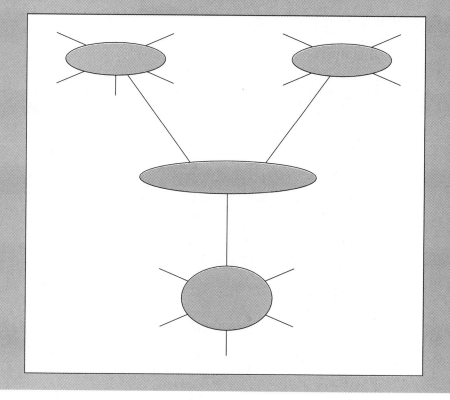

1. Write your topic in the center circle.

2. Divide your topic into at least three major ideas or groups, and write the title of each idea or group in one of the branching circles.

3. From each branching circle, list ideas, people, or things that support or are examples of the major idea or group.

4. Write nonstop, briefly, about each idea or group.

5. Put a checkmark next to your main purpose for writing on this topic.

_____ To reflect   _____ To persuade

_____ To inform   _____ To speculate

WRITING TOGETHER

Clustering is an effective prewriting strategy when you're working on a writing project with another person. Often ideas and examples come more readily when two people work together and bring their different perspectives to a common topic.

With a classmate do the following:

1. Write your topic in the center circle.

2. Divide your topic into at least three main ideas or groups, and write the title of each division in the branching circles.

3. From each branching circle, list ideas, people, or things that support or are examples of the idea or group.

4. Either together or individually, write nonstop, briefly, about each cluster.

5. As a team, develop a working thesis statement for this paper.

6. Together determine the most effective method of ordering your ideas and examples to support that working thesis statement.

DRAFTING

THE GENERAL VERSUS THE SPECIFIC

To write effectively, you must know the difference between general language and support and specific language and support. *General* language and support give readers just an overview of what you, the writer, intend to discuss. *Specific* language and support give readers a more detailed description of what you intend to discuss.

The term *food* is general. It can mean any type of food—food for cattle, food for people, food for fish. The term *food* is so general that it could generate hundreds of different images for your audience. The words *bread, milk,* and *meat* are not as general as the term *food,* but they are still general because readers can think of different examples of bread (white, wheat, rye), different types of milk (mother's milk, cow's milk, goat's milk), and different kinds of meat (beef, poultry, pork). *Russian rye bread, sweetened condensed milk,* and *beef teriyaki* are more specific terms and more specific examples of *bread, milk,* and *meat.*

The level of detail also can vary in the examples you use to support your ideas. You'll find that it is much easier to describe your ideas, attitudes, and experiences to your readers if you use specific examples. For instance, the following paragraph uses only general language with vague support:

> I'm frustrated with dating. First, it's expensive. Second, its confusing. Finally, it's stressful.

Because the language and the examples are general, readers have only a vague idea of what the writer thinks dating is like. By using specific language and detailed examples, Kevin is able to give his readers a clear picture of why he finds dating frustrating:

> I dread weekends because dating is frustrating. First, dating is expensive. Two weeks ago, I decided to save money by cooking dinner for my date and another couple. I spent all day cooking enchiladas, tortillas, beans, Spanish rice, and *biscochitos.* That meal cost me $43. After dinner, we went bowling ($12) and had ice cream sundaes ($6.37)—that date cost me $61.37. I probably spend a minimum of $30 for each date, so if I date once a week, that's easily $120 a month. Second, dating is confusing because nothing is certain. For

example, during last week's movie, my date puts her hand on my knee; I agonize whether this hand is a "clue." Should I simply place my hand on hers? Should I hold her hand? Should I put my arm around her? At the end of the date she says she has had a good time. I worry whether she's only being polite but isn't interested or if she did have a good time and wants me to ask her out again. And finally, dating is stressful. I remember, for instance, once being so nervous that I spit hot chocolate onto my date. I have also tripped and fallen on my date's front step because I was so worried about the kiss. Therefore, I think I'll have a peaceful weekend and not date.

Of course details in and of themselves are rarely useful. They have to relate to the larger idea. What makes Kevin's details about the cost of dating, his experiences at the movies and the door, and his nervousness important is their connection to the bigger picture—why Kevin finds dating frustrating.

Figure 6.3 shows the relationship between general and specific. Jackie used this inverted triangle to come up with specific examples of a general term, *relationship*.

FIGURE 6.3

General-to-specific inverted triangle

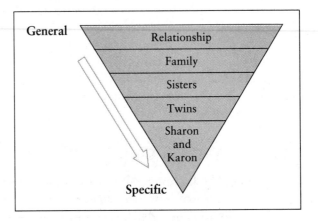

At the top of the inverted triangle is the most general term, *relationship*. As Jackie moves down the triangle, the terms become more specific. *Family* is more specific than *relationship* but more general than *sisters*. And *twins* is more specific than *sisters* but less specific than *Sharon* and *Karon*. Yet there is a connection between the general term *relationship* and the more specific *Sharon* and *Karon*.

Jackie realizes that her readers don't know her twin sisters, that she has to use specific examples to describe them. One of those examples has to do with their taste in music, a difference Jackie feels says a lot about their personalities. Sharon's favorite song is Reba McIntire's "For Herself"; she wants to change her life, to take more control of situations. Karon's favorite piece is Vladimir Ashkenazy's performance of Chopin's Nocturne in F-sharp Major. Karon, like this piece, is more relaxed; she's more content with her life.

If an idea is important, give your readers enough detail to establish clearly what you mean. Levi recognizes that his topic, the Kobe earthquake, is general. He also recognizes that the vast amounts of available information, experiences, and research on the earthquake would be too general for his paper. But he does want to give an overview of how extensive the deaths were for the earthquake. Levi decides to describe just one make-shift morgue that contained the bodies of earthquake victims.

> Three days after the earthquake, the gym floor was covered with dead bodies lined up in straight rows running from one wall to the other. The floor was twice as wide as a basketball court, and it was a few feet longer. There were at least two hundred corpses in the room. A dead dog lying on a blanket next to someone showed me that death was not biased. The remains of small children as well as the elderly and middle aged were among the numbers. Family members and friends sat at the feet of those they knew. Flowers and candles burning incense were next to heads of most bodies. Their poignant incense smell somewhat hid the rotten stench of death that filled the room.

Levi knows that the more specific his examples, the easier his message is to understand. So he uses the specific example of Mrs. Takahashi to illustrate the deep anguish of one because of the earthquake:

> Mrs. Takahashi removed the blankets from off the bodies and sat staring at them for a few minutes. She went first to Takehiro and began caressing his forehead and rubbing her fingers through his hair. Taking the boy in her arms, she held him to her breast and rocked him back and forth as a mother does with her baby. She then laid her son down and moved over by her daughter. "Isn't she beautiful," she said lifting her daughter into her arms. She began to caress Kazumi's face tenderly.

PRACTICE   Below is a paragraph that uses general language and support. Rewrite the paragraph, adding specific details and examples to support the general statements.

       Alvin Toffler believes that human relationships can be divided into three main categories: long-duration, medium-duration, and short-duration relationships. Long-duration relationships extend throughout one's lifetime. Medium-duration relationships last for a number of years. And finally, short-duration relationships may last a few minutes to a few years.

_____

_____

_____

_____

_____

_____

_____

_____

_____

_____

_____

_____

_____

EXPLORING YOUR OPTIONS

To generate concrete examples for your ideas, complete the inverted triangle below. Insert your topic, your most general idea, in the widest part of the triangle. Continue to focus your ideas until you come up with a specific concrete example.

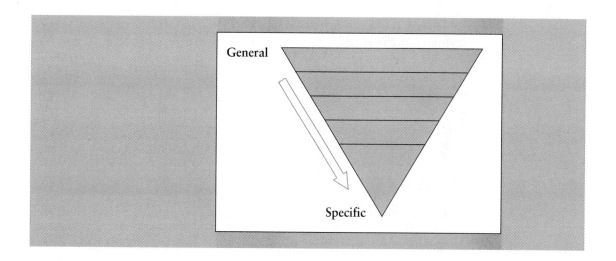

COMPARISON AND CONTRAST

Using comparison and contrast is a common type of analysis. You compare and contrast many times during the day—when you decide what cereal to buy, which clothes to wear, which television show to watch, which topic to write about. Because you compare and contrast so often, you probably tend to do this kind of analysis subconsciously. But when you're writing, you should compare and contrast consciously, to help meet the purpose of your paper.

Here are four reasons for comparing and contrasting when you write:

To explain something your readers probably don't know by comparing it with something they probably do know (living in a nontraditional family, for example, compared with living in a traditional family)

To convince your readers that one item or idea is better than another (a nonphysical punishment such as sitting on a chair as opposed to physical punishment like a spanking)

To show how two seemingly similar things or people really are different in important ways (yourself compared to your sister)

To show how two seemingly different things or people really are similar in important ways (governments and families)

You'll find comparison and contrast most effective when you're trying to prove a point. In the paper he's working on now, Lenny has decided to compare his childhood hero and his current hero, to show how his attitudes toward heroes have changed. Lenny's childhood hero was Popeye; his current hero is his own father. As a basis for comparison, Lenny plans to use specific examples that show how his heroes react to frustration, their partners, and their children. First, though, he has to decide how to organize his discussion.

Patterns of Organization

Two major methods of organizing a paper that compares and contrasts are the block pattern and the point-by-point pattern.

Block pattern   The block pattern emphasizes the subjects of the comparison and contrast. This is a sample outline of Lenny's paper showing the block pattern:

Subject 1 (Popeye)

> Characteristic 1 (Frustration)
>
> Characteristic 2 (Partner)
>
> Characteristic 3 (Children)

Subject 2 (Dad)

> Characteristic 1 (Frustration)
>
> Characteristic 2 (Partner)
>
> Characteristic 3 (Children)

This block pattern emphasizes the two subjects: Popeye and Dad. In the first half of the paper Lenny discusses Popeye; in the second half he writes about his dad.

> My heroes have changed over the years because of how they treat frustration, partners, and children. My first memorable hero was Popeye. I remember watching every Saturday morning to see how Popeye would solve his problems with the big, mean Brutus. Popeye constantly was being thrown through the air or twisted into different shapes by the bully Brutus. When Popeye couldn't take it anymore, he'd open his spinach can, muscles would bulge, and he'd smash Brutus. Popeye solved his problems through force. Popeye also treated his partner Olive Oyl with force. Most episodes he would stretch her away from Brutus and carry her off to safety. And I remember wanting to be Popeye's son, Sweet Pea, because Popeye would throw the laughing baby to the moon.

My own strong father, on the other hand, never used force or physical strength. I remember one evening when our car ran into an angry neighbor's fence. Dad calmly invited the mad neighbor in for some cookies, and they talked it out. Dad and Mom also talked about everything each night as they would cook dinner and do dishes together. And finally, Dad didn't throw me to the moon, but he'd set me on his lap and read to me, talk to me, and hold me. Popeye may have been my childhood hero, but Dad is my true hero.

This organization gives the readers a general overview of one subject before going on to the next. It works well for short papers with several subjects. But by forcing readers to wait until the end of the paper to make the comparison, the block pattern also forces readers to remember all they have read about earlier subjects.

Point-by-point pattern   The point-by-point pattern emphasizes the characteristics being compared and contrasted. It focuses more on the specifics or details of the comparison than on the general subjects. Here's a sample outline of Lenny's paper, showing the point-by-point pattern:

Characteristic 1 (Frustration)

> Subject 1 (Popeye)
>
> Subject 2 (Dad)

Characteristic 2 (Partner)

> Subject 1 (Popeye)
>
> Subject 2 (Dad)

Characteristic 3 (Children)

> Subject 1 (Popeye)
>
> Subject 2 (Dad)

This organizational pattern emphasizes the characteristics of the two heroes, how they deal with their frustration, their partners, and children. Each point is discussed in turn with examples of how Popeye and Dad demonstrate that particular characteristic:

My heroes have changed over the years because of how they treat frustration, partners, and children. My first memorable hero was Popeye. I remember watching every Saturday morning to see how Popeye would solve his problems with the big, mean Brutus. Popeye constantly was being thrown through the air or twisted into different shapes by the bully Brutus. When Popeye couldn't take it anymore, he'd open his spinach can, muscles would bulge, and he'd smash Brutus. Popeye solved his problems through force. My own strong father, on the other hand, never used force or physical strength. I remember one evening when our car ran into an angry neighbor's fence. Dad calmly invited the mad neighbor in for some cookies, and they talked it out. Popeye also treated his partner, Olive Oyl, with force. Most episodes he would stretch her away from Brutus and carry her off to safety. Dad and Mom, however, quietly talked about everything each night as they would cook dinner and do dishes together. And I remember wanting to be Popeye's son, Sweet Pea, because Popeye would throw the laughing baby to the moon. But Dad didn't throw me to the moon; rather he'd set me on his lap and read to me, talk to me, and hold me. Popeye may have been my childhood hero, but Dad is my true hero.

The point-by-point organization allows readers to make comparisons as they read; they don't have to wait until the end of the paper.

✓ CHECKLIST: COMPARISON AND CONTRAST

1. Do you compare or contrast your topic with a clear purpose?

2. Do you give each item equal space?

3. Do you explain your comparison or contrast with clear examples?

4. Do you use the block pattern or the point-by-point pattern?

COMPARISON AND CONTRAST: AN EXAMPLE

In the following paragraph, Richard Rodriguez contrasts his public life with his private life. His public life is conducted mostly in English, while his private life is mainly in Spanish. Notice that his contrast focuses on the way in which he connects language to his associations with others.

Public and Private

For me there were none of the gradations between public and private society so normal to a maturing child. Outside the house was public society; inside the house was private. Just opening or closing the screen door behind me was an important experience. I'd rarely leave home all alone or without reluctance. Walking down the sidewalk, under the canopy of tall trees, I'd warily notice the—suddenly—silent neighborhood kids who stood warily watching me. Nervously, I'd arrive at the grocery store to hear there the sounds of the *gringo*—foreign to me—reminding me that in this world so big, I was a foreigner. But then I'd return. Walking back toward our house, climbing the steps from the sidewalk, when the front door was open in summer, I'd hear voices beyond the screen door talking in Spanish. For a second or two, I'd stay, linger there, listening. Smiling I'd hear my mother call out, saying in Spanish (words), "Is that you Richard?" all the while her sounds would assure me: *You are home now; come closer; inside. With us.*

PRACTICE

1. Rodriguez claims that he has two lives and two languages: public and private. In your own words, describe how those two lives and languages are evident for Rodriguez.

   _____

   _____

   _____

   _____

2. Do you have two lives and languages—both public and private?

   a. Describe your public life.

   _____

   _____

   _____

   _____

   b. Describe your public language.

   _____

   _____

_____

_____

c. Describe your private life.

_____

_____

_____

_____

d. Describe your private language.

_____

_____

_____

_____

3. Show the similarities or the differences between your public life and language with your private life and language.

_____

_____

_____

_____

_____

_____

Comparison and Contrast and Aims

As these assignments suggest, you can use comparison and contrast whatever the aim of your writing.

Reflect

Reflect on the differences in your life since your parents' divorce. How did you feel about your family life before you were aware of your parents' difficulties? What were your feelings after the divorce? Explain how those differences have led you to a deeper understanding of the effect divorce has had on your family.

Grandparents can play a significant role in a person's life. Compare and contrast two of your grandparents, explaining how they've influenced your life.

Inform

Two common emotions that often are confused are infatuation and love. Cite specific examples of each emotion to help your readers understand the similarities and differences between the two.

Consider the marriages of two couples you know. Compare or contrast the marriages to explain the characteristics that strengthen or weaken the relationships.

Persuade

Parents sometimes use physical punishment to discipline their children. Contrast the effects of physical punishment (spankings, being locked in a room) with those of nonphysical punishment (sitting on a chair, the loss of privileges). Write an article for the local newspaper, persuading parents to use nonphysical punishment.

Two of your friends—both teenagers—are planning to get married this summer. Write a letter to the couple in which you contrast teenage marriages with later marriages and encourage your friends to wait.

Speculate

Many of us have had experiences in our childhood that we do not want our children to have. Explain, for example, the effects of living with parents who are verbally abusive. Contrast your experiences by writing about what life would have been like in a home where verbal abuse was not commonplace.

Single parenting can be difficult. Compare the lives of two single parents. How would you function in similar circumstances?

EXPLORING YOUR OPTIONS

You now are ready to write the first draft of your essay. You already have determined the following:

Your topic: _____

Your main writing aim: _____

Your main ideas:

Idea 1: _____

Idea 2: _____

Idea 3: _____

Specific support for your main ideas:

Support for idea 1: _____

_____

_____

_____

Support for idea 2: _____

_____

_____

_____

Support for idea 3: _____

_____

_____

_____

Set aside a block of time, and write your first draft. Don't worry about being right or wrong. The object is to get your ideas onto paper.

REWRITING

SUPPORTING EVIDENCE

When you write, you don't have to know all there is to know about your topic, but you should know something about it. In Chapter 1 we talked about three kinds of knowledge: personal, indirect, and researched. Each kind of knowledge can give you the authority you need to write about your topic credibly.

Kinds of Knowledge

Personal Knowledge   Personal knowledge is the experience you've had with a topic. Because of that experience, you become, in a sense, an authority on the subject. For example, the student Levi Liljenquist was living in Kobe, Japan at the time of the earthquake; therefore, that event establishes him as an authority on that experience.

Personal experience is valuable experience. But seldom would you rely only on personal examples in college writing assignments. Examples drawn from personal experiences become more effective when they are used together with indirect and researched knowledge.

Indirect Knowledge   Indirect knowledge is the experience someone else has had with your topic. It's impossible for you to have personal experience with every topic you write about, but you can use the experience of others to support your thesis. Indirect knowledge is important because the people you use as examples are, in a sense, authorities on your topic. Bob Greene, for instance, relies on indirect experience in his essay "Four Words" (at the beginning of this chapter on page 194). Greene is writing about someone else's experience; he uses Atsuko Saeki as the authority on her experience of having the four words "You can do that" to affect her life positively.

Researched Knowledge   Researched knowledge comes from reading books and magazines, watching documentaries, and interviewing experts. It is gleaned from the work of people whom others recognize as authorities on your topic. Researched knowledge often is strong support for college writing assignments. Robert J. Trotter uses researched knowledge as the basis for his essay "How Do I Love Thee?" (at the beginning of this chapter on page 196). Trotter is describing the research Robert J. Sternberg, a professor of psychology and education at Yale University, has done on love relationships.

Proving Your Authority

Your readers need evidence of your authority; they need proof that you are knowledgeable. In other words, you have to back up your assertions with concrete support. That support can take the form of facts, statistics, opinions, examples, and the words of other authorities.

Suppose you write a vague, general statement: *Divorce affects children.* To make this statement believable, you need proof or evidence. One method of proving that divorce affects children is with a *fact:*

> In 1991, 66.9 percent of American homes had two parents; this means that one-third of American homes had just one parent.

Or you could use *statistics* for evidence:

> In 1991, 22 percent of America's children lived alone with their divorced mother; 3 percent lived alone with their divorced father.

Opinion is also an effective support, as long as the opinion is substantiated by experience, observation, or a recognized authority:

> A social worker believes that ten years after a divorce, most fathers will be entirely absent from the lives of their children.

And *examples* provide support:

> Clay describes traveling three hours to visit his father two weekends each month after his parents' divorce.

Finally, other *authorities* are a source of evidence:

> Dr. Richard A. Gardner, a child psychiatrist, insists that children be told they are not the reason for their parents' divorce.

By using facts, statistics, opinions, examples, and other authorities, we've given substance to the statement that divorce affects children.

One purpose of rewriting is to verify the evidence you've used in your writing. This means deleting ineffective examples, adding more specific or convincing proof, and rearranging weak evidence for stronger emphasis. But first you need a means of evaluating the evidence you use to prove your assertions.

To begin, read your draft, looking specifically at the types of proof you use. As you read, underline or put a checkmark next to each fact, statistic, opinion, example, and authority cited in the paper.

Now evaluate each piece of evidence. Look at how much support you have for each assertion. Where it's not enough, add more. Look at the effectiveness of the evidence. If it's not effective, take it out. Constantly ask yourself if each new example helps establish you as an authority on the topic. Then think about information you can include to make your writing more authoritative and confident.

In his paper, Levi uses several different kinds of support to establish his authority. Levi relies on personal knowledge to describe the Kobe earthquake. As Levi starts writing his paper, he describes the earthquake in first person (see his prewriting paragraph on page 200), but he soon questions whether he should be the focus of this college paper. Although his final draft doesn't include direct references to Levi himself, as readers we clearly understand that he is taking us through his experiences with the earthquake at the hospital, church, and morgue. The information about Mrs. Takahashi grieving for her two children comes from indirect knowledge, from Levi's interactions with and observations of Mrs. Takahashi. Levi is not a parent, and he has not experienced the death of a close family member, but he indirectly learns of that experience through Mrs. Takahashi. Finally, Levi relies on researched knowledge by using facts and statistics to give an overview of the devastation caused by the earthquake.

To write effectively, you have to establish yourself as an authority on your topic. You have to have the confidence both in yourself and in your writing to let others know that you know what you're writing about. You can do this by combining your personal, indirect, and researched knowledge in the facts, statistics, opinions, examples, and other authorities you use to support your assertions.

STUDENT ESSAY

Below is a draft of Levi Liljenquist's essay. Levi is from Texas and has lived two years in Japan. Levi is majoring in history. As you read the draft, ask two basic questions:

- How does Levi succeed in fulfilling his purpose for writing this essay?

- How can Levi strengthen this draft?

Mrs. Takahashi

Levi begins with facts and statistics to acquaint readers with the earthquake.

The Kobe, Japan earthquake, one of the most disastrous in the country's long history, occurred at 5:45 on the morning of January 17, 1995. The tragic event left 5,500 dead, 25,000 injured, 300,000 homeless, 50,000 destroyed buildings, and caused over 60 billion U.S. dollars worth of damage.

He uses personal experience to establish himself as an authority on this event.

We arrived at the hospital to find it in disarray. All the hospital rooms were full, so new patients were laid in the reception area where nurses were taking care of them. The nurses were far outnumbered by the injured; many lay in helpless consciousness with open wounds and bleeding gashes. We weaved our way through the mass of bodies to the reception desk. We asked for Kazumi Takahashi, a fifteen-year-old girl we had recovered from the rubble, but the receptionist couldn't help us. We decided to search every floor of the building to find the girl and her parents. After looking in every room of the three-story hospital, we gave up our search and decided to go home.

As we headed out the main entrance of the hospital, we found Mr. Takahashi sitting in the entry way next to Kazumi's corpse. He acknowledged us. We did not want to allude to his daughter who was obviously dead, so we asked if Takehiro, his older son we also pulled from the building, was doing alright. He told us his son was in serious condition and probably would not live much longer. He also said that all the crematoriums in Kobe were filled, and he had no place to take his daughter's body.

We received permission to put the body in a church not far from the hospital. We drove to the church where we carried the young body to a small upstairs room. Although Kazumi was only fifteen and very skinny, her limp body was heavy and hard to move. She had probably been dead since the time of the quake and was already growing stiff. We carried her as carefully as possible to the small room, laid her in the middle of the floor, and covered her with a blanket.

My friend traveled with Mr. Takahashi back to the hospital to observe the condition of Takehiro. They returned two hours later with his lifeless body in the bed of a truck. We took the body up the stairs and laid him next to his sister.

He uses a specific incident and indirect knowledge to illustrate the death resulting from the earthquake.

Mrs. Takahashi removed the blankets from the bodies and sat staring at them for a few minutes. She went first to Takehiro and began caressing his forehead and rubbing her fingers through his hair. Taking the boy in her arms, she held him to her breast and rocked him back and forth as a mother does with her baby. She seemed deep in thought, and I was sure she must be remembering how she had held him close as a child.

She then laid her son down and moved over by her daughter. "Isn't she beautiful," she said lifting her daughter into her arms. She began to caress Kazumi's face tenderly. Staring into the face of her daughter, Mrs. Takahashi began telling me about Kazumi. Kazumi had been her favorite child. She always helped her mother in the kitchen when she returned home from school. "She loved to play the piano and sing. Before she went to bed at night, we would talk as I brushed her hair," she said remembering fondly.

Mrs. Takahashi held the head of her daughter close to her breast and slowly rocked back and forth. She released the head tenderly, looked into her eyes, and lovingly placed the head back on the floor. She reached down and grasped her daughter's tiny hand. As she held it, tears began to run down her cheeks. "*Tsumetai, Tsumetai,*" "It's cold, It's cold," she said in a tone of hopelessness and sorrow. She held the hand, caressing it lightly with her own. As she continued rubbing the hand, it gradually began to grow warm, and some of the stiffness also left. Mrs. Takahashi, noticing the temperature change, began rubbing it more energetically. "It's getting warm," she said with a tinge of hope in her voice. She placed the hand between hers and rubbed harder. "She's not dead; she's asleep," she said, sounding like a little girl playing with her dolls. She took the child's other hand and began rubbing it also. "She's just asleep; we just have to wait for her to wake up. She'll be okay in the morning," she said trying to convince herself. Dropping the hand, she grabbed the girl by the shoulders. She began shaking the shoulder and crying out desperately, "Wake up, wake up!"

She took her daughter in her arms again and rocked her gently back and forth. As she rocked her eyes were fixed on the wall in front of her. The death of her children was hard to bear, especially as she deeply contemplated the improbability of ever seeing them again. Questions like "Where are they now? Are they safe?" could be seen on the face of this sad, broken-hearted mother.

He uses general description and personal experience to show the larger extent of deaths because of the earthquake.

Three days after the earthquake, the gym floor was covered with dead bodies lined up in straight rows running from one wall to the other. The floor was twice as wide as a basketball court, and it was a few feet longer. There were at least two hundred corpses in the room. A dead dog lying on a blanket next to someone showed me that death was not biased. The remains of small children as well as the elderly and middle aged were among the numbers. Family members and friends sat at the feet of those they knew. Flowers and candles burning incense were next to heads of most bodies. Their poignant incense smell somewhat hid the rotten stench of death that filled the room.

Levi concludes with a personal observation of how the earthquake has affected him.

I have seen such scenes on T.V. before and have never been affected by them, and now, when I hear the death count, over 5,500 killed, or see other disasters, I think only of Mrs. Takahashi.

EXPLORING YOUR OPTIONS

The purpose of this activity is to identify the number and types of evidence you use in your essay. It isn't necessary to use *all* types in each paper.

1. List examples from your personal knowledge you used in this draft.

_____

_____

_____

_____

2. List examples from your indirect knowledge you used in this draft.

_____

_____

_____

_____

3. List examples of the researched knowledge you used in this draft.

_____

_____

_____

_____

4. List the facts and statistics you used in this draft.

_____

_____

_____

5. List the opinions you cited in this draft.

_____

_____

_____

6. List the other authorities you cited in this draft.

_____

_____

_____

7. After identifying the number and types of evidence you used in this draft, think about other information you might add to make your writing more authoritative and confident.

WRITING WITH COMPUTERS

Use the computer to visually represent the types of authority you use in your draft.

1. Highlight and **bold** all facts or statistics you use for support.

2. Highlight and <u>underline</u> all opinions you use for support.

3. Highlight and *italicize* all examples you use for support.

4. Highlight and use CAPS for all authorities you use for support.

5. Now evaluate each piece of evidence. Look at how much support you have for each assertion. Where it's not enough, add more. Look at the effectiveness of the evidence. If it's not effective, take it out. Think about other information you might add to make your writing more authoritative and confident.

WRITING TOGETHER

1. Exchange your paper's draft with a classmate.

2. Circle the personal knowledge your classmate uses in the draft.

3. Box the indirect knowledge your classmate uses in the draft.

4. Underline the researched knowledge your classmate uses in the draft.

5. Discuss the effectiveness of the kinds of knowledge you each use in your paper drafts.

EDITING

CORRECTING AMBIGUOUS MODIFIERS AND PRONOUNS

A *modifier* is a word, a phrase, or a clause that clarifies information about a word in a sentence. To be effective, modifiers must be close to the word or words they modify. Modifiers are confusing when they are misplaced or dangling.

Misplaced Modifiers

Modifiers that are not close to the words they modify are misplaced:

> The <u>hiker</u> with a pair of binoculars <u>observed</u> the deer quietly munching wildflowers.

In this sentence, *hiker* is the subject and *observed* is the verb. The other phrases are modifiers. The phrase *with a pair of binoculars* describes the hiker; *quietly munching wildflowers* describes the deer. Notice that the modifiers are close to the words they modify (*with a pair of binoculars* is near *hiker,* and *quietly munching wildflowers* is near *deer*). If the modifiers were not located near the words they modify, there might be some confusion. For example:

> The hiker observed the deer quietly munching wildflowers with a pair of binoculars.

In this sentence, the deer is munching wildflowers and has the binoculars. Of course this doesn't make sense, and most readers eventually would figure out that the hiker has the binoculars and that the deer is eating. But why make them work at it? And what about the reader who has no experience with a topic to draw on?

When you write, be sure that the modifiers describe those words that you want them to describe. Here are two more examples:

> Jumping through the bushes, we saw two rabbits.

> At seventeen my grandfather decided to retire.

In the first sentence, "we," not the rabbits, are jumping through the bushes. In the second, "my grandfather" decided to retire when he was seventeen, not when I was seventeen. Here's how the sentences should read:

> We saw two rabbits jumping through the bushes.

> When I was seventeen, my grandfather decided to retire.

Dangling Modifiers

A modifier needs a word to modify; otherwise it's a dangling modifier. A modifier "dangles" when the person or object that performs the action (the natural subject) is missing from the sentence:

> With a little free time, the fishing was excellent.

> After screening the applicants, the decision was made.

In these sentences, there is no word for the modifiers to modify. *With a little free time* does not describe the fishing; it describes the person doing the fishing. And there are no words in the sentence that refer to that person. In the second sentence, "the decision" did not screen the applicants; the person or people who did the screening aren't mentioned in the sentence.

The easiest way to correct a dangling modifier is to insert into the sentence the person(s) or object(s) that perform the action:

When *I* had a little free time, the fishing was excellent.

After screening the applicants, *we* made the decision.

Ambiguous Pronoun References

Just as modifiers should be placed close to the words they modify, pronouns should be placed near their antecedents. Remember that an antecedent is the word that a pronoun refers to. Your objective here, too, is to avoid confusion. Look at this example:

I put the oatmeal on the table, took off my apron, and began to eat it.

In this sentence, technically I'm eating my apron because the word *apron* is the closest antecedent for the pronoun *it*. *It* here can refer to three words: *oatmeal, table,* or *apron.* We can fix the problem by replacing the pronoun or by rewriting it altogether:

I put the oatmeal on the table, took off my apron, and began to eat the oatmeal.

I put the oatmeal on the table, took off my apron, and began to eat.

In the next example, the pronouns *him* and *his* cause the confusion:

The professor told him that his article was going to be published.

We don't know the professor's gender. Is a male professor addressing another male? Did the professor write the article that's going to be published? Or did the person the professor is talking to write the article? We don't know which of the two people the words *him* and *his* refer to. The sentence may be clear in context (with other sentences) but by itself, it's not clear. It needs clarification:

The professor told him, "Your article is going to be published."

The professor told him, "My article is going to be published."

EXERCISE 1   In these sentences you'll find misplaced or dangling modifiers. Some you can correct simply by placing the modifier next to the word it modifies. Other sentences may require rewriting.

1. Lincoln Park is the most interesting park in the city that I have seen.

2. Putting on the brake quickly, the car screeched to a stop.

3. At the age of fourteen, my sister was born.

4. Unwrapping gift after gift, the puppy had a great time playing with all the tissue paper.

5. After a three-year absence, the trees were full grown.

6. Excited and eager to go, the bus was in front of the building waiting for us.

7. Almost too excited to eat, the letter was read over and over.

8. I decided to give the clothes to a charity that I had no use for.

EXERCISE 2   In some of these sentences you'll find misplaced or dangling modifiers. Some you can correct simply by placing the modifier next to the word it modifies. Other sentences may require rewriting.

Badly in need of affection, grandparents often render numerous acts of kindness to their grandchildren. They sometimes don't fully appreciate those kind acts. Sitting on their knees, being held in their arms, and hearing soft voices, grandparents can provide a sense of security to a troubled child. Because of their added years and experience, grandchildren benefit from the attention. Grandparents need not live near them to offer emotional support. Letters and brief phone calls remind them that they're remembered. Creating bonds early in their lives, grandparents can have a lasting influence on their grandchildren. And as they grow older, they will remember them during times of their own loneliness.

EXERCISE 3   Using the draft from your current essay, do the following:

1. Identify ten sentences that contain modifiers. Draw arrows to connect the modifiers with the words they describe.

2. Identify five sentences that contain pronoun references. Draw arrows to connect the pronoun to their antecedents or words they represent.

OPTIONS FOR WRITING

Reflect

1. Children frequently are misunderstood by parents. Think back to a time when you were misunderstood by a parent. What has that experience taught you about child-parent relationships? What effect has that experience had on you? How has that experience colored your perceptions of childhood and parenthood? How could the situation have been handled differently?

2. Family customs—table experiences, cleaning procedures, holiday celebrations, vacations, morning and evening routines, religious or ethnic rituals—mark individual families. Compare two customs that are unique to your family, and explain how these customs encourage family unity.

Inform

3. Conduct surveys to determine the extent of date rape on campus. Ask students about their definitions of and experiences with date rape. Then talk to college counselors or hotlines about the warning signs, frequency, severity, and effects of date rape. Discuss with campus security ways to protect oneself and ways for victims to get

legal advice. Then write a section in the student handbook informing students about date rape.

4. The stepfamily is fast becoming a "traditional" family in our society. But just because two families are joined by marriage doesn't mean that family members get along. From your own observations or on the basis of an interview with several stepfamilies, draw up some basic guidelines for successfully joining two families in one unit. Write an article for the school newspaper in which you explain your guidelines.

Persuade

5. Convince several men or women whom you know to reevaluate their perceptions of gender roles. For example, encourage male friends to take responsibility for changing their children's diapers and for cooking dinner. Persuade a female friend to consider majoring in a predominantly male field such as engineering, animal husbandry, or law enforcement.

6. Talk to local social workers and foster families about the qualifications, responsibilities, and challenges of being a foster parent. Write a paper persuading families in your community to look into the possibility of offering foster care for children.

Speculate

7. Speculate on the qualities you would like to see in an ideal mate. Focus on the characteristics that are essential, not simply desirable. Then think of someone you know who exhibits those attributes. Describe your ideal someone (a dangerous activity—the partner of your expectations rarely exists outside those expectations!).

8. Write a position paper explaining to others (but mostly to yourself) fair discipline practices that you would want to use in your own family. Be specific: Choose incidents from your childhood or your own children's lives. Explain why certain methods of discipline were or are effective. Where discipline failed, discuss why and suggest an alternative. Consider focusing your paper on a single age group. Disciplining a three-year-old is different from disciplining a seventeen-year-old.

Chapter 7

LAW

Violence and crime have become a way of life in many American homes, neighborhoods, and communities. In this chapter we look at different aspects of the law, among them legal procedures, legal assistance, crime, and neighborhood crime prevention programs.

To prepare for this chapter's theme, the law, answer the following questions:

- How are laws meant to benefit people?
- How can people better protect themselves from those who break laws?

READINGS on *Law*

After a Burglary

Albert Scardino

In 1984, Albert Scardino won a Pulitzer Prize for editorial writing. He is now an editor of the New York Times. *In this essay, Scardino describes how a burglary affected him and his family.*

I heard glass break, but it didn't wake me enough to crawl out from under the comforter on the coldest night of the winter. I heard voices, but they were too remote for me to realize they came from our living room. It wasn't until the telephone receiver hit the floor in the kitchen that I accepted the idea that someone I didn't know had found his way in.

It was Christmas Eve, in Savannah, Ga. For weeks I had been working myself into the spirit of the season—open, warm and generous, especially in my feelings toward my two children. My 4-year-old son was about to receive his first bicycle. We had bought the only 10-foot tree on the lot to fill the bay window of our Victorian house and had hung twin wreaths on the double doors facing one of the busiest streets in the neighborhood.

By the time I forced myself out from under the covers, I could already hear the footsteps of the intruder in the hallway. His shadow came down the hall in front of him, then he turned to look through the doorway of our bedroom. He was skinny and wore a military jacket and running shoes. My throat was frozen. I grunted at him, more out of desperation than out of any sense that I could defend us, "Get out of here."

It caught him off guard. He loped back toward the front of the house, not running so much as withdrawing defiantly. He had a partner in the living room who had helped him gather all of the Christmas presents in a pile. The two of them slipped out the window empty-handed, and I started down the hall behind them, feeling very awkward in my underwear. I stopped and yelled for my wife to call the police, then dodged up to the front of the house. The cold was pouring in through the open window. The presents, so full of private joys and personal expressions, were stacked on a dirty blanket the intruders must have brought with them.

The police came and went. We began to close up our lives. We barricaded the window and unplugged the Christmas tree, then retreated to our bedroom to comfort the children. They finally calmed down enough to return to their own rooms, and my wife and I sat on our bed reconstructing every detail. Why had she not heard the glass break, she wondered? How did I pull myself out of my sleep to respond at all, when she heard nothing until my yell? I told her how my voice had caught in my throat, how angry it made me that there was no panic on the intruder's face when he heard me grunt at him, how guilty I felt for letting someone else into our lives. Because we share so many family responsibilities—I do most of the cooking, she buys most of the presents—it surprised us both that the job of facing a robber fell automatically to me.

By then it was 5 o'clock in the morning. My wife heard a noise in the front of the house. I thought it must have been the wind, but I stepped quietly through the kitchen to be sure. There they were again, the two of them, slowly forcing their way back through the same window. In a panic, I dialed the police. I was describing the clothing of one of them when he heard me and looked up from his work.   6

"Get out," I grunted again from the dark kitchen. He cursed at me, then casually, insultingly crawled back out of the window. What would I have used to defend myself if he had attacked? The phone? A chair? The door? The police arrived in 30 seconds, but the partners had vanished.   7

Suddenly I wasn't 22 anymore. My life seemed so much more vulnerable and my family made it seem so much more valuable. I wanted to hold a gun again to make the sides even. If they knew they no longer had the upper hand, maybe they would respect my boundary. They had left the second time only because they could not see how naked I was.   8

I had no desire for revenge, only for privacy. The next night I sat up with my gun across my knees, sure that they intended to return and determined not to let them catch me unprepared again.   9

They never came back, but they really never left. I now hear every sound, a window rattling, a voice on the sidewalk out front, a whimper from a child's room. At the slightest disturbance I'm out of bed and searching the drawer of the bedside table for a shell or two. I know all the statistics about the likelihood that the gun in my closet will accidentally be used against me rather than against a robber, and I'm almost ashamed to have given in to the impulse to keep it around because of two brief encounters.   10

We built a new latticework[1] fence to block entry to the garden alongside the house. We decided to plant holly and roses to discourage anyone from getting close to the windows. Last Christmas, a year later, I bought my 7-year-old daughter a BB gun, a Daisy; "Ask Dad, he had one," the box reminded me. In January we began the long course of instruction in the safe use of firearms, a course my father had started with me at that age.   11

Earlier this year a career change brought us to New York City, a move that, strangely enough, helped restore my sense of security. Though only the statisticians[2] can believe it, New York's crime rate in most categories is no higher than Savannah's. That fact probably does not comfort me, but moving away from the scene of the crime did. I am no longer overwhelmed by the urgency to teach my daughter to defend herself with a gun. When we complete the   12

---

[1]**latticework:** made of interwoven strips of wood or metal
[2]**statisticians:** people who compile numerical information

move away from Savannah at the end of the school year, I plan to return the shotgun to my father's attic, but I will continue to teach my daughter how to use one. If she ever loses her invincibility,[3] I want her to be able to make her own decision about whether to have a gun around.

My wife and I drank coffee and talked until dawn. That's when I went to my father's house and took out the shotgun I had not held since 1968. It would have been unusual for a boy to grow up in the South 20 years ago without becoming familiar with guns. We hunted almost every weekend in the fall and winter and practiced on clay pigeons the rest of the year. But the images from Vietnam and the suicide of a close friend had made me think there was no longer any need for a gun in my life. Being 22 and invincible had been sport enough.

13

---

[3]**invincibility:** inability to be hurt; strength

Questions and Issues to Consider

Writing Process   1. Scardino uses details to involve his readers. List the details Scardino uses in the first four paragraphs.

2. Identify any one sentence in Scardino's essay that you find powerful. Explain how that sentence is significant to the rest of the essay.

Aims of Writing   3. What is Scardino's purpose in this essay? Why does he relate his experience as a burglary victim? To reflect on the incident? To inform us of the burglary? To persuade us to take an action? Some or all of the above? What is his primary purpose?

Critical Thinking   4. Scardino writes about wanting a gun both to give himself more confidence and to scare burglars. He also mentions buying a BB gun for his daughter. Do you think people should have guns in their homes? Support your position with reasons.

The Ways of Meeting Oppression
Martin Luther King, Jr.

Martin Luther King, Jr. (1929–1968) was the leading spokesperson for civil rights during the 1950s and 1960s before he was assassinated in 1968. In 1964, he was awarded the Nobel Prize for Peace. In the following essay, taken from his book Stride Toward Freedom *(1958),* *King classifies three ways oppressed people have reacted to their oppressors.*

O ppressed people deal with their oppression in three characteristic   1
ways. One way is acquiescence:[1] the oppressed resign themselves to their doom. They tacitly[2] adjust themselves to oppression, and thereby become conditioned to it. In every movement toward freedom some of the oppressed prefer to remain oppressed. Almost 2800 years ago Moses set out to lead the children of Israel from the slavery of Egypt to the freedom of the promised land. He soon discovered that slaves do not always welcome their deliverers. They become accustomed to being slaves. They would rather bear those ills they have, as Shakespeare pointed out, than flee to others that they know not of. They prefer the "fleshpots of Egypt" to the ordeals of emancipation.

There is such a thing as the freedom of exhaustion. Some people are so   2
worn down by the yoke of oppression that they give up. A few years ago in the slum areas of Atlanta, a Negro guitarist used to sing almost daily: "Been down so long that down don't bother me." This is the type of negative freedom and resignation that often engulfs the life of the oppressed.

But this is not the way out. To accept passively an unjust system is to   3
cooperate with that system; thereby the oppressed become as evil as the oppressor. Noncooperation with evil is as much a moral obligation as is co-operation with good. The oppressed must never allow the conscience of the oppressor to slumber. Religion reminds every man that he is his brother's keeper. To accept injustice or segregation passively is to say to the oppressor that his actions are morally right. It is a way of allowing his conscience to fall asleep. At this moment the oppressed fails to be his brother's keeper. So acqui-escence—while often the easier way—is not the moral way. It is the way of the coward. The Negro cannot win the respect of his oppressor by acquiescing; he merely increases the oppressor's arrogance and contempt. Acquiescence is interpreted as proof of the Negro's inferiority. The Negro cannot win the respect of the white people of the South or the peoples of the world if he is willing to sell the future of his children for his personal and immediate com-fort and safety.

A second way that oppressed people sometimes deal with oppression   4
is to resort to physical violence and corroding[3] hatred. Violence often brings about momentary results. Nations have frequently won their independence in battle. But in spite of temporary victories, violence never brings permanent peace. It solves no social problem; it merely creates new and more compli-cated ones.

---

[1]**acquiescence:** agreement without protests
[2]**tacitly:** silently
[3]**corroding:** gradual eating away

Violence as a way of achieving racial justice is both impractical and   5
immoral. It is impractical because it is a descending spiral ending in destruction for all. The old law of an eye for an eye leaves everybody blind. It is
immoral because it seeks to humiliate the opponent rather than win his understanding; it seeks to annihilate[4] rather than to convert. Violence is immoral
because it thrives on hatred rather than love. It destroys community and makes
brotherhood impossible. It leaves society in monologue rather than dialogue.
Violence ends by defeating itself. It creates bitterness in the survivors and bru-
tality in the destroyers. A voice echoes through time saying to every potential
Peter, "Put up your sword." History is cluttered with the wreckage of nations
that failed to follow this command.

If the American Negro and other victims of oppression succumb to the   6
temptation of using violence in the struggle for freedom, future generations
will be the recipients of a desolate[5] night of bitterness, and our chief legacy to
them will be an endless reign of meaningless chaos. Violence is not the way.

The third way open to oppressed people in their quest for freedom is the   7
way of nonviolent resistance. Like the synthesis[6] in Hegelian philosophy, the
principle of nonviolent resistance seeks to reconcile the truths of two oppo-
sites—the acquiescence and violence—while avoiding the extremes and
immoralities of both. The nonviolent resister agrees with the person who acqui-
esces that one should not be physically aggressive toward his opponent; but he
balances the equation by agreeing with the person of violence that evil must be
resisted. He avoids the nonresistance of the former and the violent resistance of
the latter. With nonviolent resistance, no individual or group need submit to
any wrong, nor need anyone resort to violence in order to right a wrong.

It seems to me that this is the method that must guide the actions of the   8
Negro in the present crisis in race relations. Through nonviolent resistance the
Negro will be able to rise to the noble height of opposing the unjust system
while loving the perpetrators of the system. The Negro must work passionately
and unrelentingly for full stature as a citizen, but he must not use inferior
methods to gain it. He must never come to terms with falsehood, malice, hate,
or destruction.

Nonviolent resistance makes it possible for the Negro to remain in the   9
South and struggle for his rights. The Negro's problem will not be solved by
running away. He cannot listen to the glib suggestion of those who would urge
him to migrate en masse to other sections of the country. By grasping his great
opportunity in the South he can make a lasting contribution to the moral
strength of the nation and set a sublime[7] example of courage for generations
yet unborn.

By nonviolent resistance, the Negro can also enlist all men of good will   10
in his struggle for equality. The problem is not a purely racial one, with

---

[4]**annihilate:** destroy
[5]**desolate:** lonely
[6]**synthesis:** combining of elements into one
[7]**sublime:** inspiring

Negroes set against whites. In the end, it is not a struggle between people at all, but a tension between justice and injustice. Nonviolent resistance is not aimed against oppressors but against oppression. Under its banner consciences, not racial groups, are enlisted.

◆ ～

Questions and Issues to Consider

Writing Process   1. Why do you think King discusses the three methods of meeting oppression (acquiescence, violence, and nonviolent resistance) in that particular order?

2. List the examples King uses to illustrate the three different ways of meeting oppression. Which examples are general, and which are specific?

Aims of Writing   3. What is King's purpose in writing this essay? How does classifying the three types of resistance to oppression serve this purpose?

Critical Thinking   4. Consider the negative aspects of nonviolent resistance. What do you think King would have to say about these?

PREWRITING

ENHANCING PERCEPTIONS

As a writer, your ability to look at a general topic from different points of view enhances your perceptions of both the topic and your audience. The process you use is a series of questions and brief written responses. The product is a limited topic and a clear understanding of why you're writing about that limited topic.

The questions below suggest different points of view on the topic of gun control. As you read them, replace the words *gun control* with your own general topic.

1. How does age affect a person's attitude toward *gun control?* Does a child look at *gun control* differently than a teenager? an adult? an older person?

2. How do economic conditions affect a person's attitude toward *gun control?* Does someone living below the poverty level look at *gun control* differently than someone living on a low income? a middle income? a high income?

3. How does education affect a person's attitude toward *gun control?* Does someone who dropped out of high school look at *gun control* differently than someone with a high school diploma? a college degree? a graduate degree?

4. How does ethnic background affect a person's attitude toward *gun control?* Does a person from one ethnic background look at *gun control* differently than someone of another ethnic background?

5. How does political stance affect a person's attitude toward *gun control?* Does a Democrat look at *gun control* differently than a Republican? an Independent? a Libertarian?

6. How do religious beliefs affect a person's attitude toward *gun control?* Does someone who practices one religion look at *gun control* differently than someone who practices another religion?

7. How does culture affect a person's attitude toward *gun control?* Does someone from North America look at *gun control* differently than someone from South America? from Europe? from the Middle East? from Asia?

Your answers to these questions broaden your perception of both your topic and your audience. At the same time, the very specific ideas are a source of a more limited topic for your paper and an understanding of your purpose for writing about that topic.

Two students, Shelly Walker and Venita Walker, have decided to write a paper together. They have chosen the general topic of gangs. To enhance their perceptions of their topic and their audience, they wrote brief answers to the questions above, replacing *gun control* with *gangs.* Here are several of Shelly and Venita's responses:

1. How does age affect a person's attitude toward *gangs?*

Age is an important factor in gangs. Shelly remembers in her elementary school in California how impressed some of her classmates were when older students would walk by wearing gang colors. Venita recalls that some friends in

Michigan started joining gangs in early junior high school. Young people are easily impressed by gangs because of the hope for acceptance. Teenagers also view gangs as a source of power and strength. However, most adults are afraid of gangs because they perceive gangs as being lawless and out of control.

2. How do economic conditions affect a person's attitude toward *gangs?*

We assume economy is another significant factor relating to gangs. From our experience, most gang members come from poor backgrounds; many of them are living below the poverty level. These members see the gang as a way to obtain more money and power, although they often obtain it illegally and violently. We believe gangs become less prevalent among the young the higher the economic level. We're not sure because we also wonder about syndicated crime organizations, where the economic levels are extremely high. We think we'll stick with the gangs we're familiar with from our communities, and they're generally from poor backgrounds.

3. How does education affect a person's attitudes toward *gangs?*

Venita remembers hearing somewhere that a large percentage of gang members are functionally illiterate. Many members seek acceptance in gangs because they're not accepted at school. We have begun to wonder if education could be a means of addressing gangs. We want to know if some elementary schools have special programs for students who wear gang colors or tend to lean toward gang membership. Certainly we hope there are community programs to educate the public about gangs. Shelly remembers several school assemblies on gangs following the Los Angeles riots. We think something can be done to improve gang issues through education, but we don't yet know what.

4. How does ethnic background affect a person's attitude toward *gangs?*

```
     When we initially asked ourselves this
question, we thought we had pat answers. But
the more we think about this, we begin to
realize that most if not all ethnic groups
have individuals involved in gangs. Also, com-
munity ethnic leaders would undoubtedly want
to do all they can to solve the many problems
contributing to and resulting from gangs.
```

After Shelly and Venita answered these questions, they realized that they feel most strongly about gangs and education. They aren't sure yet where their paper is going, but they want to examine the role of public education in solving gang-related problems. They assume that their purpose for writing this paper is to inform their audience. (A draft of Shelly and Venita's paper begins on page 252.) Remember not to worry about where the prewriting is taking you. As Shelly and Venita were writing, they went off on a tangent that produced another topic for them. Discover your topic in your own writing.

EXPLORING YOUR OPTIONS

1. Write your general topic on the line below.

   _____

2. Inserting your general topic, write four of the questions listed above. Then write brief responses to those questions.

   Question: _____

   _____

   Response: _____

   _____

   _____

   _____

_____

_____

Question: _____

_____

Response: _____

_____

_____

_____

_____

_____

Question: _____

_____

Response: _____

_____

_____

_____

_____

Question: _____

_____

Response: _____

_____

_____

_____

_____

_____

3. Read your responses and choose one aspect of your topic that you would like to explore further. Write that more limited topic on the line below.

_____

4. In a single sentence describe what you hope to accomplish in this paper.

_____

_____

5. Put a checkmark next to the aim that best describes your reason for writing this paper.

_____ To reflect   _____ To persuade

_____ To inform   _____ To speculate

WRITING TOGETHER

Working with someone is another effective method of enhancing perceptions. Team up with a classmate and choose a general topic. Work individually on the Exploring Your Options activity above. Then share your responses with each other. Look at the similarities and differences between your individual responses. Then, together, write responses like Shelly and Venita did. When you've finished, talk about collaborating on this writing assignment.

DRAFTING

CRAFTING SENTENCES

Good sentences should say something specific; at the same time they should be simple and brief.

Say Something

Perhaps most essential to a good sentence is that it say something meaningful. Of course the purpose of a draft is to explore ideas, not to sharpen your writing. But especially when the purpose of a paper is to introduce or explain information, your thinking and writing need to be sharply focused. As you write, keep asking yourself these questions:

What am I trying to say in this sentence?

Am I saying anything meaningful or new to my reader in this sentence?

Am I saying anything in this sentence that can help my reader understand my topic?

These two sentences are "blurry":

Television violence affects children.

Family violence is increasing.

The statements are generalizations; few people would argue with them. Unfortunately, few people would even think about what they mean. The sentences lack substance; they require no thought.

One method for turning a vague sentence into a focused sentence is to ask yourself a question about the statement and then answer the question. For example, take the sentence *Television violence affects children.* You could ask yourself, What do I mean when I say that television violence affects children? Or, Why does television violence affect children? Or, Who says television violence affects children? Or, What are the effects of television violence on children? Obviously a single sentence can't answer all these questions. It's your responsibility to choose the most important question (or questions) on the basis of your topic and purpose and then to answer it in a sentence. If your purpose for writing is to discuss the effects television violence has on children, you'd draft the sentence to answer the question, What are the effects of television violence on children? Instead of a content-poor statement— *Television violence affects children*—you'd end up with a meaningful statement, like this:

One effect of television violence on children is that they come to believe that violence can solve their problems, that whoever has a weapon or is stronger can get what he or she wants.

Be Specific

Good sentences are also specific. The sentence *It is hot* is not specific. The word *hot* doesn't tell the reader anything. Hot to an ice cube is 33 degrees Fahrenheit. Hot to a welder is 1500 degrees Fahrenheit. Hot to someone living in Palm Springs, California, may be 126 degrees; hot to someone living in Salmon, Idaho, may be 95 degrees; and hot to someone living in humid Houston, Texas, may be 85 degrees. The word *hot* isn't specific. But by adding details and examples, you can help a reader understand exactly what you mean when you write, "It is hot."

Here's an example from Joseph Kane's essay, "A Dose of Discipline for First Offenders." Kane addresses the use of military-style discipline and boot camps for young offenders. He begins a paragraph with this statement:

The remainder of the day is filled with menial labor. . . .

The statement is general; it doesn't tell the reader exactly what that labor is. But Kane goes on to clarify the statement with specific details:

wacking weeds, swabbing floors, painting walls, marching in formation

Be Simple

Good sentences are also simple. We live in a complex world of highly technical information that sometimes confuses more than it clarifies. An example: the booklet state and local governments publish before elections in which they explain the ballot. Usually there are two descriptions of each ballot question. The first is the official description, an often-convoluted version that uses the language and phrasing found in state constitutions or statutes. The second—a simple version—is written with the common citizen in mind. This version isn't simple-minded; it's just clear and easy to understand. The words are simpler; the sentence construction is easier to follow; and the examples are short and to the point. Usually the more simply something is written, the easier it is to understand.

Joseph Kane also writes simply. Look at his description of correctional officer Eddie Cash, who is shouting at the new inmates:

By now Cash is soaking with sweat and stomping the floor. His neck veins are popping and his eyes are bulging as he works his way from inmate to inmate, delivering a series of blistering, nose-to-nose tongue-lashings.

Kane uses simple, yet specific, words that are clear and easy to understand on the first reading.

Be Brief

Closely associated with being simple is being brief. Although varied sentence lengths and sentence types are important to good writing, the value of a brief clear sentence cannot be overemphasized. Readability studies show that writing that contains short words, short sentences, and short paragraphs is easier to read than writing that contains long words, long sentences, and long paragraphs. Of course, there are excellent examples that are exceptions, but the basic principle is sound. The longer and more complicated the sentence, the easier it is for a reader to misunderstand your meaning.

In his essay "After a Burglary," Albert Scardino uses details, but he uses them sparingly. For example, look at this sentence from the second paragraph:

My 4-year-old son was about to receive his first bicycle.

Scardino tells us about his son's age and the gift, but he doesn't elaborate unnecessarily. There's no reason to tell us that the bicycle is 20 inches high, is painted a blue metallic color, and has training wheels—so he doesn't. Now look at this sentence from paragraph 5:

The police came and went.

Scardino chooses not to describe in detail how the police arrived at his home after the burglary or what they did there. We don't need to know the details of the police report. Because he wants to emphasize the incident itself and how it has affected him and his family, he simply and briefly states, "The police came and went."

PRACTICE

Draft the following sentences so that they say something specifically, simply, and briefly.

1. Drunk driving is a serious problem.

_____

_____

_____

_____

2. Alcohol is often a contributing factor in divorce.

_____

_____

_____

_____

3. American cities are plagued with violence.

_____

_____

_____

_____

4. Gun control laws are controversial.

_____

_____

_____

_____

5. Americans have the right to bear arms.

_____

_____

_____

_____

EXPLORING YOUR OPTIONS

Write your limited topic on the line below.

_____

Now draft three sentences about your paper's topic. The sentences should say something specifically, simply, and briefly. These sentences can provide support in your draft.

1. _____

_____

_____

2. _____

_____

_____

3. _____

_____

_____

EXPLAINING A PROCESS

A *process* is *how* something works or *how* something is done. The steps taken to organize a neighborhood watch program or to report a theft are examples of processes.

Determining the Process

Before you write the description of a process, answer these five basic questions:

1. **What is this process?**   This is the first and most basic question. To determine what the process is, define it as simply as possible. For example:

   A neighborhood watch program is an anticrime program organized and maintained by a group of concerned responsible citizens within a neighborhood.

2. **Who performs this process?**   The next question to consider in your description of a process is who performs it. This question helps you analyze your audience and adjust the level of your writing to your

readers' experience. A neighborhood watch program in a high-crime area probably would be very different from a program in a low-crime area.

3. **Why is this process performed?** Why the process is necessary is different from what the process is. Here you look at why the process is performed, the reason the process is carried out. For instance, a neighborhood watch program is established to help neighbors work together to prevent crime in their neighborhood.

4. **What are the chief steps in this process?** You've determined what the process is, who performs it, and why it's necessary. Now you have to determine the major steps in the process. The major steps in establishing a neighborhood watch program are gathering information, forming committees, contacting law enforcement agencies, and implementing the program.

5. **From what point of view is the process being described?** The last question has to do with point of view. Usually you write from the perspective of the person performing the process. But occasionally, you examine a process from another viewpoint. For example, you might describe a neighborhood watch program from the viewpoint of an organizer, a law enforcement officer, a victim, an elderly person, or a criminal.

Once you've answered these questions, you're ready to write your description of a process. The organization is simple: you begin by explaining the first step of the process, then explain the second step, and so on until you've described all of the steps.

Explaining a Process

Introduction
  1. What is this process?
  2. Who performs this process?
  3. Why is this process performed?
  4. What are the chief steps in this process?
  5. From what point of view is the process being described?
Step 1
Step 2
Step 3
Step 4
Conclusion

✓ CHECKLIST: EXPLAINING A PROCESS

1. Do you know the process?

2. Are the instructions complete?

3. Are the instructions in proper order?

4. Are the instructions easy to read?

5. Do you have a clear and complete introduction?

EXPLAINING A PROCESS: AN EXAMPLE

In the following paragraph, Grace Lichtenstein explains the process of brewing beer. Notice that her explanation progresses step by step from growing the barley to putting the beer into cans, bottles, or kegs.

Brewing Coors

Like other beers, Coors is produced from barley. Most of the big Midwestern brewers use barley grown in North Dakota and Minnesota. Coors is the single American brewer to use a Moravian strain, grown under company supervision on farms in Colorado, Idaho, Wyoming and Montana. At the brewery, the barley is turned into malt by being soaked in water—which must be biologically pure and of a known mineral content—for several days, causing it to sprout, and producing a chemical change—breaking down starch into sugar. The malt is toasted, a process that halts the sprouting and determines the color and sweetness (the more roasting, the darker, more bitter the beer). It is ground into flour and brewed, with more pure water, in huge copper-domed kettles until it is the consistency of oatmeal. Rice and refined starch are added to make mash; solids are strained out, leaving an amber liquid malt extract, which is boiled with hops—the dried cones from the hop vine which add to the bitterness, or tang. The hops are strained, yeast is added, turning the sugar to alcohol, and the beer is aged in huge red vats at near-freezing temperatures for almost two months, during which the second fermentation takes place and the liquid becomes carbonated, or bubbly. (Many breweries chemically age their beer to speed up production; Coors people say only naturally aged brew can be called a true "lager.") Next, the beer is filtered through cellulose filters to remove bacteria, and finally is pumped into cans, bottles, or kegs for shipping.

PRACTICE   Answer the following questions based on Lichtenstein's explanation of the beer-brewing process.

1. What is this process?

_____

_____

_____

2. Who performs this process?

_____

_____

_____

3. Why is this process performed?

_____

_____

_____

4. What are the chief steps in this process?

_____

_____

_____

5. From what point of view is the process being described?

_____

_____

_____

Process and Aims

As these writing assignments suggest, you can use the explanation of a process whatever the purpose of your writing.

Reflect

If you've been the victim of a crime, explain how the crime happened or how you handled the consequences of the crime.

From your observations of others, explain how alcohol changes an individual's behavior.

Inform

Explain how a home security system works.

Explain how an individual in your community should report family violence to the authorities.

Persuade

Write an article for the school newspaper convincing female students who have been the victims of sex crimes to seek legal and emotional counseling by explaining how to obtain these services.

Write a letter in which you persuade a friend who drinks to give an alcohol-free party; make your case by explaining how to have fun without alcohol.

Speculate

Programs to prevent illegal aliens from entering the United States often are ineffective. Speculate on how another program might work more effectively, and describe the process in a letter to the editor.

Juvenile crime is at an all-time high, and parents are often at a loss as to what to do. Consider a family you know whose child is involved in crime. What do you think this family could do to help the child? Write your response to your classmates.

EXPLORING YOUR OPTIONS

You now are ready to write the first draft of your essay. You already have determined the following:

Your limited topic: _____

A single sentence expressing what you hope to accomplish in this paper:

_____

_____

_____

Your chief writing aim: _____

Your major supports:

_____

_____

_____

_____

Set aside a block of time, and write your first draft. Don't worry about being right or wrong. The object is to get your ideas on paper.

REWRITING

RECONSTRUCTING SENTENCES

Before you can rewrite a sentence that isn't clear or meaningful, you have to rethink it. One way to rethink a sentence is to use sentence reconstruction. Writers reconstruct a sentence by adding to it, deleting from it, or rearranging its parts, or *kernels*. (Think of an ear of corn and the way each kernel is arranged in a row. Each part of a sentence is like a kernel, each sentence is like a row of kernels, and a paragraph is all the rows of kernels combined.) Break the sentence into its individual kernels and then rebuild the kernels in different patterns.

Here's an example:

Parents should teach drug awareness to their young children.

This sentence has four kernels:

1. Parents have children.
2. The children are young.
3. Parents teach their children.
4. Drug awareness should be taught.

These four kernels can be reconstructed in various ways:

Drug awareness should be taught to young children by their parents.

Parents should teach their young children drug awareness.

Young children should be taught drug awareness by their parents.

Although the basic meaning of these sentences is the same, notice how the emphasis changes.

A more complicated sentence has more reconstruction possibilities:

Although conflicts often occur daily between parents and children, love and trust still should be the central emotions of the relationship.

There are twelve possible sentence kernels here:

1. Conflicts occur.
2. Conflicts occur often.
3. Conflicts occur daily.
4. Conflicts occur between parents and children.
5. Love is an emotion.
6. Trust is an emotion.
7. Love should exist in a relationship.
8. Trust should exist in a relationship.
9. Love should be a central emotion in a relationship.
10. Trust should be a central emotion in a relationship.
11. Love should exist between parents and children.
12. Trust should exist between parents and children.

And there are several ways to reconstruct the original sentence:

> Love and trust between parents and children can overcome daily conflicts.

> Parents and children who are experiencing conflict also can experience love and trust.

> Relationships between parents and children are marked by multiple emotions ranging from anger and disappointment to love and trust.

> Despite their conflicts, parents and children still should love and trust each other.

> Regardless of frequent conflicts, love and trust should be the foundation of the relationship between parents and children.

Again, although the basic meaning of these sentences is the same, notice how the emphasis changes.

Reconstructing a sentence means examining its core and then rewriting it so that it says exactly what you want it to say. Reconstruction also can be used to break up a long complicated sentence into a short clear statement. For example, the original sentence about love and trust between parents and children is twenty-one words long:

> Although conflicts often occur daily between parents and children, love and trust still should be the central emotions of the relationship.

This reconstruction is just eleven words long. Notice how clear and easy to read it is:

> Love and trust between parents and children can overcome daily conflicts.

Sentence reconstruction also is a way of joining smaller sentences together, both to avoid choppy writing and to add variety to your writing.

PRACTICE

The following sentence comes from an essay by Shelly Walker and Venita Walker. It's a description of Jim Brown's Amer-I-Can program:

> Brown invites gang members off the street to his Hollywood Hills home, where the program takes place.

1. Write five kernel statements from the sentence.

    a. _____

    b. _____

    c. _____

    d. _____

    e. _____

2. Reconstruct or rearrange the kernels in two different ways:

    a. _____

       _____

       _____

       _____

    b. _____

       _____

       _____

       _____

STUDENT ESSAY

Below is a draft of Shelly Walker and Venita Walker's essay. Shelly is from California and is majoring in general studies. Venita is from Nevada and is majoring in behavioral and social sciences. As you read the draft, ask two basic questions:

- How do Shelly and Venita succeed in fulfilling their purpose for writing this essay?

- How can Shelly and Venita strengthen this draft?

Los Angeles Gang Control

Los Angeles is plagued with gang violence. The city has been referred to as the "gang capital" of the United States and with good reason. Between the period of January to October 1991, there were

520 gang-related murders. Gang membership in Los Angeles has doubled in the past five years, bringing the total to 950 gangs involving 100,000 youth (Clark, 1991, p. 755). Yet Los Angeles is experiencing some success with three current methods used to control gang violence: parental laws, individual efforts, and police crackdowns.

Parental Laws

A stricter parenting law, entitled California State Penal Code 272, appeared in 1989. Under this law, police arrested Gloria Williams, a single mother of three, because of the criminal activity of her 15 year old son. Her home contained evidence that she condoned her son's affiliation with the gang. For example, a photo album showed incriminating pictures of Williams with her children aiming guns at each other while they were wearing the signature colors of the Crips gang and making gang hand gestures. The walls were covered with gang graffiti that suggested the home was a gang headquarters (Thompson, 1989). The stricter parenting laws now hold parents responsible for their children's gang participation. If a parent is convicted, he or she may face up to a year in jail with a fine of $2,500. Punishing parents may make them take their responsibilities more seriously.

Individual Efforts

In addition to stricter laws, many individuals are working with government agencies and police programs to help control gangs. One program, founded by ex-football player Jim Brown, is *Amer-I-Can.* Brown invites gang members off the street to his Hollywood Hills home, where the program takes place. At this neutral location, Brown and Amer-I-Can offer self-esteem and personal responsibility classes, employment workshops, and job placement services conducted by former gang members (Katz, 1991). Brown has compiled a handbook that outlines the values of positive thought, goal setting, family relationships, and job-seeking skills. Members of opposite gangs often meet each

Shelly and Venita's thesis statement divides their paper into three major sections.

They document a specific incident to illustrate this method.

Shelly and Venita write simple, easy-to-understand sentences.

other and share their feelings of guilt, fear, and hope. Brown has an optimistic view of the program. He says, "This could be the most important move-ment in the last 200 years. We know these young men with their negative power turned positive can change our communities. This is the source . . . the hope of America" (Leerhsen, 1991, p. 58).

Police Crackdowns

They support their statements with specific details.

The police have also initiated their own pro-grams to crack down on Los Angeles gangs. For example, they have "gang sweeps." Hundreds of police sweep through Los Angeles every weekend looking for gang members and violence. In just one weekend sweep in June 1990, 34 illegal guns were confiscated, 298 vehicles were impounded, and over $10,000 in believed drug money was taken (Gilbert, 1990). Police also use roadblocks to decrease gang violence. The announced roadblocks work much like sobriety checkpoints where police stop every third car to hand out flyers and ask for information and suggestions concerning gangs. Police only take action when they see drugs or weapons (Holgun, 1991). Most citizens welcome the neighborhood sweeps and roadblocks.

There are no easy answers to gang prevention and control. However, through the combined efforts of parents, individuals, and the police, citizens may begin to make their streets safer.

Shelly and Venita use APA documentation (see the Appendix).

Works Cited

Clark, Charles S. (1991, October 11). Youth gangs. *CQ Researcher,* pp. 755-771.

Gilbert, Holly. (1990, June 16). Nationwide roundup nets Crips, Bloods. *The Oregonian.* News-bank, Law, 1990, 58:F5.

Holgun, Rick. (1991, August 8). Roadblocks to curb gangs to be set up in Paramount. *Los Angeles Times.* Newsbank, Law, 1991, 94:A5.

Katz, Jesse. (1991, September 24). Jim Brown taps potential of "baddest cats" in city. *Los Angeles Times.* Newsbank, Law, 1991, 106:E2.

Leerhsen, Charles. (1991, June 17). Going like
    gangbusters. *Newsweek,* pp. 58–59.
Thompson, Ginger. (1989, May 31). Mother arrested
    under gang law denies blame. *Los Angeles Times.*
    Newsbank, Law, 1989, 73:A3.

EXPLORING YOUR OPTIONS

Select two sentences from your essay that don't clearly express your purpose, that are long or complicated or confusing, that are repeatedly choppy and short, or that seem dull and dead. Reconstruct these sentences by doing the following:

1. Write the first sentence on the lines below:

    _____

    _____

    _____

    _____

2. Write possible kernel statements from the sentence above.

    a. _____

    b. _____

    c. _____

    d. _____

    e. _____

    f. _____

    g. _____

3. Reconstruct or rearrange the kernels in two different ways.

    a. _____

    _____

_____

_____

b. _____

_____

_____

_____

4. Write the second sentence on the lines below:

_____

_____

_____

_____

5. Write possible kernel statements from the sentence above.

a. _____

b. _____

c. _____

d. _____

e. _____

f. _____

g. _____

6. Reconstruct or rearrange the kernels in two different ways.

a. _____

_____

b. _____

_____

_____

_____

7. Reread your reconstructed sentences and incorporate into your essay the sentences that clearly express your purpose.

WRITING TOGETHER

1. After completing the above Exploring Your Options exercise, exchange with a classmate one of the original sentences that you selected to reconstruct.

2. Write possible kernel statements for each other's sentences.

3. Reconstruct or rearrange the kernels in two different ways.

4. Compare the reconstructed sentences with your partner's reconstructed sentences.

5. Discuss the effectiveness of each sentence.

WRITING WITH COMPUTERS

1. Use the three sentences you drafted in the above Exploring Your Options as the beginnings for three possible paragraphs.

2. Draft on the computer three developed paragraphs for your paper that say something specifically, simply, and briefly.

3. Incorporate these paragraphs into your draft by cutting and pasting.

EDITING

ECONOMY AND PARALLELISM

You can simplify your writing by writing economically and by keeping form, time, person, and number parallel.

Economy

When your writing is economical, you're using fewer words to say what you want to say. Every time you write *red* instead of *red in color,* *today* instead of *in this day and age,* and *now* instead of *at the present time,* you're saving words.

You can economize in your writing by crossing out extra words in a sentence or by replacing longer phrases with shorter phrases or single words. In the examples below, I have made the sentences more economical by crossing out unnecessary words. At the end of each example is the number of words that have been eliminated from the sentence.

~~In order~~ to feel wanted, each ~~and every one~~ of us needs a friend. (5 words cut)

~~My personal~~ experience has taught me ~~the fact~~ that children need parents' love. (4 words cut)

~~In his opinion~~ most ~~of the~~ children ~~in our country are~~ spend~~ing entirely~~ too much time watching ~~programs presented on~~ television. (13 words cut)

Here's a list of expressions that you can make more economical by substituting shorter expressions or cutting unnecessary words:

Poor	*Good*
with the purpose of	to
for the purpose of	so that
in the interest of	for
not far from	near
in the midst of	among
in the region of	around
over and above	beyond

Poor	Good
next to	by
on top of	on *or* above
with regard to	regarding
an unexpected surprise	a surprise
at the present time	now
in this day and age	today
at that point in time	then
green in color	green
round in shape	round
due to the fact that	because
each and every	each
very unique	unique
past history	past *or* history
she is a person who	she
in order to	to
important essentials	essentials
free gift	gift
surrounded on all sides	surrounded
in the field of mathematics	mathematics
there is no doubt but that	no doubt
repeat again	repeat
ask the question	ask
refer back	refer
two different kinds	two kinds
end result	result
usual custom	custom

Usually the more economical the writing, the easier it is to understand. But don't cut out too many words in your effort to be brief. Clarity is more important than brevity. If it takes a few more words to clarify an idea, use more words.

Parallelism

Parallelism, like economy, helps simplify writing. *Parallelism* is the use of similar grammatical forms in sentences. Look at these two sentences:

> For fun, my family likes swimming, hiking, and to play golf.

> For fun, my family likes swimming, hiking, and golfing.

The first sentence is not parallel. Notice the *-ing* endings on the words *swimming* and *hiking;* the parallelism is broken with *to play golf.* The second sentence is parallel. *To play golf* has been replaced with *golfing.* You can also make the first sentence parallel by changing *swimming* and *hiking* to *to swim* and *to hike:*

> For fun, my family likes to swim, to hike, and to play golf.

Parallelism applies to time, person, and number as well as to form.

> The book on parenting explains different discipline strategies and gave practical suggestions.

This sentence is not parallel because of the shift in time. The first verb, *explains,* is in the present tense; the second verb, *gave,* is in the past tense. The sentence should be rewritten with both verbs in the present tense or both verbs in the past tense:

CHOOSING THE RIGHT PRONOUN

	Number	
Person	*Singular*	*Plural*
First person	I	we
Second person	you	you
Third person	he	they
	she	people
	one	
	anyone	
	a person	

The book on parenting *explains* different discipline strategies
and *gives* practical suggestions. (present tense)

or

The book on parenting *explained* different discipline strategies
and *gave* practical suggestions. (past tense)

Parallelism also demands consistency in person and number. *Person* is how the writer refers to the speaker or the person being spoken
of (see Chapter 5, page 186). You can write in the first person, second
person, or third person. Each person also is described by number—
singular or plural.

Here's an example of a sentence that isn't parallel in person:

When you say no in a dating situation, I mean no.

This sentence shifts from the second person *you* to the first person *I*.
You can fix it by using the first person pronoun consistently or the second person pronoun consistently:

When *you* say no in a dating situation, *you* mean no (second
person pronoun)

or

When *I* say no in a dating situation, *I* mean no. (first person
pronoun)

Sentences also should be parallel in number:

If he wants to spend more time traveling, they need to budget
their time.

This sentence agrees in person—both *he* and *they* are third person
pronouns. But the sentence is not parallel in number: *he* is singular,
and *they* is plural. To make this sentence parallel, make the number
agree:

If *he* wants to spend more time traveling, he needs to budget
his time. (singular)

or

If *they* want to spend more time traveling, *they need to budget
their* time. (plural)

EXERCISE 1   Make the following sentences economical and parallel by cutting unnecessary words or by making the sentences agree in form, time, person, and number.

1. Redmond City is a city that established community watch programs during the spring in April 1997.

2. The community watch program were with regards to the increased cases of criminal activity.

3. Due to the fact that the criminals felt unafraid, community citizens decided to make changes.

4. The mayor is a woman who campaigns to make the city safer.

5. The city at this point in time of the beginning of the community watch program needed to alert citizens.

6. The citizens organized their committees and start to implement plans.

7. Television stations record at that time citizens patrolling their communities to protect their neighborhoods.

8. There is no doubt that much of the improvements in the community resulted because of people's participation in community watch programs.

EXERCISE 2   Make the sentences in the following paragraph economical and parallel by cutting unnecessary words or by making the sentences agree in form, time, person, and number.

It seems Americans are surrounded on all sides by aggression. We need to ask the question, Do we benefit from aggression? In a study of aggression, we find that aggression is a part of a struggle to resolve stressful and threatening events in the hopes of learning to adapt. There is not any doubt that not all aggression was bad. Each and every one of us has positively directed aggression to reach our many and various goals. However, aggression that inflicts physical and emotional damage is violence. Verbally attacking people, dominating others, and to actually push someone are examples of violent aggression. Violence is a learned aggression. For example, parents who violently punish children for violent acts are teaching you violent behavior. Yet there is hope due to the fact that if violence can be learned, perhaps it also can be unlearned.

EXERCISE 3   Using the current draft from your essay, do the following:

1. Identify ten of your longest sentences. Make them economical and parallel by cutting unnecessary words or by making the sentences agree in form, time, person, and number.

2. Identify five sentences that use parallelism. Label the elements that are parallel.

OPTIONS FOR WRITING

Reflect

1. Write about a time in your life when you were the victim of a crime. Don't emphasize the crime itself; instead, focus on the consequences of the crime, how it's affected you physically, emotionally, socially, or mentally. In your writing use specific, concrete examples.

2. At some time—either knowingly or unknowingly—you've broken a law. Perhaps you drove over the speed limit, made an illegal turn, ran a light, or failed to come to a complete stop at a stop sign. Describe what happened, and then discuss whether you think of yourself as a "law-abiding citizen."

Inform

3. Interview a police officer to gain insight into the profession. Explain how the officer views his or her role in the community, or describe the process he or she went through to become an officer.

4. Identify a legal assistance program in your community, and talk with staff members to determine the types of cases the program handles and the people the organization helps. Then write an article for the school paper telling the campus and the community about the program.

Persuade

5. Speak to people at senior citizens' centers, law enforcement agencies, the Better Business Bureau, or the Chamber of Commerce to learn about the ways in which the elderly are victimized. Explain why the elderly are vulnerable. Then develop a series of steps they can take to protect themselves, and persuade a group of senior citizens to use them.

6. How successful are neighborhood watch programs in your community? What is the crime rate in your neighborhood? Consult with authorities to determine how a neighborhood can become more involved in crime prevention. Then write a letter to your neighbors—using facts and figures—to persuade them to develop and implement a neighborhood watch program.

Speculate

7. Imagine what life is like for a member of a gang. Focus on the individual's attitudes, education, experience, roles, activities, friends, family, or living conditions as you explain how he or she became involved in a gang.

8. From court records reported in your local newspaper, choose a single case—a case of driving under the influence, shoplifting, or burglary, for example. Write an essay from either the criminal's or the victim's point of view in which you describe the crime, its motivation, and its consequences.

Chapter 8
Media

Each of us is influenced by the media. We see 30-second commercials or giant billboard and miniature print ads. We read magazine and newspaper articles. We listen to music and radio talk shows. We surf computer networks, retrieve electronic mail, and play computer and video games. And we view television, videos, and films. Media surrounds and sometimes envelops us. Each of us should recognize the influence media can and does have on us individually and collectively. We need to consciously be aware of individual responsibility in evaluating and selecting the media's power to influence us.

To prepare for this chapter's theme, media, answer the following questions:

- How does the media influence your daily life?
- How can individuals be more responsible for media's impact on their lives?

READINGS on *Media*

Turn Off the TV before It Ruins Us
David Nyhan

David Nyhan is a columnist and associate editor for the Boston Globe. *In this 1996 article, Nyhan uses facts, statistics, reasoning, and emotion to persuade readers to consider the influence television has on their lives.*

I'm not a doctor, but I play one when I'm talking about TV. 1

And the American Medical Association and I agree: Television is 2 bad for kids.

Young people not only would kill to watch TV; they do kill from staring 3 goggle-eyed at the box, a truly infernal machine[1] that delivers two hundred thousand acts of violence to the typical youngster's brain pan before he's old enough to drive.

Every kid in America, on average, witnesses sixteen thousand murders on 4 TV before reaching the ripe old age of eighteen. And you wonder why they throw candy wrappers on the sidewalk or refuse to give an old lady a seat on a crowded bus? Geddoudda here, witch, or I'll blow you away!

Four hours a day is what the average kid watches. That twenty-eight hours 5 per week, over the year, is more time than he spends in school (less than one-fourth of the day for less than 180 days.)

The AMA has studied the phenomena[2] of self-hypnotic television con- 6 sumption and concluded: Aaaaarrrrrrgh!!!

Did you know that wherever television-watching is introduced, homicide 7 rates double within a decade and a half? The babies born to households where TV was just coming in grow up (if they're lucky) to be fifteen-year-olds in communities with twice as many homicides.

Little kids who OD on TV kick and punch and bite much more frequently 8 than the little monsters who do not have their sensitivities dulled by the repetitive and mindless violence of the cathode ray projector.[3]

How bad does it get for a teenager who watches a lot of TV? He or she is 9 fatter, sicker, more likely to drink and smoke and drug, and more likely to engage in premature sexual conduct that can be harmful to him or the kid he's messing with.

---

[1] **infernal machine:** an explosive device intentionally meant to harm or destroy
[2] **phenomena:** an unusual or significant event
[3] **cathode ray projector:** television

TV is an open sewer running into the minds of the impressionable, and   10
progressively desensitized, young. It is a conveyor belt of cynicism, of self-
gratification, of violence-inducing behavior, of role modeling gone wrong, of
tasteless drivel. The more meretricious[4] the content, the more successful the
sale of same. TV is repackaged dross on video for the ages, syndication rights
reserved.

It is ruining the country. Our society's rot owes more to television than any   11
other single cause. As the dominant medium, it overwhelms the periodic,
valiant, and ultimately futile appeals to a higher morality and a more inspirational way of dealing with the rest of humanity.

Television makes everyone cynical, more convinced that no one is honest,   12
no one pure, no one even admirable. All the politicians are crooks, the athletes crooks, the journalists cynics, the businessmen greedheads, the clergy
corrupt, the movie stars perverse.

Six out of ten family meals take place under the baleful glare of a working   13
TV set. More than half of America's kids have TV sets in their bedrooms, where
they can pig out on whatever vile[5] fare is lowest common denominator of the
day.

We already have 1.6 million Americans behind bars. That's almost 2 per-   14
cent of our total employment rate. Most of them are young, most are unedu-
cated, and most are coming out, eventually, to a community near you. They
watched too much TV when they were kids, raised in single-parent, often
violence-racked households where they got cuffed around when they weren't
staring at some stupid television program.

Does it get any better if we shut off the tube and ask them to listen to   15
music? Not much. Three out of four of the top-selling CDs of 1995 use cuss
words and exalt guns, rape, or murder, according to a *Providence Journal-
Bulletin* report.

Between grades seven to twelve, teenagers drain in 10,500 hours of rock   16
music—that's more hours than they spent in class in all the years between second grade and graduating from high school.

The impact on our kids of electronic media—ranging from the soporific[6]   17
to the truly horrific—is the single biggest problem our society faces. It's a much
bigger deal than the deficit or taxes or "job-loss anxiety" labels tossed about in
the election campaigns.

The degrading of our human capital by the corrosive moral erosion of   18
television and the related video-audio industries is a challenge of immense
significance. The politicians nibble around the edges for slivers of political
advantage.

But the dumbing-down of a generation, the deadening of moral sensitivity   19
in millions of youngsters, is a much greater threat than anything rumbling in
the Middle East. Our real problem is the Middle West, and the rest of Middle

---

[4] **meretricious:** vulgar
[5] **vile:** disgusting
[6] **soporific:** lulling to sleep

America. Our kids are bathed in filth, in trivia, in meaningless violence, in false happy endings, in cynical nattering from false media gods.

It's a disease. It requires prevention. And vaccination. And, occasionally, something drastic, like amputation. In my family we still talk about one Super Bowl eve when my sister got so mad at the stupefied gazes on the faces of her four kids that she lugged the TV set into her car, drove to the reservoir, and tossed it in, leaving it sitting cockeyed and unplugged on the ice she forgot to take into account.   20

The AMA is on the right side on this one. Our future is rotting, one channel at a time.   21

Questions and Issues to Consider

Writing Process   1. Identify a passage in Nyhan's article that affects you and explain why it affects you. What details do you remember after reading the essay?

2. Discuss Nyhan's use of statistics and examples to support his position. How effective are those examples and sources?

Aims of Writing   3. Nyhan is writing to persuade readers to consider his position. Identify passages in which he uses objective reasoning and passages that are emotional. How do the reasoned examples affect you? How do the emotional examples affect you?

Critical Thinking   4. Consider the amount of time and types of programs you watch each day on television. Describe the influence television has on your life.

Universal E-mail: Worthy of a 'New Frontier' Commitment
Max Frankel

Max Frankel writes a weekly column on communications for The New York Times Magazine. *In this 1996 article, he recognizes the powerful influence e-mail can have on individuals; therefore, he recommends that the federal government make e-mail available to all Americans just as telephones and the postal system are.*

I t doesn't quite have the ring of John F. Kennedy's vow, 35 years ago this   1
month, to land a man on the moon "before this decade is out." But
you'd think a President or candidate for President would by now have hurled
a similar challenge, with the promise of raising the nation's literacy, its computer skills and its technical prowess: E-mail for All by 2010!

As millions of Americans already know, E-mail is electronic mail that can   2
be sent by anyone with a computer and telephone to everyone similarly
equipped, anywhere on earth, almost instantaneously, at virtually no cost. It is
by far the most popular feature of the Internet, that amorphous[1] network of
computer networks. E-mail's digital messages can be coolly deliberate, like a
letter, or warmly spontaneous, like a phone call. They can be sent at any hour
and read at the receiver's convenience. They can be addressed to a single person or simultaneously to thousands—thousands chosen by the sender for some
shared interest or thousands who asked for a certain type of mail.

Although E-mail will eventually carry moving pictures and oral messages,   3
it is now mostly written—typed, to be precise, on keyboards. Its messages are
sliced up and wrapped inside small electronic packets, all of which pick their
way along the best available Internet routes to an electronic postal station,
where they reassemble and wait in storage for an addressee—like frankel@
times.com—to check in to read them. E-mail travels as fast as a fax but arrives
in much more versatile form. It can be long or short, studied, searched or
skimmed, instantly answered or copied, relayed, edited or destroyed.

E-mail lets you court a lover, proclaim a credo[2], organize a rally or circu-   4
late a recipe. City Hall can use it to schedule trash collections; politicians can
use it to take a poll. E-mail can order groceries or offer clothing discounts to
selected customers. It is certain to become a vital new instrument of commerce and the creator of vibrant[3] electronic communities.

But like conventional telephone and postal service, E-mail will never ful-   5
fill its social and commercial promise until it is universal. The more people it
can reach, the greater its value to all. The already visible danger is that E-mail
will become the preserve[4] of the affluent and educated classes, bypassing large
segments of the population—much as paper mail and telephones once
bypassed rural America. Now, as then, the market alone seems unable at first
to serve its own best interest.

It took a decree of Congress to require the Postal Service "to bind the   6
Nation together through the personal, educational, literary and business correspondence of the people . . . in all areas and . . . all communities." As a
result, paper mail became a powerful stimulus to road building, railroading
and aviation. Similarly, governments imposed universal service on telephone

---

[1] **amorphous:** shapeless or formless
[2] **credo:** statement of religious belief
[3] **vibrant:** vigorous and lively
[4] **preserve:** safe place

companies, requiring them to overcharge urban customers so as to subsidize the extension of phone lines to farflung rural areas.

That mail and phone services can now be profitably privatized and dereg- 7
ulated is not an argument against government intervention and leadership. On the contrary, it is proof of the value of government incubation.

A recent Rand study, with research supported by the Markle Foundation, 8
concluded that in the foreseeable future the free market is likely to deliver E-mail to only half of America. Without a government-led drive toward universality, some E-mail systems may prove to be incompatible with others. And without induced subsidies,[5] perhaps from Internet access fees, the computer industry may never produce the inexpensive technologies that would enable television sets, telephones and computer games to bring E-mail into the home. Interim[6] subsidies and technologies would also be needed if less-affluent citizens are to get their E-mail outside the home, in apartment lobbies, libraries and schools.

There appear to be no technical barriers to achieving universal E-mail 9
once that goal has been proclaimed. Indeed, experiments in a few specially wired communities show that E-mail arouses people's interest in other computer services. In Blacksburg, Va., it has stimulated many to learn more complicated computer skills, to use the Internet for more sophisticated transactions and to create two dozen Net-related businesses.

House Speaker Newt Gingrich was not nearly as "nutty" as he thought 10
when he mused out loud about subsidizing laptops for poor ghetto kids. But he was only scoring debating points and soon abandoned his own insight about how computers threaten to further divide American society.

If political leaders would reflect on the subject, they would recognize a 11
vast constituency[7] of the computerless and computer-challenged. They would recall the rich history of conservatives as well as liberals using government to advance and enlarge the nation's communications and transportation industries. They would summon Microsoft's Bill Gates and I.B.M.'s Lou Gerstner and the other titans of technology who so often deplore our inadequate schooling and seek their commitment to universal E-mail. The computer companies and their charities need to be challenged to underwrite cheaper terminals, to recycle older terminals and to invent pay terminals, like pay phones, for public spaces. They should be asked to consider charging modest fees for profitable private uses of the Internet—a government offspring—to subsidize the Net's penetration of every community.

President Kennedy, of course, could invoke the specter of *Sputnik*[8] and 12
cold war divisions to urge a race against the Russians to the moon. But he set a loftier goal than missile superiority. "Now it is time to take longer strides," he said, "time for a great new American enterprise." We face the more abstract

---

[5] **subsidies:** financial assistance
[6] **interim:** temporary
[7] **constituency:** voters
[8] ***Sputnik:*** a Soviet satellite sent into orbit in 1957

specter of technological partition, a society of computer elites and illiterates drifting apart and losing touch. And we, too, could use a great new enterprise. E-mail for all won't guarantee how well we speak to one another, but it can keep us talking and growing richer together.

＊～＊

Questions and Issues to Consider

Writing Process   1. Identify where Frankel informs readers of a problem affecting them and a possible solution to that problem.

2. Describe how Frankel considers his readers' questions or concerns about the issue.

Aims of Writing   3. Frankel is writing to persuade. Underline the support he uses such as studies, examples, comparisons, opinions. How effective is his support?

Critical Thinking   4. Consider people you know. How many of them have access to computers and e-mail? How have computers and e-mail affected you? Respond to Frankel's article by discussing types of communicating the article does not.

PREWRITING

VOICE PROJECTION

When you feel uncertain about a topic, try to imagine how other people would respond to the topic. *Voice projection*—exploring a topic through other people's voices—can help you clarify your own thoughts and feelings. Voice projection is similar to the work a ventriloquist does with a puppet. The ventriloquist generates the ideas, the sound, and the style, but it's the puppet's imagined personality that directs the ventriloquist's responses.

Suppose you're writing an essay on the topic of honesty. You'd begin by making a list of different people. For example:

Business partner	Employer	Police officer
Child	Friend	Politician

Consumer	Grandparent	Religious leader
Doctor	News reporter	Student
Employee	Parent	Teacher

Now choose at least two people from the list, and imagine how they would react to a situation in which honesty comes into play. Try to determine their thoughts, experiences, and feelings. Then project their voices: Write short paragraphs in their voices.

Let's say you've assumed the voice of a four-year-old who climbed onto the kitchen counter and accidentally broke the cookie jar. When a parent asks what happened, the child either tells the truth or, hoping to escape punishment, makes up a story. Put yourself in that child's place. Determine how and why the child reacts a particular way.

Or assume the voice of someone who has found a purse in the parking lot at the mall. Would you turn the purse into the authorities or keep it? Imagine you're someone hoping to sell your own car. Do you tell prospective buyers everything that you believe is wrong with the car? Or imagine that you're someone calculating your own income taxes. Do you report all wages and tips? Think about how these people feel and how and why they react the way they do.

After you explore "your people's" responses, explore your own feelings. How would you react in a similar situation? Do you think your own reactions are right? wrong? justifiable? As you begin to place different people in different situations, you should begin to look at your topic differently.

For example, two students, Kristi Hansen and Jared Williams, have decided to write about pornography on the Internet. They don't know yet how they will approach the topic, so they try voice projection to generate ideas. They choose to respond from the points of view of a parent and an advocate of the First Amendment and freedom of expression. Jared writes first as the parent:

> I want free speech, and I'm against cen-
> sorship, but I want to protect my daughter
> against Internet pornography. My 8-year-old
> daughter unknowingly has access to Internet
> pornography. When I watch my 8-year-old
> daughter sit down at the computer, click on
> the Internet, and type *www.disneychannel.com*
> after watching a commercial on the Disney
> Channel, I suddenly realize that she can type
> in or search for and retrieve anything on the

Internet. One day she accidentally pulled up indecent information through innocent words linked to pornographic phrases. As a father, I'm concerned. Sure, we could discuss and enforce guidelines like we do with television and videos (no more than two hours a day and no R-ratings), and we could restrict her use of the computer to when we're with her. But she often goes to the computer to e-mail her friends or her grandparents; she sees a television ad on recycling and wants to go to that homepage, or surf for information about a favorite athlete or celebrity. I want my daughter to have access to the computer and to the information highway. I don't want to place too many restrictions on her, but I do want unquestionably obscene and pornographic material to be blocked from her. Therefore, I guess I am for censorship—I want pornography off the Internet so my daughter can surf.

Kristi's response is written from the point of view of a First Amendment, freedom of expression advocate:

I'm not advocating pornography. I'm not a sleaze. I don't even watch R-rated movies. But people have the right to freedom of speech, of thought, of press, of expression. I agree that pornography is degrading. I agree that children should not have access to material that is clearly meant for adults. But I also believe that the rights of the many outweigh the rights of the few. I'm very uncomfortable with the idea of others policing what I do have access to—that's my responsibility. As far as pornography on the Internet, I personally don't want to view it, so I won't. To safeguard children against pornography, parents could subscribe to or purchase filtering programs that restrict computer access. Sure that's a form of censorship, but that is self-imposed censorship and discipline rather than governmental

`censorship—thereby protecting the First
Amendment.`

While working on these paragraphs, Kristi and Jared remember reading an article earlier about a pedophile sending pornography to a 12-year-old boy. They decide to focus their paper on censoring pornography on the Internet through governmental involvement. Their main purpose is to persuade. (A draft of Kristi and Jared's paper begins on page 295).

EXPLORING YOUR OPTIONS

To help generate ideas and examples for your paper, do the following voice projection activity.

1. On the line below, write your general topic.

    _____

2. Choose two people from the list on page 272 or from a list of your own.

    _____

    _____

3. Write a paragraph about your topic from each person's point of view.

    Person 1

    _____

    _____

    _____

    _____

    _____

    _____

    _____

    _____

    _____

Person 2

_____

_____

_____

_____

_____

_____

_____

_____

4. From these paragraphs, choose one aspect of your topic that you want to write about. This is your limited topic. Write it on the lines below.

_____

_____

5. Put a checkmark next to the aim that best describes your reason for writing.

_____ To reflect   _____ To persuade

_____ To inform   _____ To speculate

WRITING WITH COMPUTERS

1. Use your general topic as a search word on the Internet.

2. Scan the listings to determine differing points of view on your general topic.

3. Make a list of what you consider to be major arguments for different sides of your issue.

4. Add items and ideas to that list that appear as possible Internet links.

5. After creating an Internet list of positions and arguments on your general topic, determine your own position and write a paragraph representing your views.

6. Select another point of view discovered on the Internet and write a paragraph representing that view.

DRAFTING

COORDINATING AND SUBORDINATING IDEAS

Paragraphs are made up of sentences that deal with the same subject. There are no hard-and-fast rules governing paragraphs. But you do have a responsibility as a writer to present the information within the paragraph in small units that are easy to understand. To create these small units, you have to understand the writing principles of coordination and subordination. *Coordination* is the process of grouping larger pieces of information that are of equal importance. *Subordination* is the process of grouping smaller units of information that are used in large part to support and explain a larger point.

Suppose you're writing a paper on the topic *prejudice*. You've decided to write on four types of prejudice: racial, cultural, gender, and religious. These four types are equal in that they represent large general categories of prejudice. Therefore they *coordinate* with one another. Now, let's say that you decide to divide your discussion of gender prejudice into two parts: the gender prejudice found in sexist language and the gender prejudice found in role expectations. These parts or subgroups are *subordinate* to the broader category of gender prejudice.

The same principles of coordination and subordination apply as the groups become narrower. For example, the category *home* both coordinates with the categories *work* and *school* and subordinates to the broader subgroup of prejudice found in role expectations. And *home* can be subordinated into smaller coordinated units like *female* and *male*.

To visualize coordination and subordination, use a formal outline. Here's a formal outline for the topic *prejudice in the media:*

Prejudice in the Media

I. Racial

II. Cultural

III. Gender

    A. Sexist language

    B. Role expectations

        1. Print advertisements

           a. Female

           b. Male

        2. Television commercials

           a. Female

           b. Male

        3. Television programs

           a. Female

           b. Male

        4. Films

           a. Female

           b. Male

        5. Music videos

           a. Female

           b. Male

IV. Religious

This formal outline shows the relationships between coordinating and subordinating items. For example, all of the items grouped by Roman numerals (I, II, III, IV) are equal, or coordinating. The capital letter entries (A, B) under a particular item are subordinate to the

Roman numeral entry; at the same time, they are equal (coordinated) with each other. All the Arabic numeral entries (1, 2, 3) are subordinate to the capital letter entries but coordinate with one another. And finally, the lowercase letter entries (a, b) are subordinate to the Arabic numeral entries but coordinate with each other.

The purpose of coordination and subordination is to help you organize your ideas logically and clearly. Jared, for example, uses coordination and subordination in the prewriting paragraph he wrote for the essay on Internet censorship. In this paragraph he's writing as if he is a parent:

> I want free speech, and I'm against censorship, but I want to protect my daughter against Internet pornography. My 8-year-old daughter unknowingly has access to Internet pornography. When I watch my 8-year-old daughter sit down at the computer, click on the Internet, and type *www.disneychannel.com* after watching a commercial on the Disney Channel, I suddenly realize that she can type in or search for and retrieve anything on the Internet. One day she accidentally pulled up indecent information through innocent words linked to pornographic phrases. As a father, I'm concerned. Sure, we could discuss and enforce guidelines like we do with television and videos (no more than two hours a day and no R-ratings), and we could restrict her use of the computer to when we're with her. But she often goes to the computer to e-mail her friends or her grandparents; she sees a television ad on recycling and wants to go to that homepage, or surf for information about a favorite athlete or celebrity. I want my daughter to have access to the computer and to the information highway. I don't want to place too many restrictions on her, but I do want unquestionably obscene and pornographic material to be blocked from her. Therefore, I guess I am for censorship—I want pornography off the Internet, so my daughter can surf.

The first sentence in this paragraph is the topic sentence: It states the subject of the paragraph—censoring Internet pornography. The paragraph is divided into two equal coordinating parts. One part is about the daughter's innocent ability to access questionable material on the Internet; the other is about the father's concern. An outline of the major divisions in this paragraph would look like this:

I. I want free speech, and I'm against censorship, but I want to protect my daughter against Internet pornography.

   A. My 8-year-old daughter unknowingly has access to Internet pornography.

   B. As a father, I'm concerned.

Jared subordinates descriptive details to each of his major divisions—the daughter's access to Internet pornography and the father's concern. Each detail about the daughter's access coordinates with the other details about her access, and each detail about the father's concern coordinates with the other details about his concern. Here's the paragraph outline again, this time with the details added:

I. I want free speech, and I'm against censorship, but I want to protect my daughter against Internet pornography.

   A. My 8-year-old daughter unknowingly has access to Internet pornography.

      1. When I watch my 8-year-old daughter sit down at the computer, click on the Internet, and type *www.disneychannel.com* after watching a commercial on the Disney Channel, I suddenly realize that she can type in or search for and retrieve anything on the Internet.

      2. One day she accidentally pulled up indecent information through innocent words linked to pornographic phrases.

   B. As a father, I'm concerned.

      1. Sure, we could discuss and enforce guidelines like we do with television and videos (no more than two hours a day and no R-ratings), and we could restrict her use of the computer to when we're with her.

      2. But she often goes to the computer to e-mail her friends or her grandparents; she sees a television ad on

recycling and wants to go to that homepage, or surf
for information about a favorite athlete or celebrity.

3. I want my daughter to have access to the computer
and to the information highway.

4. I don't want to place too many restrictions on her, but
I do want unquestionably obscene and pornographic
material to be blocked from her.

5. Therefore, I guess I am for censorship—I want
pornography off the Internet, so my daughter can surf.

Notice that the outline shows clearly how Jared's ideas and examples
coordinate with and subordinate to one another.

PRACTICE

1. Write a paragraph that supports this topic sentence: *Television has
a positive influence on people in three ways.*

_____

_____

_____

_____

_____

_____

_____

_____

2. Write an outline that shows how the sentences in the paragraph
coordinate with or are subordinate to one another.

_____

_____

_____

_____

_____

_____

_____

_____

EXPLORING YOUR OPTIONS

1. Write a possible topic sentence for your paper.

_____

_____

2. Write a paragraph supporting that topic sentence.

_____

_____

_____

_____

_____

_____

_____

3. Write an outline that shows how the sentences in the paragraph coordinate with or subordinate to one another.

_____

_____

_____

_____

_____

_____

_____

PERSUASION

You use persuasion to convince, motivate, or gain the agreement of another individual or group.

Using Persuasion

It's important to understand five guidelines for using persuasion effectively: (1) know your audience, (2) know your position, (3) provide support, (4) be objective, and (5) use formal organization.

1. **Know your audience.** Persuasive writing, perhaps more than any other type of writing, should focus on a particular audience. After all, the reason you're using persuasion is to convince someone of something. Don't underestimate your audience's intelligence. But be familiar with your audience's limitations: Is there some information your audience has not received yet? Once you understand your audience, think about which approach will work best. For instance, suppose you want to persuade someone to buy a particular product. Your approach is going to be different if the person you're writing to is someone who has money to buy the product than if you're writing to someone with very little money.

2. **Know your position.** The more certain you are of your topic and of your position, the more convincing your writing. If you haven't worked problems out in your mind, chances are you won't be able to help your readers work out problems in their minds. Of course, you don't want to give the impression that you know everything, because you don't. For instance, if you're planning to write a paper on rating music (CDs and tapes), but you haven't thought about the topic much before now—it's not clear to you, for example, exactly what specifically should be rated—you probably should change topics. Even if you do have a strong background in or feelings for music through experience or research, be realistic. Recognize that there probably is at least one aspect of the issue that you haven't considered fully.

3. **Provide Support.** You've reached your conclusions after much thought, experience, observation, and research. Your convictions are strong. But so are your readers' convictions. Your readers aren't going to accept what you say simply because you say it. This means that you have to explain each reason you have for thinking the way you do. If your topic is violence in cartoon programming and you

simply state that you are in favor for or against it, you're not being persuasive. It's your support—in the form of examples, statistics, sources, and experiences—that does the convincing.

4. **Be objective.** You're not going to convince your readers by ranting about just one side of an issue. People react much more positively to a rational, balanced discussion. Remember: For every issue there are at least two valid points of view. Logically, each point of view isn't all right or all wrong. Recognize the strengths and weaknesses of each position. Suppose the issue is restricting talk show sensationalism. Even if you fully support the idea, you should recognize that a blanket restriction that covers every situation and guest is not necessarily an effective method of stopping sensationalism or of changing people's attitudes about talk shows.

5. **Use formal organization.** The way you organize a persuasive argument is important. Even if you're just writing a letter to convince a friend to come visit, persuasion is more powerful within the framework of the time-tested formal organization that is attributed to Aristotle. This formal persuasive organization itself consists of five parts: (1) state your position, (2) offer your proof, (3) acknowledge your reader's views, (4) offer alternatives to your reader's views, and (5) show your position's superiority.

   Suppose you're writing a letter to the school administration to encourage the school to fund a drug awareness media campaign on campus. Here's one way you could use the persuasive organization:

(1) **State your position.** Both you and your reader need to understand what you're trying to do, so begin by concisely stating your purpose. Most often a simple direct sentence works best: "I'm writing this letter to ask for administrative support for a drug awareness media campaign."

(2) **Offer your proof.** The administration gets lots of requests for its support. Just because you ask for help doesn't mean that the administration is going to give you help. You must have valid reasons. Use examples, statistics, scenarios, case studies, and other authorities to convince your reader that your request is valid. To collect support for a drug media campaign, survey students about drug abuse on campus. Interview campus security for statistics on the number of drug-related incidents over the last few years. And explain how other schools have successfully implemented a drug awareness media campaign.

(3) **Acknowledge your readers' views.** No matter how valid and reasonable your position, there always are other viewpoints. Be aware of and understand those viewpoints. For example, an administration that's concerned about a shrinking application rate may not want to emphasize a drug abuse media campaign on campus. Or the administration may not have the money or the time budgeted for what it considers a special interest group. Or the administration may want to limit funding to academic programs.

(4) **Offer alternatives to your readers' views.** After you anticipate your readers' viewpoints, explain why those viewpoints aren't right (at least in this context). Then offer more support to develop your own position. For instance, if the administration has budget constraints, appreciate its problem, acknowledge its interest in the students, and offer an alternative. Perhaps the administration can encourage student organizations to fund and participate in a drug awareness media campaign.

(5) **Show your position's desirability.** Finally, emphasize your position again by restating the primary reasons you need your readers' support. This summary solidifies your stance and reminds your reader again of why you're writing and what you want them to do. Remind the administration of its obligation to educate students, and show how a drug awareness media campaign could help fulfill this obligation.

✓ CHECKLIST: PERSUASION

1. Do you try to understand your readers' position?

2. Do you know your own position?

3. Do you clearly state your position?

4. Do you provide support for your position based on thought, experience, observation, and research?

5. Are you objective and reasonable?

6. Do you use a formal organization?

PERSUASION: AN EXAMPLE

In the following paragraph, Donna Woolfolk Cross is writing to persuade readers to recognize that advertising is institutionalized lying. Notice how she supports her topic with an example and explanation.

Institutional Lying

The fact is that advertising is institutional lying. The lies are tolerated—even encouraged—because they serve the needs of the corporate establishment. . . . By now the falsity—either direct or inferential—of most television commercials is a matter of well-documented fact. Most people accept that ads are not true and yet, because they do not understand the methods by which they are influenced, are still taken in. Can *you* detect the deception behind the following statement?

"All aspirin is not alike. In tests for quality, Bayer proved superior."

Most people assume this means that Bayer aspirin has been shown to relieve pain better than other aspirin. In fact the "tests for quality," which were conducted by Bayer and not an independent testing agency, showed that Bayer was superior, in its own manufacturer's opinion, because the tablets were whiter and less breakable than the other aspirins tested. Nevertheless, this claim is so effective that a recent FTC survey revealed that forty percent of consumers believe Bayer is the most effective aspirin.

PRACTICE   Use Cross's paragraph to respond to the following.

1. In a single sentence, state Cross's position.

_____

_____

_____

2. Explain how her use of the Bayer example supports her position.

_____

_____

_____

_____

3. Cross acknowledges that the Bayer corporation is telling the truth. Explain how it is telling the truth.

_____

_____

_____

_____

4. Describe how Cross explains the use of the corporation's honesty to mislead the public.

_____

_____

_____

_____

5. Explain how Cross uses a final example to persuade her readers that her position (that advertising is institutionalized lying) is superior to the corporation's contention that it is being honest.

_____

_____

_____

_____

WRITING TOGETHER

1. Write a sentence clearly identifying the position you want to take on your paper's topic.

2. Exchange sentences with a classmate.

3. Each of you now write a paragraph taking an opposing stance than that of your classmate.

4. Share the responses with each other and discuss the different points of view.

5. Determine what support each paper will need to help persuade the opposing reader.

Persuasion and Aims

As the following writing assignments suggest, you can use persuasion whatever the purpose of your writing.

Reflect

Remember a time when you did volunteer work for an individual or an organization. Use that experience as the basis for writing a letter to the newspaper persuading others in your community to be volunteers.

Describe someone in your neighborhood who has had a positive influence on someone else's life. This person may have done something quietly, yet it may also be newsworthy. Write a tribute to that individual in which you persuade other neighbors to become more involved in other people's lives.

Inform

Write an article for parents of pre-teenage children informing them of possible advantages and disadvantages of video games in a child's life. Use specific examples to illustrate your position. Then persuade parents to participate more in their children's video activities.

In an essay, encourage your classmates to appreciate the personal freedoms they take for granted. Give them examples of other cultures or societies that restrict individual rights.

Persuade

Identify a product that you feel should not be on the market. Write a letter to others encouraging them not to buy or use the product. Be sure to explain your reasons.

Television and television advertising are often the subject of much criticism. Write a letter to your college newspaper or to members of the PTA in your city defending the *positive* effects or value of television. Cite particular programs or commercials as examples.

Speculate

Convince your classmates that they have buying power. Describe what you think would happen if people stopped buying a particular product that you feel is harmful to individuals or to the environment.

Develop a proposal for your college administration to make computer literacy courses graduation requirements. Be sure to discuss how those courses will affect students' performances in and out of the college classroom.

EXPLORING YOUR OPTIONS

You now are ready to write the first draft of your essay. You already have determined the following:

Your limited topic: _____

Your purpose for writing this paper: _____

_____

Your topic sentence: _____

_____

A paragraph supporting that topic sentence:

_____

_____

_____

_____

_____

_____

_____

_____

Set aside a block of time, and write your first draft. Try not to worry about being right or wrong. The object is to get your ideas on paper.

REWRITING

RECONSTRUCTING PARAGRAPHS

Sometimes a paragraph doesn't feel right, doesn't say what you want it to say, or is only one or two sentences long. (You can write a very powerful paragraph with just a couple of sentences. Usually, however, especially if you're a beginning writer, a short paragraph means undeveloped ideas.) In Chapter 7 we looked at reconstructing sentences; here we look at a way to reconstruct individual paragraphs.

You begin by determining the subject of the paragraph:

1. **Isolate the paragraph, and read the paragraph twice.** Choose just one paragraph to work on. Isolate the paragraph: Read it twice without reading the paragraph before or after it. Without information from other paragraphs, you're better able to see whether your targeted paragraph can stand alone.

    Jared and Kristi, for example, have identified a short paragraph in their first draft that they want to develop more. Here is the isolated paragraph.

    > Vast availability of indecent material on the Internet exposes innocent children to pornography. Thomas E. Weber of the *Wall Street Journal* writes that Internet search directories are now including advertisements for X-rated materials that would have been banned from newspapers and television and are now available through simple search links. Children have access to these directories and are innocently being exposed to pornographic and improper material.

2. **Summarize the ideas or examples in the isolated paragraph in a single brief sentence.** This summary helps you focus on the topic of the paragraph; it also suggests a topic sentence. Write this single-sentence summary (topic sentence) at the top of another sheet of paper. Here's Jared and Kristi's single-sentence summary of their paragraph:

    > Children unknowingly access indecent material through Internet search directo-

```
ries because children aren't aware of the
evils lurking behind certain word meanings.
```

Once you've determined the subject of your isolated paragraph, you need to examine how well you support or develop that subject in the subsequent sentences. To examine the paragraph's support, try the following:

3. **Treat the summary sentence as the beginning of a new paragraph, and list as many examples, statistics, definitions, and proofs as you can to illustrate the summary sentence.** Use this listing activity, like other listing activities, to generate as many ideas as possible to draw from when you're rewriting the paragraph. When your list is done, choose several good examples. Jared and Kristi's list includes details on children innocently accessing indecent material on Internet search directories:

<u>Misinterpreted words</u>	Penguins sex
<u>Cartoon wolf</u>	<u>Key word searches</u>
<u>Lycos, Infoseek, Yahoo!</u>	Cyberporn
Advertisements	<u>Sussex, England</u>
<u>Computer links</u>	Suggestive home pages

4. **With the summary sentence functioning as a topic sentence, write a paragraph incorporating the new examples.** As you write the paragraph, concentrate on providing the necessary details to make the examples as clear as possible. Explain the relationships the examples share with one another and with the topic sentence. This is Kristi and Jared's rewrite. Notice how they use their summary as a topic sentence and incorporate the underlined examples and details from the list.

```
    Children unknowingly access indecent
material through Internet search directo-
ries because children aren't aware of the
evils lurking behind certain word meanings.
For example, one child while doing a school
report on wolves found a tuxedo-clad car-
toon wolf pointing to the words "Live Nude
Girls!" with photographs of bare-shouldered
women to complete the pitch. And another
```

student researching Sussex, England, was
exposed to pornographic links because of
the misinterpreted key word *sex* in *Sussex*.
Children have access to these directories
and are innocently being exposed to pornographic and improper materials.

5. **Reread the new paragraph to see that it clearly and accurately
   expresses what you want it to.** If it doesn't, work on individual sentences until you're satisfied with what you've written. After reading
   the paragraph, Jared and Kristi revise it again by adding a source
   from an authority:

Children unknowingly access indecent
material through Internet search directories because children aren't aware of the
evils lurking behind certain word meanings.
For example, one child while doing a school
report on wolves found a tuxedo-clad cartoon wolf pointing to the words "Live Nude
Girls!" with photographs of bare-shouldered
women to complete the pitch. And another
student researching Sussex, England, was
exposed to pornographic links because of
the misinterpreted key word *sex* in *Sussex*.
Thomas E. Weber of the *Wall Street Journal*
writes on this very issue. He explains that
popular and trusted Internet search directories such as Lycos, Infoseek, Excite, and
Yahoo!, used by millions of Internet users
"to sift the Web for information," are
beginning "to drum up business for merchants selling X-rated fare." He states,
"Advertisements for pornography, long banished from broadcast outlets and newspaper
movie listings and relegated to 'alternative' magazines, are finding a remarkably
warm reception at some of the most prominent, mainstream outposts on the World Wide
Web." Children have access to these directories and are innocently being exposed to
pornographic and improper material.

You've determined the subject of the paragraph and good support for that subject. Now, you're ready to incorporate the rewritten paragraph into your paper. Sometimes you can put the paragraph back where it came from. But sometimes the rewritten paragraph suggests changes to the paragraphs around it. Before incorporating the reconstructed paragraph, do the following:

6. **Read the paragraphs immediately before and after the targeted paragraph.** As you read, ask if the previous paragraph adequately prepares the reader for the information in the reconstructed paragraph. Then ask yourself if the paragraph that follows successfully builds on the main idea of the reconstructed paragraph. If you find that the paragraph before doesn't prepare for, or that the paragraph after doesn't build on, the reconstructed paragraph, consider rethinking those paragraphs as well.

   Jared and Kristi read the paragraph that precedes their rewritten paragraph. It's about certain individuals' argument that since pornography is everywhere, it doesn't matter if it's also on the Internet. The paragraph also establishes that there are large amounts of indecent material on the Internet. Jared and Kristi want a smoother transition into the rewritten paragraph, so they decide to emphasize the key word *availability,* using that word in the last sentence of the previous paragraph and the first sentence of their rewritten paragraph. When they read the paragraph that follows the rewritten paragraph, they decide they want to tie the idea of innocent subject links to the idea of choice. They pick up the word *choose* from the next paragraph and use it in the closing sentence to bring the ideas together.

   Jared and Kristi rephrase the topic sentence and write a new closing sentence for the rewritten paragraph. They now have reconstructed a paragraph that flows from the previous paragraph into the following one:

> The large availability of pornographic
> material on the Internet intrudes upon the
> rights of the innocent. Children unknow-
> ingly access indecent material through
> Internet search directories because chil-
> dren aren't aware of the evils lurking
> behind certain word meanings. For example,
> one child while doing a school report on
> wolves found a tuxedo-clad cartoon wolf

pointing to the words "Live Nude Girls!"
with photographs of bare-shouldered women
to complete the pitch. And another student
researching Sussex, England, was exposed to
pornographic links because of the misinterpreted key word *sex* in *Sussex*. Thomas E.
Weber of the *Wall Street Journal* writes on
this very issue. He explains that popular
and trusted Internet search directories
such as Lycos, Infoseek, Excite, and
Yahoo!, used by millions of Internet users
"to sift the Web for information," are
beginning "to drum up business for merchants selling X-rated fare." He states,
"Advertisements for pornography, long banished from broadcast outlets and newspaper
movie listings and relegated to 'alternative' magazines, are finding a remarkably
warm reception at some of the most prominent, mainstream outposts on the World Wide
Web." Children have access to these directories and are innocently being exposed to
pornography and are innocently choosing
improper material.

7. **Read the reconstructed paragraph in connection with the complete essay.** Finally, determine how the reconstructed paragraph works within the entire essay. Chances are that a strong reconstructed paragraph is going to suggest improvements in other areas of the essay.

Reconstructing paragraphs is time-consuming; you may not be able to reconstruct every paragraph in a paper. But if you choose several of your weakest paragraphs and rebuild them and make the necessary changes to fit them into your original draft, you will find that your writing and ideas become clear, more concise, and easier to read.

STUDENT ESSAY

Below is a draft of Kristi Hansen and Jared Williams's essay. Kristi is from Idaho and is majoring in computer information systems. Jared is from Oregon and is majoring in business management. As you read the draft, ask two basic questions:

- How do Kristi and Jared succeed in fulfilling their purpose for writing this essay?

- How can they strengthen this draft?

A Wolf Isn't a Wolf:
Censoring Pornography on the Internet

In 1995, John Keith of Boston began to send pornographic electronic mail to a twelve-year-old boy. Keith's correspondence included explicit descriptions of pornographic pictures that he had found off the Internet. Luckily, the authorities were alerted, and in 1997, the offender pleaded guilty in a federal court (U.S. Attorney's Office, 1997, p. 1). Many wonder if such a crime is a rare occurrence. The U.S. Justice Department says it is currently working on one hundred Internet-related crimes involving children that "could have been avoided by limiting where children surf" (Tejada, 196, p. R14). In view of this topic, Senator Herbert Kohl remarked, "The yellow-brick road to a dazzling future of instant information and global interconnection is now a dank pit of sleaze, murder, and terror" (qtd. in Sussman, 1996, p. 62). Since pornography on the Internet is becoming a serious problem, we need to enact national laws against electronic pornography, and we need to involve parents in their children's use of the Internet.

One argument against censorship says that since pornography is everywhere anyway, it doesn't matter if it's on the Internet too. Just because pornography is already available through other means, doesn't justify its spread on the Internet. Richard A. Detwieter remarks that a growing number of private citizens and politicians claim that the Internet is the "latest and grossest violator of moral standards," appearing "not on some sleazy

Kristi and Jared state their position.

They use authorities and examples to support their position.

back street, but right in the home of every American with a phone line and computer. As such, they
say, it should be regulated just as porn shops and
broadcast media are" (Detwieter, 1996, p. A40).
Mike Hoskins, a member of "Clubs and Vice" police
unit, states that "there is material [produced for
and distributed] on the Internet that is clearly
obscene," and similar offenders are frequently
arrested if they produce that kind of material in
other media, such as videos, floppy disks, CD-
ROMs, books, or magazines—so why not those on the
Internet? (qtd. in Akdeniz, 1996, p. 5). The over-
whelming availability of pornographic material,
which has been established as detrimental to society, is not a valid justification for allowing its
spread through the Internet.

The large availability of pornographic material
on the Internet intrudes upon the rights of the
innocent. Children unknowingly access indecent
material through Internet search directories
because children aren't aware of the evils lurking
behind certain word meanings. For example, one
child while doing a school report on wolves found
a tuxedo-clad cartoon wolf pointing to the words
"Live Nude Girls!" with photographs of bare-
shouldered women to complete the pitch. And
another student researching Sussex, England, was
exposed to pornographic links because of the misinterpreted key word *sex* in *Sussex*. Thomas E.
Weber of the *Wall Street Journal,* writes on this
very issue. He explains that popular and trusted
Internet search directories such as Lycos, Infoseek, Excite, and Yahoo!, used by millions of
Internet users "to sift the Web for information,"
are beginning "to drum up business for merchants
selling X-rated fare." He states, "Advertisements
for pornography, long banished from broadcast outlets and newspaper movie listings and relegated to
'alternative' magazines, are finding a remarkably
warm reception at some of the most prominent,
mainstream outposts on the World Wide Web." Children have access to these directories and are

innocently being exposed to pornography and are innocently choosing improper material.

Kristi and Jared acknowledge their opponent's concerns.

Those opposing Internet censorship argue that Internet pornography is constitutionally legal because it allows people the freedom to choose. Freedom of choice does not account for innocent bystanders who type in a word completely unrelated to obscenity and get assaulted by hard-core material such as a young student doing a report on penguins typing in the key words *penguins sex* and being linked to pornographic sites (Weber, 1997, B10). And when we typed in the word *pornography* to search the Internet for sources, the first ten titles included a link for cyberporn promising free sex pictures and chat, a link for sex movies, a link for adult videos with the labels "20,000 Adult Videos" and "Warning: Totally Uncensored," and a link on marketing pornography on the Internet ("Excite Search Results: Pornography," 1997, pp. 1-2).

Most anyone who uses the Internet is aware that pornography abounds on-line. Nebraska Democrat Senator James Exon maintains, "It is not an exaggeration to say that the worst, most vile, most perverse pornography is only a few click-click-clicks away from any child on the Internet" (qtd. in "Case," 1997, p. 1). And Indiana Republican Senator Dan Coats claims, "The Internet is like taking a porn shop and putting it in your children's bedroom and then saying, 'Do not look'" (qtd. in "Case," 1997, p. 2). Because of these attitudes, the federal government is placing more emphasis on protecting minors than on any infringement of the First Amendment rights of adult users on the Internet. In fact, President Clinton declares, "I remain convinced . . . that our Constitution allows us to help parents . . . to prevent children from being exposed to objectionable material transmitted through computer networks" (qtd. in "Case," 1997, p. 2).

They provide suggestions for parents.

In addition to national laws, parents must continue to take responsibility for their children's involvement with the Internet. Organizations such as the Virginia-based anti-pornography group Enough is Enough encourage parents to spend quality time with their children to prevent children from depending on computer technology for recreation or for communicating on-line to others for companionship, to keep the computer in a public area of the house, to watch computer service bills to see how much time children spend on-line, and to keep children out of "chat" or "CB" sections of the Internet ("Take Action at Home," 1997, p. 2). And parents can teach children safe behavior on the Internet, develop acceptable use policies in the home, and act responsibly ("Child Safety on the Internet," 1997, p. 1).

<aside>Jared and Kristi restate their position in the conclusion.</aside>

The Internet's large, variable audience means there is a good chance that children will be subjected to pornography. Pornography is detrimental to society and especially to children. Because pornography is available in large quantities on the Internet, national legislation for censorship is needed to protect individual liberty, health, the economy, and morality and to aid parents in fulfilling their responsibilities in protecting their children. Censorship does not violate the First Amendment, but the great availability of electronic pornography limits a citizen's right not to choose to view such material. National laws prohibiting the transfer of pornography via the Internet need to be created, ratified, and enforced. And parents must take an active role in protecting their children from objectionable material on the Internet.

References

<aside>Jared and Kristi use APA documentation (see the Appendix).</aside>

Akdenziz, Y. (1996, December 5). UK Police ban of 133 news groups. <http://www.leeds.ac.uk/laws/pgs/yaman/newsban.htm> (1997, May 22).

Child safety on the Internet. (n.d.) <http://www.voicenet.com/~cranmer/censorship.html> (1997, August 1).

Detwieter, K. (1996, June 28). Democracy and decency on the Internet. *Chronicles of Higher Education,* p. A40.

Enough is Enough. (n.d.) Take action at home: Safeguard your home from computer pornography. <http://www.familyhost.com/inaugural/eie/action.htm> (1997, August 1).

Excite search results: Pornography. (n.d.). <http://www.excite.com/search.gw? trace=1&search=pornography> (1997, August 1).

Sussman, V. (1995, May 22). Hate, murder and mayhem on the net. *U.S. News and World Report, 118* (20), 62.

Tejada, C. (1996, December 9). The Internet are my kids safe? *Wall Street Journal,* p. 14R.

The case for the Communication Decency Act. (1997, May 13). <http://www.cnn.com/us/9702/eda.scotus/for/index.html> (1997, May 5).

U.S. Attorney's Office. (1997, May 20). Malden man pleads guilty to possession of child pornography, U.S. Attorney reports. <http://biz.yahoo.com/prnews/97/05/20/mitbx_5.html> (1997, May 21).

Weber, T. (1997, January 16). Net interest. *Wall Street Journal,* p. B10.

They use print and
electronic sources.

EXPLORING YOUR OPTIONS

1. Identify a problem paragraph in your own paper.

2. Read the paragraph at least twice.

3. Summarize the ideas and examples in a single brief sentence.

_____

_____

_____

4. Treat the summary sentence as the beginning of a new paragraph, and list as many examples, statistics, definitions, and proofs as you can to illustrate the summary sentence.

    _____   _____

    _____   _____

    _____   _____

    _____   _____

5. Using the summary sentence as a topic sentence, rewrite the paragraph, incorporating the new examples.

    _____

    _____

    _____

    _____

    _____

    _____

    _____

6. Reread the new paragraph to see that it clearly and accurately does what you intended it to do.

7. Read the paragraphs immediately before and after the targeted paragraph.

8. Make whatever changes are necessary so that the new paragraph connects easily with the paragraphs before and after it.

WRITING TOGETHER

Sometimes rewriting can be difficult because you're too close to your own writing. Reworking someone else's essay is much easier. Team up with a classmate and help each other rewrite a particularly difficult paragraph.

1. Identify a problem paragraph in your own paper.

2. Trade with each other, and read the other's paragraph at least twice.

3. Summarize the ideas and examples in a single brief sentence.

4. Treat the summary sentence as the beginning of a new paragraph, and list as many examples, statistics, definitions, and proofs as you can to illustrate the summary sentence.

5. Using the summary sentence as a topic sentence, rewrite the paragraph, incorporating the new examples.

6. Reread the new paragraph to see that it clearly and accurately does what you intended it to do.

7. Read the paragraphs immediately before and after the targeted paragraph.

8. Return the reconstructed paragraph to your partner, and discuss the suggested changes.

EDITING

USING PUNCTUATION CORRECTLY

Punctuation makes writing easier to read. In this section we focus on basic punctuation rules. Use them to refresh your memory and as a resource for writing and editing on your own.

Semicolon ;

A semicolon has three possible uses: between two closely related independent clauses, before conjunctive adverbs or transitional phrases, and between items in a series that contains commas.

Use a semicolon between two closely related independent clauses.

James Brady <u>was hit</u> by an assassin's bullet; he <u>supports</u> gun control.

Semicolons are helpful in correcting run-on sentences (see Chapter 3).

Use a semicolon before conjunctive adverbs or transitional expressions. Conjunctive adverbs join two independent clauses or complete sentences. When you use a conjunctive adverb to connect two sentences, you must use a semicolon to indicate the sentence break. Notice that a comma usually follows the conjunctive adverb (see the introductory element comma rule in Chapter 2).

Many <u>people</u> in urban areas or changing neighborhoods <u>fear</u> the rising crime rate and the breakdown of law and order; *therefore,* these frightened <u>people</u> <u>are buying</u> guns.

COMMON CONJUNCTIVE ADVERBS

accordingly	however	nonetheless
also	indeed	otherwise
besides	instead	similarly
consequently	likewise	therefore
finally	meanwhile	thus
furthermore	moreover	
hence	nevertheless	

When you use a transitional expression to join two complete sentences, you must use a semicolon to indicate the sentence break. Transitional expressions—*for example, for instance, in addition,* and *now*—indicate relationships between sentences:

<u>Aggression</u> <u>has helped</u> people survive; *for example,* <u>it</u> <u>can motivate</u> people to act.

Use a semicolon between items in a series that contains commas.

Violent crimes have escalated against children; youth; women; the emotionally, mentally, or physically handicapped; and the elderly.

Urban violence has increased in Detroit, Michigan; Atlanta, Georgia; Houston, Texas; Seattle, Washington; and Washington, D.C.

Notice the semicolon that precedes the *and* before the final item in each series.

Colon :

Use a colon after a complete sentence to introduce a list or a brief explanation. The colon in this example introduces a list of reasons for opposing gun control:

> <u>People</u> who oppose gun control <u>offer</u> the following reasons: that the right to bear arms is a constitutional right and that guns protect people from danger.

Don't use a colon after the words *namely* or *such as; a* colon means *namely* or *such as.* Use one or the other, not both.

> Incorrect: People who oppose gun control legislation offer reasons such as: . . .

> Correct: People against gun control legislation offer reasons such as . . .

Dash —

Use a dash to indicate an abrupt change of thought or to emphasize what follows.

> The eighty-seven-year-old great-grandmother feels safe in her home—when she's holding her gun.

> The parents—with three young children—feel guns are too dangerous for their home.

Dashes rarely are used in college writing, especially in the sciences and social sciences, but they can be effective. To create a dash, type two hyphens with no space between them.

Parentheses ( )

Use parentheses to set off information that may be helpful or interesting to readers but that is not central to the message of the sentence.

> Violence on television (for instance, in movies, in cartoons, and on news broadcasts) can frighten small children.

In this sentence, the parenthetical information—"for instance, in movies, in cartoons, and on news broadcasts"—could be deleted, and the sentence still would be clear:

> Violence on television can frighten small children.

However, the parenthetical information helps the reader by providing examples of the types of television programs that display violence.

Quotation Marks " "

Quotation marks are used primarily to set off direct quotations, to indicate that a word or phrase is being used in a special way, and to identify the titles of short works.

Use quotation marks around direct quotations. The most common use of quotation marks is to indicate a speaker's exact words:

My grandmother said, "I love you. Now be good."

The quotation marks enclose everything the speaker says. The introduction to the quotation is set off with a comma.

Don't use quotation marks with an indirect quotation:

My grandmother said that she loves me and that I should be good.

Use quotation marks around words with special meanings. To indicate that a word or phrase is being used in an unusual way, place the word or phrase in quotation marks:

Government agencies sometimes refer to deliberate misrepresentations of truth or lies as "misinformation."

In this case *misinformation* means more than a casual misunderstanding of some information; it means a conscious decision to mislead the public.

Use quotation marks to set off the titles of essays, chapters, short stories, poems, songs, television episodes, or other short works.

Dr. Martin Luther King, Jr. wrote an influential essay entitled "Pilgrimage to Nonviolence."

Robert Frost's poem "Mending Wall" questions whether good fences make good neighbors.

Using Quotation Marks with Other Punctuation

Put commas and periods inside quotation marks.

After reading Countee Cullee's poem "Incident," we discussed racial prejudice.

People often misunderstand the ideas Robert Keith Miller writes about in his essay "Discrimination Is a Virtue."

Put semicolons and colons outside quotation marks.

Alice Walker writes about being blind in one eye in her essay "Beauty: When the Other Dancer Is the Self"; because of her experience, I have begun to think about myself differently.

We plan to discuss the following issues suggested in Robert Frost's poem "Home Burial": gender differences, grief, poor communication, and marital strife.

Put question marks and exclamation points inside quotation marks if they apply only to the quoted material and not to the entire sentence.

His boss asked, "Are you being honest?"

He immediately answered, "Of course I am!"

In the first example, the quoted information is a question, so the question mark is inside the quotation marks. In the second, the employee's quoted answer is emphatic, so the exclamation point comes inside the quotation marks.

Put question marks and exclamation points outside quotation marks if they apply to the overall sentence in which the quoted material appears.

Did she say, "That's only gossip"?

He has no right to say, "I thought it was true"!

In the first example, the entire sentence is a question introduced by "Did she say," so the question mark is outside the end quotation mark. The same principle applies to the second sentence, where the entire sentence receives the emphasis of the exclamation point.

Italics and Underlining

Italics and underlining serve the same purpose. If you use a word processor, you may be able to print out italic type. If you type or write by hand, you can indicate italicized material by underlining it.

Use italics (or underlining) to indicate the titles of individually produced works. Titles of books, plays, magazines, newspapers, films, paintings, statues, record albums, CDs, tapes, and radio or TV series should be italicized (or underlined):

> Robert Pirsig's book *Zen and the Art of Motorcycle Maintenance* is more than an account of a motorcycle road trip.
>
> *The Fisher King* is a movie about people coping in today's society.
>
> *Newsweek* has devoted an issue to cheating in colleges and universities.

Use italics (or underlining) to show emphasis. Usually emphasis should come with word choice, not with punctuation. However, occasionally it is appropriate to stress a word or phrase by using italics (or underlining):

> *You* are the one who makes a difference in your own life.
>
> Do *not* let gossip enter the conversation.

Use italics (or underlining) to refer to words or letters used as words or letters.

> The word *dog* is spelled *d-o-g*.

Ellipsis Points . . .

Use ellipsis points to signal omissions from quoted material. If you have to omit material from quoted information, let the reader know you've left something out by inserting ellipsis points in its place. For example, a sentence from an essay by Michael Demerset entitled "The Fine Art of Putting Things Off" reads:

> There is a difference, of course, between chronic procrastination and purposeful postponement, particularly in the higher echelons of business.

Suppose you decide not to use the phrases *of course* and *particularly in the higher echelons of business* in your quotation. To show the omissions, you would use ellipsis points:

> There is a difference . . . between chronic procrastination and purposeful postponement. . . .

Notice that ellipsis points are *three* periods separated by spaces. The first point at the beginning of the second omission is a sentence period, not an ellipsis point.

Brackets [ ]

Use brackets to interject your own comments into quoted material or to clarify words within a quotation.

> He [Joe Jensen] road [rode] 23 miles on horseback to return the two bits [25 cents].

Notice the misspelling of *rode*. By seeing the correct spelling in brackets, readers know that the mistake was in the original passage. Another way to show that an error was made in the original is to write the Latin word *sic* (which means "thus") in brackets:

> He road [*sic*] 23 miles on horseback to return the two bits.

Apostrophe '

The apostrophe has two main functions: to indicate possession and to indicate the omission of letters or numbers.

Use an apostrophe to show possession. The placement of an apostrophe to indicate possession depends on whether the owner word is singular or plural. If the word is singular, show possession with *'s:*

Joan's gratitude	anybody's guess
my friend's dog	the athlete's strength

If the word is plural, add an apostrophe after the *s (s')*.

the neighbors' attitudes	the girls' bikes
the Johnsons' car	the athletes' strength

If the owner word is singular and ends in the letter *s*, add *'s* to show possession:

Kris's self-control	Charles's suit

If a plural word doesn't end in *s*, indicate possession with *'s:*

men's ideas	children's ideas
women's ideas	people's ideas

Possessive pronouns do not require an apostrophe.

POSSESSIVE PRONOUNS

my	your	its	their
mine	yours	her	theirs
our	his	hers	whose
ours			

Use an apostrophe to indicate that letters or numbers have been omitted. The most common use of apostrophes to show omissions are *contractions,* two words condensed into one. The words *should not* become *shouldn't*: the apostrophe signals the omission of the letter *o.* Place the apostrophe exactly where the letters are left out:

I am	I'm
you are	you're
it is, it has	it's
they are	they're

Some pronoun contractions sound like possessive pronouns. Don't confuse them:

It's (not *its*) a virtue to be patient.

They're (not *their*) listening to each other.

Who's (not *whose*) spreading those rumors?

You're (not *your*) self-reliant.

Capital Letters

Capitalize the first word of every sentence. Any word that follows a sentence period should begin with a capital letter. (*Note:* The periods that follow abbreviations like *Mr.* and *Ms.* are not sentence periods.)

The senior citizens are sponsoring a fund-raising project. They want to help finance a gym for the youth center.

Capitalize the first word of every direct quotation.

The mayor asks, "How can we improve our city's neighborhoods?"

"We can have a city clean-up week," responds a citizen, "and the city can set up special dropoff locations for hazardous wastes like paints, batteries, and oil."

Capitalize the first, last, and important words in a title. Prepositions, conjunctions, and the words *a, an, the,* and *to* do not require capitals in a title:

Everything You Need to Know about Your Community is a valuable book for concerned citizens.

Capitalize the names of people, places, languages, races, and nationalities.

Aunt Belva	Finnish	African American
Uruguay	English	Hispanic

Capitalize the names of months, days of the week, and holidays.

March	Thursday	Memorial Day

Don't capitalize the names of seasons:

summer	autumn	winter

Capitalize the title of a relationship or a position when it replaces or follows a person's name.

I'll ask Mayor Boyle for her support.

I'll also ask Dad to become involved in community projects.

Ron Messer, President of Sunshine, Inc., will help finance the playground.

Capitalize the titles of particular people, places, or items, but do not capitalize general terms.

The President of the United States supports environmental programs.

The president of the corporation supports environmental programs.

The city created a greenbelt on the Snake River.

The city created a greenbelt on the river.

We are from the Midwest.

We drove south.

She's taking Ecology 203 and Political Science 304.

She's taking courses in ecology and city government.

The Upper Valley Community College faculty donated trees to the new city park.

The community college faculty donated trees to the new city park.

Capitalize the personal pronoun *I*.

EXERCISE 1   Correctly punctuate and add capitalization to the following sentences.

1. walter lippmann has said that the mass media paint an imagined world that influences what men and women will do and say at any particular moment

2. mr lippmann a distinguished political analyst has written the book public opinion

3. in a newspaper article entitled the long arm of what you watch michael medved the cohost of pbss sneak previews discusses the relationship between entertainment and violence.

4. medved says that we are unaware of the impact of a single 30 second ad

5. george gerbner and his research associates have determined that heavy television viewers those who watch more than four hours a

day have different attitudes and beliefs than light viewers those who watch less than four hours a day

6. these researchers claim heavy viewers express more racially prejudiced attitudes overestimate the number of people employed as physicians lawyers and athletes and perceive women as having more limited abilities and interests than men

7. two professors of psychology at the university of california santa cruz say that we seldom ask ourselves questions such as why are they showing me this story on the evening news rather than some other one is the world really this violent and crime ridden

8. bernard cohen a political scientist observes the mass media may not be successful much of the time in telling people what to think but it is stunningly successful in telling its readers what to think about

EXERCISE 2   Below is a passage from Dr. Martin Luther King's "I Have a Dream" speech without punctuation. Punctuate and add capitalization to the passage.

five score years ago a great american in whose symbolic shadow we stand signed the emancipation proclamation this momentous decree came as a great beacon light of hope to millions of negro slaves who had been seared in the flames of withering injustice it came as a joyous daybreak to end the long night of captivity but one hundred years later we must face the tragic fact that the negro is still not free one hundred

years later the life of the negro is still sadly crippled by the manacles of
segregation and the chains of discrimination one hundred years later
the negro lives on a lonely island of poverty in the midst of a vast ocean
of material prosperity one hundred years later the negro is still lan-
guished in the corners of american society and finds himself an exile in
his own land so we have come here today to dramatize an appalling
condition in a sense we have come to our nations capital to cash a
check when the architects of our republic wrote the magnificent words
of the constitution and the declaration of independence they were sign-
ing a promissory note to which every american was to fall heir this
note was a promise that all men would be guaranteed the unalienable
rights of life liberty and the pursuit of happiness it is obvious today
that america has defaulted on this promissory note insofar as her citizens of color are concerned instead of honoring this sacred obligation
america has given the negro people a bad check a check which has
come back marked insufficient funds but we refuse to believe that the
bank of justice is bankrupt we refuse to believe that there are insufficient funds in the great vaults of opportunity of this nation so we have
come to cash this check a check that will give us upon demand the
riches of freedom and the security of justice we have also come to this
hallowed spot to remind america of the fierce urgency of now this is no
time to engage in the luxury of cooling off or to take the tranquilizing
drug of gradualism now is the time to make real the promises of democ-

racy now is the time to rise from the dark and desolate valley of segregation to the sunlit path of racial justice now is the time to open doors of opportunity to all of gods children now is the time to lift our nation from the quicksands of racial injustice to the solid rock of brotherhood

EXERCISE 3   Using the current draft of your essay, do the following:

1. Correctly punctuate five sentences using semicolons.

2. Correctly punctuate a sentence using a colon.

3. Correctly punctuate a sentence using quotation marks.

4. Correctly punctuate a sentence using parentheses.

5. Identify five sentences that contain apostrophes. Label the reasons for using apostrophes.

6. Identify five sentences that contain internal capitalization. Label the reasons for using capitalization.

OPTIONS FOR WRITING

Reflect

1. Think back to television programs you watched while you were growing up. Describe one or two programs that you remember watching faithfully. Explain how these programs may have helped shape your attitudes toward yourself, toward others, and toward life.

2. Pick a favorite cassette tape or CD from your collection—one that you've owned for a few years—and play one song. As you listen, write down the associations or memories that come to mind. What were you doing when you first heard the song? What other people, places, or events does it remind you of? Now write an essay discussing the influence music has had on your life by using a single song or artist as your extended example.

Inform

3. Find a recent issue of a magazine you like to read—*Time, Science Digest, Ebony, Newsweek, Sports Illustrated, Ms., Rolling Stone, Glamour, Jet, New Yorker,* and so forth. Your purpose is to determine current trends in magazine advertising. Using only the full-page ads as your subject, collect at least three ads and take notes on their important features: use of color, design, personalities, slogans, or whatever else occurs frequently. What conclusions can you draw from your investigation?

4. Local governments are run by average hard-working citizens—by clerks, engineers, and maintenance personnel—who are rarely recognized by the media. Identify and interview a public employee in your town or county about his or her function in and contributions to the local government. Write an article for the local newspaper in which you pay tribute to a single public employee.

Persuade

5. Examine your neighborhood to determine ways it could be improved. Perhaps an older person's home needs repair or painting, a playground or park needs upkeep or new equipment, or a vacant lot needs cleaning up. Make tentative plans for a single project. Then write a letter to a local radio or television station persuading them to run a public service announcement persuading your community to get involved in the project. Describe benefits, costs, and alternatives.

6. Consult with your local United Way or other charitable organization representative to learn how they use the media to get their messages out to the community. Evaluate their media presentations, and write an essay on how persuasive and informative these campaigns are. Now persuade someone you know to make a contribution to that organization.

Speculate

7. As a student you have been standing in long lines to use the campus computer center to type your class assignments, e-mail your parents, and research on the Internet. You recognize that there simply are not enough computer facilities on campus. Write a letter to the administration proposing a solution to this problem.

8. "Let the buyer beware" is a time-honored maxim for all consumers. Write a letter to the Better Business Bureau explaining some consumer problem or rip-off that you've recently experienced and suggest a solution that will prevent others from being exploited.

APPENDIX

—~—

Researching and Documenting

RESEARCHING

Here are some basic guidelines for doing research.

Choose a general topic. Begin with a topic that is broad enough to explore yet narrow enough to give you some focus. For example, the topic homelessness is more specific than the topic poverty but not as limited as the topic homeless men under age twenty-five on State Street.

Use the *Library of Congress Subject Headings* index. The *Library of Congress Subject Headings* index makes research easier by standardizing the terms libraries use to catalog information. To use the LOC index, simply locate your topic, say homelessness, in the alphabetized volumes. On the next page is shown a page from the index. On it you can find the entry *Homelessness*. The subject homelessness is divided into three general categories: BT, RT, and NT. The initials *BT* stand for "broader terms" (*housing, poverty*); the initials *RT* stand for "related terms" (*homeless persons*); and the initials *NT* stand for "narrower terms" (*domicile in public welfare, housing—effects of wars on, relief stations [for the poor]*).

The LOC index also is useful in other ways. For instance, after the entry *homelessness* is the abbreviation *May Subd Geog*, which means "may be subdivided geographically." This is helpful if you are researching homelessness in your own state. You would look up the state in the LOC index to see if there's an entry *homelessness*.

The LOC index also lists general call numbers to direct you to specific locations within the library. For example, in the entry *Homeless Students* is *LC5144–LC5144.3,* the range of call numbers under which you will find books on homeless students.

Read general references. Begin reading background information about your topic in general reference books—the *Encyclopedia Americana,* the *New Encyclopaedia Britannica, Compton's Encyclopedia,*

Home service insurance
  USE Industrial life insurance
Home sharing
  USE Shared housing
Home shopping
  USE Teleshopping
Home sites
  USE Homesites
Home sounds
  USE Household sounds
Home storage
  USE Storage in the home
Home study courses
  USE Correspondence schools and courses
      Self-culture
      Singing—Methods—Self-instruction
Home swapping
  USE Home exchanging
Home teaching by parents
  USE Home schooling
Home training in Christian education
  USE Christian education—Home training
Home training in Jewish religious education
  USE Jewish religious education—Home
      training
Home training in religious education
  USE Religious education—Home training
Home video systems (May Subd Geog)
  BT Home entertainment systems
      Television
  NT Camcorders
      Direct broadcast satellite television
      Television cameras
      Television display systems
      Video tapes
      Videocassette recorders
Home video systems industry
  (May Subd Geog)
  ⸢HD9696.T46-HD9696.T464⸣
  BT Television supplies industry
Home visit programs
  USE Home-based family services
Home visiting (Church work)
  USE Visitations (Church work)
Home visiting (Religious education)
  USE Visitations (Religious education)
Home visiting in Christian education
  USE Visitations in Christian education
Home workshops
  USE Workshops
Homebirth
  USE Childbirth at home
Homebound, Library services for the
  USE Public libraries—Services to shut-ins
Homeland (Baltimore, Md.)
  UF Baltimore (Md.). Homeland
Homeland (Theology)
  UF Fatherland (Theology)
      Native land (Theology)
  BT Theology, Doctrinal
Homeland in literature
Homelands (South Africa)
  ⸢DT1760⸣
  UF Bantoetuislande (South Africa)
      Bantu Homelands (South Africa)
      Bantustans (South Africa)
      Black Homelands (South Africa)
      South African Homelands (South
          Africa)
      Tuislande (South Africa)
Homeless adults
  USE Homeless persons
Homeless aged (May Subd Geog)
  ⸢HV4480-HV4630⸣
  UF Aged, Homeless
  BT Aged
      Homeless persons
Homeless camps (May Subd Geog)
  UF Camps for the homeless (Camp sites)
      Car camps for the homeless
      Homeless car camps

  BT Camp sites, facilities, etc.
Homeless car camps
  USE Homeless camps
Homeless children (May Subd Geog)
  UF Children, Homeless
  BT Children
      Homeless persons
  NT Abandoned children
      Runaway children
Homeless people
  USE Homeless persons
Homeless persons (May Subd Geog)
  UF Homeless adults
      Homeless people
      Street people
  BT Persons
  RT Homelessness
  NT Church work with the homeless
      Homeless aged
      Homeless children
      Homeless students
      Homeless veterans
      Homeless women
      Homeless youth
      Libraries and the homeless
      Police services for the homeless
      Rogues and vagabonds
      Shelters for the homeless
      Social work with the homeless
      Tramps
      Underground homeless persons
  — Mental health services
      (May Subd Geog)
  — — Law and legislation
      (May Subd Geog)
  — Services for (May Subd Geog)
  — — Law and legislation
      (May Subd Geog)
Homeless persons and libraries
  USE Libraries and the homeless
Homeless persons' gardens
  (May Subd Geog)
  ⸢SB457.4.H64⸣
  UF Gardens of the homeless
  BT Gardens
Homeless persons shelters
  USE Shelters for the homeless
Homeless persons' writings
  UF Writings of homeless persons
      Writings of the homeless
  BT Literature
Homeless persons' writings, American
  (May Subd Geog)
  ⸢PS153.H (History)⸣
  ⸢PS508.H (Collections)⸣
  UF American homeless person's writings
  BT American literature
Homeless students (May Subd Geog)
  ⸢LC5144-LC5144.3⸣
  UF Homelessness (Students)
      Students, Homeless
  BT Homeless persons
      Students
Homeless veterans (May Subd Geog)
  UF Veterans, Homeless
  BT Homeless persons
      Veterans
Homeless women (May Subd Geog)
  UF Bag ladies
      Shopping bag ladies
  BT Homeless persons
      Tramps
      Women
Homeless youth (May Subd Geog)
  UF Youth, Homeless
  BT Homeless persons
      Youth
  RT Street youth
Homelessness (May Subd Geog)
  BT Housing
      Poverty

  RT Homeless persons
  NT Domicile in public welfare
      Housing—Effect of wars on
  — Law and legislation (May Subd Geog)
  — Religious aspects
  — — Buddhism, ⸢Christianity, etc.⸣
Homelessness (Students)
  USE Homeless students
Homelessness in literature (Not Subd Geog)
Homem de Pessoa de Saa family
  (Not Subd Geog)
  UF Homen de Pessoa de Saa family
Homemaker service
  USE Visiting housekeepers
Homemakers (May Subd Geog)
  BT Persons
  NT Displaced homemakers
      Househusbands
      Housewives
Homemaking centers
  USE Home economics centers
Homemaking departments
  USE Home economics centers
Homemates
  USE Roommates
Homen de Pessoa de Saa family
  USE Homem de Pessoa de Saa family
Homeo box genes
  USE Homeobox genes
Homeobox genes
  ⸢QH447.8.H65⸣
  UF Homeo box genes
      Homeotic genes
  BT Genes
Homeomorphisms
  ⸢QA614 (QA613.7)⸣
  BT Manifolds (Mathematics)
      Topological spaces
      Transformation groups
  NT Isotopies (Topology)
Homeopathic hospitals
  USE Homeopathy—Hospitals and
      dispensaries
Homeopathic pharmacy
  USE Pharmacy, Homeopathic
Homeopathic physicians (May Subd Geog)
  UF Homeopaths
  BT Physicians
  — Biography
      UF Homeopathy—Biography
Homeopathic research
  USE Homeopathy—Research
Homeopathic veterinary medicine
  (May Subd Geog)
  ⸢SF746⸣
  UF Animals—Diseases—Homeopathic
          treatment
      Domestic animals—Diseases—
          Homeopathic treatment
      Livestock—Diseases—Homeopathic
          treatment
      Veterinary homeopathy
      Veterinary medicine, Homeopathic
      ⸢Former heading⸣
  BT Alternative veterinary medicine
      Homeopathy
Homeopaths
  USE Homeopathic physicians
Homeopathy (May Subd Geog)
  ⸢RX⸣
  UF Homoeopathy
  BT Alternative medicine
  SA subdivision Homeopathic treatment
      under individual diseases and
      groups of diseases, e.g. Cancer—
      Homeopathic treatment
  NT Electrohomeopathy
      Homeopathic veterinary medicine
      Medicine, Biochemic
      Obstetrics, Homeopathic
      Pharmacopoeias, Homeopathic

and *World Book Encyclopedia.* These sources offer both general background on your topic and specific terms, concepts, statistics, and authorities. Also, larger entries often conclude with a bibliography of important sources and a list of the names of leading authorities in that particular field.

Use specialized references. Once you have background information on your topic, use specialized reference books to locate more specific information. These specialized reference books include discipline-specific dictionaries and encyclopedias.

Begin limiting your topic. To begin limiting your topic, ask yourself, "Is there a question I could ask about my topic that could be answered in a research paper?" That question becomes your *issue question*—the working thesis statement—for your paper. To develop an issue question, try this approach:

1. On a piece of paper, write your general topic.

2. Choose an area of interest. As you read general background information about your topic, choose an area that interests you. For example, while you're reading about homelessness, you realize that you are more interested in the children of homeless families than in the homelessness associated with drug or alcohol abuse, the homelessness of people who are mentally ill, or the homelessness of veterans.

3. Form an issue question. Children of homeless families is a viable topic for research. Now frame the topic in the form of a simple question, something like, How does homelessness affect children? or What organizations provide support to the children of homeless families? This question becomes your working thesis statement.

Search card catalogs. A card catalog (which today often is computerized) lists the books available in a particular library. The system is arranged by subject, author, or book title. Make a list of several books that look promising and note the sources for future reference either on index cards or in a journal. (In the section on documenting in this appendix, we describe the correct format to use for listing sources.)

Search periodical indexes. Periodicals (magazines or journals that are distributed periodically) are important because the information in them is current. Periodical indexes list information on articles published in both general and specific periodicals. These indexes function like a card catalog. Look up (if the index is bound) or enter (if the index is computerized) your general topic. On index cards or in your journal make a note of articles that look promising. (Bound indexes frequently use abbreviations that are explained at the beginning of the index.)

Obtain sources. Find the books, journals, magazines, and newspapers you've noted, a few at a time, and scan them quickly in the library. For an overview of a book, look at the table of contents, the preface, and the index. For an article look at the headings and read the first and last paragraphs. As you scan each work, add to your bibliographical notes your comments about the value of the source—for example, "No good, doesn't pertain," "Housing statistics on page 439," or "Long article; looks good." Don't read the material yet; just scan so that you can make brief comments that will help you later, when you read and take notes on the source.

Continue to limit your topic as you research. As you scan or read, keep revising your topic, limiting it to the information you now have.

Begin taking accurate notes that you can work with. Select your best source to start taking notes. The first source you read is going to influence your thinking on the topic, so be sure that source is reliable. You probably will take more notes on the first source than on the others. (You will tend to use later sources to elaborate on, substantiate, or invalidate the facts you pick up from your first source.) Your notes should be accurate, useful, and just detailed enough. Don't waste time on unnecessary details: You're not a human photocopying machine!

Learn when to paraphrase and when to quote. You will be taking two kinds of notes from your sources: paraphrases and quotations. Both kinds of notes are useful, but as much as possible take down the information in your own words. Use exact quotations sparingly, for these special reasons:

A quotation is the best evidence to support a fact or an opinion.

The author has expressed the idea with unusual clarity, brilliance, or brevity.

The quotation is of interest in itself for its expression or content.

Take adequate but not excessive notes. The sooner you focus on an exact topic and issue question, the fewer notes you have to take. (You always take more notes than you eventually use!) Only you can tell when you have taken enough notes to write a convincing paper. But don't sacrifice clarity for brevity. Take down enough information so that you can tell what the notes mean.

If possible, take all your notes on four-by-six-inch index cards. Put only one kind of information on a card, and try to make your notes brief enough that you don't run over onto a second card. If you do, label the cards *a* and *b,* and keep them together. Don't write on the back of the index cards.

Writing a Summary

A summary is a brief restatement of a text in your own words. Like any good writing, a summary requires prewriting, drafting, rewriting, and editing. These are the major steps in writing a summary:

1. Read the text carefully. Underline (only if you own the source) major points, examples, definitions, and explanations.

2. Determine the author's purpose for writing.

3. Restate the author's thesis statement or controlling idea and purpose in your own words.

4. Summarize as briefly as you can the rest of the text by writing a one- or two-sentence summary for every paragraph or for every major section.

5. Read the draft of your summary, and then rewrite it, omitting all minor points, examples, definitions, and explanations.

6. Read your summary for accuracy and coherence.

7. Edit your summary for errors.

After you've taken a series of notes on the cards, read each card, see exactly what it says, and summarize it with a "slug," or title, at the top of the card. Don't do this immediately after taking the notes. You don't want to include material you remember from the source that is not actually on the card.

Indicate the source of each note in a corner of the card with the author's name and the relevant page number. Do this immediately, or you may forget the source of the note. Be sure to include the page reference.

Whether you paraphrase or quote directly, be exact. Don't confuse what the author says with what you would have said or with what you wish the author had said. If you want to make a comment of your own on a note card, enclose it in brackets to distinguish your comments from the words or intent of the person you're citing.

Organize your information. With a revised outline in front of you, scan your note cards and think through your topic again. Revise your outline as necessary, so that it completely and accurately represents your views and purpose for writing the paper.

Draft your paper. Write your first draft, scratching and scribbling at will. With your outline and your note cards arranged to conform to the outline, check that the draft represents your final paper in the rough.

Work toward the final draft. Continue to work toward the final draft of your paper with one eye on the revised outline and the other on your first and later drafts. Topics and subtopics should be in order and stated clearly.

Finalize your research report. Prepare a final draft of the paper. Arrange and type your bibliographical notes alphabetically by author's last name (see End-of-Text Documentation, beginning on page 327). Make a title page, table of contents, and any other elements your instructor has requested.

INTERNET RESEARCH

The Internet has become a valuable source for gathering information. Vast amounts of sources are available with the mere click of a mouse. Unfortunately, only small amounts of this material are of high quality. When publishing printed sources, say in professional journals, authors consciously focus on research, verification, and documentation to ensure professional integrity and accuracy. Before these printed articles are accepted for publication, numerous professionals evaluate the author's work to verify its quality. Whereas with electronic sources, anyone can place anything on the Internet without checking quality.

Consequently, before beginning electronic searches, be familiar with traditional forms of research and sources to provide the proper foundation for determining the quality of Internet information. To help determine the credibility of any author, answer three basic questions:

1. Is the author an authority in the field?

2. Do other authorities agree with or support the author's claims?

3. Is the document, either print or electronic, published in a reputable form? (Is it published in a book, in a professional journal, at a research center, or at a professional conference?)

Three avenues for locating Internet information are a college or university home page, an address bar, and search engines.

College Home Page

Many colleges and universities offer Internet access to students through computer labs or centers. Often these college home pages contain school-selected search tools such as links to campus and off-campus libraries, business and government sources, and other off-campus home pages. Ask your computer help desk for basic information or where to go for assistance.

Address Bar

The address bar located across the top of the Internet screen allows you to obtain information if you have a specific Internet address. For example:

http://www.hmco.com

Since it's difficult to determine the reliability of a source, some common, more authoritative domain suffixes include:

.com = business	.gov = government
.edu = college/university	.mil = military
.org = non-profit organization	.net = network

- Click on address bar to type a complete address.
- Press **Enter** and select desired links or connections to other electronic documents.

Search Engines

Search engines are a great place to start researching. Search engines are indexes or Web directories that help locate information.

- Click on the **Net Search** icon. A list of search engines will appear on the screen.
- Choose a search engine with an appropriate level of difficulty—some are easier to use than others.

Levels of Difficulty

☆ Easy—start here

☆☆ Good—somewhat challenging

☆☆☆ Difficult—not for beginners

☆ Yahoo!   ☆☆ Multiple Search

☆ Hotbot   ☆☆ CUSI Search

☆ Excite   ☆☆ Web Crawler

☆ Alta Vista   ☆☆☆ Archies

☆ Galaxy   ☆☆☆ Veronica

- Click on the search box to type your topic's keywords. Click on **Search.**

- A list will appear giving you a brief summary of the pages found on the Internet that most likely match your query.

- Click on the colored words to link you to the Internet page described.

- Once you have viewed a few web sites, you may wish to return to a previous one. To do this, use the Back/Forward icons located at the top of the screen.

Storing Research Electronic Information

There are two ways to store and save the information you gather from electronic sources. You may either print the information by clicking on the printer icon. You may also save the information to your disk to pull up later for screen viewing.

DOCUMENTING

Documentation is the process of attributing material so that readers know which ideas or words are yours and which are not. Documentation strengthens your arguments by showing that you've researched and evaluated information to arrive at your conclusions. And documentation helps protect against charges of plagiarism.

Carefully avoid plagiarism. Be sure that you're not guilty of any of the following:

Word-for-word plagiarism Word-for-word plagiarism includes the submission of another student's work as your own, the submission of any material written by someone other than yourself without proper acknowledgment (documentation), and the submission of someone's words without the proper use of quotation marks.

Patchwork-quilt plagiarism   Don't make the mistake of passing off as an original paper one that is stitched together from phrases and sentences taken from various sources. Simply rearranging someone else's phrases doesn't confer originality.

Unacknowledged paraphrased plagiarism   Restatement by means of paraphrasing or even the use of an author's idea without acknowledgment is plagiarism. The only material that doesn't need to be documented is material that consists of your own words and ideas or information that generally is known by most people.

To write an effective research paper, you must know how to document. Documentation is usually a two-part process. First is the in-text documentation, the credit you give to an author in the text of a report. Second is the end-of-text documentation, the list of bibliographical information at the end of the report.

The method of documentation you use depends on the discipline in which you're working. Most professors prefer one of two styles: MLA (Modern Language Association) or APA (American Psychological Association). The information you list in both styles is essentially the same, but the arrangement of the information differs.

In-Text Documentation

In-text documentation signals readers that you are using someone else's ideas or words. In-text documentation introduces the source and parenthetically indicates individual page numbers. Below are guidelines for incorporating in-text documentation into your research paper according to both MLA and APA styles. Notice that APA style requires the year in the in-text documentation.

1. **Signal the beginning of quotations and paraphrases with the name of the authority.**

   When you can, introduce each quotation or paraphrase with the name of the authority:

   MLA

   Ryan Jackson argues that many parents today are just not equipped for parenthood (42).

   APA

   Ryan Jackson argues that many parents today are just not equipped for parenthood (1990, p. 42).

2. **Give relevant page numbers.** Include a page number immediately after the quotation or paraphrase (as shown above) or immediately after the name of the authority:

MLA

Ryan Jackson (42) argues that many parents today are just not equipped for parenthood.

APA

Ryan Jackson (1990, p. 42) argues that many parents today are just not equipped for parenthood.

3. **If it does not appear in the text, include the authority's name in the citation.** When you do not use the authority's name to introduce the material, include the name in parentheses along with the relevant page number:

MLA

He says, "The new parent has lost the wisdom and daily support of older, more experienced family members" (Jackson 42).

APA

He says, "The new parent has lost the wisdom and daily support of older, more experienced family members" (Jackson, 1990, p. 42).

4. **Cite every borrowed item.** Every borrowed item needs a citation of some sort. Especially avoid quoting or paraphrasing a full paragraph with just one citation to the source at the very end. Every sentence with borrowed material must contain a signal to the reader: the authority's name, quotation marks, a reference page number, or a pronoun reference.

5. **Keep citations short.** Keep in-text citations short, but be sure that you provide all necessary information in the text or in the parenthetical citation.

6. **Include the title of the work whenever necessary.** When more than one work by an author is cited, the author's name, and the relevant page number aren't enough information because your bibliographical list has at least two references to the same writer. In this case, add a shortened version of the title.

7. **Use different types of introductions.** Look for variety in your introductions to short quotations and paraphrases. Here's a list of different ways of saying "The author says. . . ."

Melville sympathized . . .

Snow replies . . .

Carpenter identifies . . .

Matthew reveals . . .

Lundquist develops . . .

Wilke persuades . . .

Terence wished . . .

Ericksen refutes . . .

Scoresby insists . . .

Compton counters . . .

Andersen notes . . .

Usanga introduces . . .

Weaver sees . . .

McKay shows . . .

Wright suggests . . .

Hansen substantiates . . .

Frampton adds . . .

Brunson summarizes . . .

Woodward believes . . .

Seagers begins . . .

Taylor mentions . . .

Hopkin proposes . . .

Redding portrays . . .

Billings confirms . . .

Ohwiler reports . . .

Flint submits . . .

Tolman thinks . . .

Walker wants . . .

Carlton asks . . .

Kennedy indicates . . .

Gerzeli describes . . .

Mitchell points out . . .

Herd observes . . .

Curtis accepts . . .

Lee admits . . .

McMillan affirms . . .

Behling concludes . . .

Baker offers . . .

Wing emphasizes . . .

Armstrong ends . . .

Glick provides . . .

According to Anderson . . .

End-of-Text Documentation

At the end of your report, list the sources you quoted from or paraphrased. This list is called *Works Cited, References,* or *Bibliography.* It is arranged alphabetically by author's last name and should be set up with a hanging indent (the first line of a citation runs from margin to margin, and subsequent lines are indented five spaces for MLA and paragraph indent for APA). The format of end-of-text documentation must be exact.

Here are some of the most commonly used sources arranged first according to MLA style and then according to APA style.

A book by one author

MLA

da Costa Nunez, Ralph. *The New Poverty: Homeless Families in America*. New York: Insight Books, 1996.

APA

da Costa Nunez, R. (1996). *The new poverty: Homeless families in America*. New York: Insight Books.

A book by two or three authors

MLA

Ficker, Victor B., and Herbert S. Graves. *Deprivation in America*. Beverly Hills, CA: Glencoe, 1971.

APA

Ficker, V. B., & Graves, H. S. (1971). *Deprivation in America*. Beverly Hills, CA: Glencoe.

An edited book

MLA

Pugh, Deborah, and Jeanie Tietjen, eds. *I Have Arrived Before My Words: Autobiographical Writings of Homeless Women*. Alexandria, VA: Charles River Press, 1997.

APA

Pugh, D., & Tietjen, J. (Eds.). (1997). *I have arrived before my words: Autobiographical writings of homeless women*. Alexandria, VA: Charles River Press.

Selection reprinted in an anthology

MLA

Magnet, Myron. "The Rich and the Poor." *Writing in the Disciplines: A Reader for Writers*. 2nd ed. Mary Lynch Kennedy, William J. Kennedy, and Hadley M. Smith, eds. Englewood Cliffs, NJ: Prentice Hall, 1990. 339–350.

APA

Magnet, M. (1990). The rich and the poor. In M. L. Kennedy, W. J. Kennedy, & H. M. Smith (Eds.), *Writing in the disciplines: A reader for writers* (2nd ed., pp. 339–350). Englewood Cliffs, NJ: Prentice Hall.

Selection from a reference work

MLA

"Poverty." *The New Encyclopædia Britannica.* 15th ed. 1991.

APA

Poverty. (1991). *The new encyclopædia Britannica* (Vol. 9, pp. 652–653). Chicago: Encyclopœdia Britannica, Inc.

Article from a journal paginated by volume

MLA

Danziger, Sheldon. "Measurement of Poverty: Implications for Antipoverty Policy." *American Behavioral Scientist,* 26 (1983): 739–756.

APA

Danziger, S. (1983). Measurement of poverty: Implications for antipoverty policy. *American Behavioral Scientist, 26,* 739–756.

Article from a journal paginated by issue

MLA

Vargas, Bette. "A Test of Faith." *Essence.* 22.9 (January 1992): 33, 95.

APA

Vargas, B. (1992). A test of faith. *Essence. 22*(9), 33, 95.

Article from a weekly or biweekly periodical

MLA

Markee, Patrick. "The Dispossessed." *Nation* 14 Oct. 1996:27–29.

APA

Markee, P. (1996, October 14). The dispossessed. *Nation,* 27–29.

Article from a newspaper

MLA

Martin, Douglas. "Job in a Factory, Bed in a Box." *New York Times* 25 Dec. 1996:B1.

APA

Martin, D. (1996, December 25). Job in a factory, bed in a box. *New York Times*, p. B1.

A government document

MLA

United States. Department of Housing and Urban Development. *Priority Home!: The Federal Plan to Break the Cycle of Homelessness*. No. 0582. Washington: GPO, 1994.

APA

Department of Housing and Urban Development. (1994). *Priority home!: The federal plan to break the cycle of homelessness*. (No. 0582). Washington, DC: U.S. Government Printing Office.

Interviews

MLA

McIntire, Dorothy. Telephone interview. 24 June 1997.

APA

McIntire, D. [Telephone interview, June 24, 1997].

Movie or television productions

MLA

Squatters: The Other Philadelphia Story. Producer Charles Koppelman. The Cinema Guild, Inc., 1989.

APA

Koppelman, C. (Producer). (1989). *Squatters: The other Philadelphia story*. [Video]. New York: The Cinema Guild, Inc.

World Wide Web site

MLA

Lunde, Ron. "Who is Homeless in the United States of America?" *The Homeless Page*. (n.d.) <http://www.telport.com/~ronl/homeless.html> (18 July 1997).

APA

Lunde, R. (n.d.). Who is homeless in the United States of America? *The Homeless Page.* <http://www.telport.com/~ronl/homeless.html> (1997, July 18).

E-mail message

MLA

Smith, David E. <smith_de@llnl.com> "Homeless at Home." 16 May 1997. Personal e-mail. (18 July 1997).

APA

Smith, D. E. <smith_de@llnl.com> (1997, May 16). Homeless at home. [Personal e-mail]. (1997, July 18).

Electronic material (CD-ROM)

MLA

"Homelessness." *The Concise Columbia Encyclopedia.* CD-ROM. Columbia University Press: 1995.

APA

Homelessness. (1995). *The Concise Columbia Encyclopedia.* [CD-ROM]. Columbia University Press [Publisher].

Electronic material (online)

MLA

Giblin, Paul. "Tunnel Kids: Safe House Offers a Way Out for Nogales." *Tempe Daily News* (28 Nov. 1996). Online: "Homeless Persons." *NewsBank.* (18 July 1997).

APA

Giblin, P. (1996, November 28). Tunnel kids: Safe house offers a way out for Nogales. *Tempe Daily News* [Online]. Homeless persons. *NewsBank.* (1997, July 18).

ACKNOWLEDGMENTS

Chapter 1

p. 16–17:—"Nonnie's Day," from *Mary* by Mary Mebane. Copyright © 1981 by Mary Elizabeth Mebane. Used by permission of Viking Penguin, a division of Penguin Books, Inc.

pp. 18–20:—From Tomoyuki Iwashita, "Why I Quit the Company." *The New Internationalist*, May 1992. Reprinted by permission of Guardian/Observer News Services.

Chapter 2

pp. 48–49:Staff writers—"Advice that Can Help You Succeed on Campus," *US News and World Report*, November 25, 1985. Copyright 1985, *US News and World Report*. Reprinted by permission.

pp. 50–52:—Yuhfill, Ji-Yeon Mary, "Let's Tell the Story of All America's Cultures." Reprinted with permission of *The Philadelphia Inquirer,* 1991.

Chapter 3

pp. 83–85:—From Gale Lawrence, "Baby Birds," *The Beginning Naturalist*. Copyright © 1979 by *The New England Press, Inc.*

p. 86–87:—Excerpts from *Silent Spring*. Copyright © 1962 by Rachel Carson, renewed 1990 by Roger Christie. Reprinted by permission of Houghton Mifflin Company. All rights reserved.

Chapter 4

pp. 123–126:—From Henry Louis Gates, Jr., "A Giant Step," *The New York Times*. Copyright © 1996/90 by The New York Times Company. Reprinted by permission.

pp. 127–128:—From Elissa Ely, "Dreaming of Disconnecting a Respirator." Copyright © 1989 by Elissa Ely. Originally appeared in *The Boston Globe*. Reprinted by permission of the author.

Chapter 5

pp. 163–164:—"Salvation" from *The Big Sea* by Langston Hughes. Copyright © 1940 by Langston Hughes. Copyright renewed © 1968 by Arna

Bontemps and George Houston Bass. Reprinted by permission of Hill and Wang, a division of Farrar, Strauss & Giroux, Inc.

pp. 165–167:—From Kirsten Mullen, "Subtle Lessons in Racism," from *USA Weekend*, November 6, 1992.

Chapter 6
pp. 194–195:—Reprinted with the permission of Scribner, a division of Simon & Schuster. From *He Was a Midwestern Boy on His Own* by Bob Greene. Copyright © 1991, John Deadline Enterprises, Inc.

pp. 196–198:—From Robert J. Trotter, "How Do I Love Thee?" as found in Three Faces of Love. Originally printed in *Psychology Today*, September 1986. Reprinted with permission from *Psychology Today* magazine, Copyright © 1986 (Sussex Publishers, Inc.)

pp. 210–211:—"Private and Public Language," from *Hunger of Memory* by Richard Rodriquez. Reprinted by permission of David R. Godine, Publisher, Inc. Copyright © 1982 by Richard Rodriguez.

Chapter 7
pp. 229–231:—From Albert Scardino, "After a Burglary," *The New York Times Magazine*, June 2, 1985, p. 74. Copyright © 1985 by The New York Times Company. Reprinted by permission.

pp. 231–234:—Reprinted by arrangement with the heirs to the Estate of Martin Luther King, Jr., c/o Writers House, Inc. as agent for the proprietor. Copyright 1958 by Martin Luther King, Jr., copyright renewed 1986 by Coretta Scott King, Dexter King, Martin Luther King III, Yolanda King, and Bernice King.

Chapter 8
pp. 267–269:—From David Nyhan, "Turn off the TV before It Ruins Us," *The Boston Globe*, September 16, 1996. Reprinted courtesy of *The Boston Globe*.

pp. 269–272:—From Max Frankel, "Universal E-Mail: Worthy of a New Frontier," *New York Times*, May 5, 1996, pp. 40 & 42. Copyright © 1996/90 by The New York Times Company. Reprinted by permission.

p. 286:—Reprinted from *Mediaspeak: How Television Makes Up Your Mind* by Donna Woolfolk Cross (New York: The Putnam Publishing Group, 1983). Copyright © 1993 by Donna Woolfolk Cross.

p. 318:—From *The Library of Congress Subject Headings Index*, Vol. II, 19th Edition, 1996, p. 2451.

INDEX